THE BODIES DOWN AT BONDI

ELIZABETH BANKES

Credits

I am extremely grateful to the following friends and family for the advice and assistance they have given me when writing this book.

Anthea Savidis

Christina Austron

Edwina Harvey (edwinaseditingservices@gmail.com)

Gretchen Fitzgerald

Judith Mendoza-White

Lucy Burke

Michael Murphy

Michelle Ridge

Sarah Moeda

Steve Bankes

All characters and events in this publication are fictitious and any resemblance to real persons, living or dead, is purely coincidental.

The cover was designed by Anthea Savidis.

CHAPTER ONE

Saturday night and the sound system was blasting out *Wonderwall* as increasing numbers of revellers entered the Regent Hotel. Being near the famous Bondi beach, the pub was a popular venue for backpackers, especially those from Britain.

Some of the punters were attempting to dance and sing along to the recent Oasis hit, while others were busy eyeing up potential shags. Conversation between the groups of lads was no longer necessary. Now was the time to pick up and or find some recreational drugs for the night ahead. With luck attain both.

'Another bevvy?' Mark offered.

'Grand,' Siobhan answered, tugging at her boob tube.

'You alright?' Mark grinned. 'Bit uncomfortable?'

She rolled her shoulders then puffed up her hair with both hands. 'Got to look the part.'

'What part? Any bloke who gets you is a lucky fella,' he complimented, gently placing his arm around her shoulders.

'You don't know how lucky *you* are,' Siobhan replied, still tweaking at her top.

'Oh yeah?'

'Yes! Men can wear whatever they want while we always have to tart up.'

'And you think us queers can dress any way we want?'

Siobhan pulled away to look at Mark. 'You dress like most of the men here, except for the tradies, and you can't count them.'

Mark grinned. 'Maybe they're gay too?'

'The tradies? Don't be daft. If they are, there's no way in hell they'd admit it.' Siobhan sipped her drink before asking, 'Meeting Darcy tonight?' Mark said he was. 'Told your parents about him yet?'

The smile on Mark's face faded. 'God no. They'd never understand. Too bloody religious. They'd disown me.'

Siobhan sighed, shaking her head. 'Sounds like home. Some attitudes never change.'

With drinks replenished, they watched the social intercourse evolve. The girls picking and choosing between the lads, the dejected looks of those whose chat up lines had failed, followed quickly by 'I don't give a fuck' expression while they strutted to Blur's *Park Life*.

Mark was glad he wasn't a part of this social dance where women seemed to have the upper hand. Soon he'd meet Darcy at the Albury on Oxford Street where gay men were more open when it came to sexual desire and needs. When he'd first arrived in

Sydney it was such a relief not to hide his sexual identity as he had back in Liverpool, although the continuing AIDS epidemic hadn't won his 'lot' any favours in either country. At home in Liverpool he'd told no-one he was gay, certainly not his family nor close friends.

Nirvana's *Smells Like Teen Spirit* jogged Mark back to the present. The song had been popular in England and hearing these hits made him feel less of an outsider in his new environment. Pushing his nostalgia to one side, he turned to Siobhan. 'How come you're not working tonight? It's Saturday. Is that why you're so worried about your appearance? Out to pick up?'

'No, you eejit, not with effing Trev hanging around.' Siobhan swirled her drink thoughtfully. 'Needed a break. Said it was time of the month. There's only so much ogling a lass can take.' She sighed. 'The other night one of the bouncers decked a guy for trying to climb onto the stage. Out cold. Fecken eejit.'

'Men!' Mark grinned, throwing his hands in the air. 'What're you doing later?'

'Not sure. Wouldn't mind a bit of gear but that means being nice to himself. Pain in the arse but he comes in handy.'

Mark agreed. Trev was a bellend, but he had the drugs so had the power. He'd seen how the pub crowd kowtowed to him because he was the source of marijuana and party drugs, although that didn't stop him from being a total twat.

'Where are you meeting Darcy?' Siobhan asked.

'The Albury, Oxford Street.'

'Is everything going well with him?'

Mark paused. 'Not really. He's been a bit of a tool lately. Always at me to tell my family about him but I can't. Don't know why it's so bloody important to him.'

'Jesus, Mary and Joseph. If I told me ma and da I was a leso, not that I am, they'd slaughter me. They'd be happier knowing I'm a stripper.'

Mark laughed bitterly. The Irish were as bad as the Scousers. He wished Darcy would mind his own business as being an Aussie he had no idea what he'd put up with back home, the bullying and the taunting because he seemed a bit different.

He should never have told Darcy where his parents lived. Now Darcy knew, Mark wouldn't put it past him to contact them. The line from an Elvis song came to mind, 'Caught in a trap, I can't walk out.'

'What're you going to do? Do you love him?' she asked.

'Yes. No. I don't know. He's …'

'What?'

'Sorry. It's nothing.' He downed the dregs of his beer. 'Anyway, I'd better do the off. See you soon.' Mark kissed Siobhan on the cheek. 'Enjoy your night off.'

'Slán. Take care.'

8

Mark wove his way through the crowd of drinkers towards the exit. A couple of fellow Poms stopped him to say hiya, but he kept going. He wished he could have stayed longer with Siobhan but Darcy was being rather demanding, and if he was late he wouldn't hear the end of it.

He was nearly at the main doors when a hand grabbed his arm. 'Alright?'

Mark turned towards the voice.

'It's been a while. Avoiding me?'

Mark's face paled. 'Of course not.'

The man put his arm firmly around Mark's shoulders and drew him towards the doors. 'Got a bit of news. Let's go somewhere quiet,' he uttered, gripping Mark even tighter.

'I'm … I'm meeting …' Mark stuttered, then realised there was no point in arguing and allowed himself to be manhandled out of the pub in the direction of the sweeping curve of Bondi Beach.

CHAPTER TWO

Jim and Anh snuggled together on the couch watching a favourite British whodunit on the ABC. The show finished and Jim was about to turn off the television when the music tag for a news break stopped him. A grim-faced newsreader appeared on the screen. 'A young man's body has been found on the beach at North Bondi. If anyone has information please contact Crime Stoppers on 1800 333 000 or your nearest police station.'

'Poor bugger,' Jim said, switching off the box. 'Probably some backpacker who's had a few too many and not used to the rips and currents.' Anh agreed as she turned off the lounge lights and followed Jim upstairs.

'Are you going to ring Mark again?' Anh asked, rubbing her face with moisturiser while watching Jim's reflection in the bathroom mirror.

'Yes,' he answered, staring at his face and running a hand through his hair. 'Think I need a trim. Might get rid of some of the grey. Can't tell the St Cuthbert's boys to have a haircut when mine is over my collar.' He chuckled before his thoughts returned to

Mark. 'Funny he hasn't returned my call. Hope he's alright. …
I've got to stop acting like a parent. He *is* from Liverpool which
sounds like a bloody tough place to live.'

'Don't worry, darling. It's Saturday night. He'll be out with his
friends having fun. We'd be the last people on his mind.' Anh
handed Jim her hairbrush. 'Please,' she asked.

'You're so lucky. No grey. Still as rich and lush as when we
first met. Not like mine,' Jim complimented as he stood behind her
and gently brushed her long black hair, then pulling the thick
strands away from the back of her neck, kissed the skin.

Anh turned to him, led him into their bedroom and firmly
closed the door.

Jim woke early to find Anh standing next to their bed holding a
cup of tea, a worried look on her face. 'There's more on the news
about the man found down at Bondi. The police are still asking for
information. You'd think someone would know him,' she said,
handing Jim his tea.

Laughter from the kitchen informed Jim his sons were up. He
slowly rolled over and placed his feet on the floor. Although it was
Sunday, there was 'no rest for the wicked'. Daniel and Josh were
busy gulping Nutrigrain drenched in milk and sugar when their
father joined them. The cereal looked inviting but these days Jim
was conscious of cholesterol and weight gain. If he wanted to have

11

a few drinks then he had to cut down on other pleasures. Getting old was no place for sissies, a friend had informed him. Apparently, it was a quote from the actress Bette Davis. He'd always been trim but now in his fifties he had to take greater care. At least he still had his hair.

The phone rang. Anh paused in the doorway, glancing at Jim as he walked over to answer it. A call this early on a Sunday morning was unusual.

'Cameron speaking.'

'Jim. It's Alan Stone.'

'Alan. How're you? Am I in trouble?' he asked, grinning at his wife.

'No, of course not. Sorry about the time but I'm wondering if you've kept in touch with the young English chap who stayed with you?'

'Yes,' Jim answered cautiously. 'Why?'

'Well … You may have heard on the news about the young bloke who was found down at Bondi Beach?'

Jim's heart began to beat faster.

'The Bondi Police rang us at Waverley this morning to say they'd received an anonymous phone call last night. Some bloke with a Pommie accent saying it was Mark Dunlop's body. The name rang a bell and I remembered he'd stayed with you.'

Jim remained silent. Oh shit.

'Apparently, the body had no identification, no wallet, but I thought of your visitor. I know he hasn't been with you for a while but …' Stone paused, 'we think the body could be Mark's.'

'Oh my God. When we heard it on the news last night I have to admit Mark crossed my mind. I tried to contact him yesterday but no answer.' Jim's face crumpled. 'What happened?'

'After the police got the call, they went down to the beach, found the body at the north end where the English bloke told them it might be, then they contacted the coroner's van after securing the area, and to protect the body. By the time they got there the tide had … well you know what I mean.'

'Shit!' Jim exclaimed. Daniel and Josh jerked in shock at their father's use of the expletive. 'Did he drown?'

'Looks like it. Forensics are checking as we speak.'

Jim couldn't think of anything else to say. He listened to Stone breathe deeply. Finally, Stone asked if Jim could meet him at the Glebe morgue and identify the body.

'Oh my God, of course … How come you're involved?' Jim asked.

'Bondi got the call, but they need some assistance as they're fairly stretched dealing with tourists and backpackers as well as the usual stuff. So are you okay to meet me in Glebe this morning?'

Jim swallowed, his heart pounding. 'I can be there within the hour.'

'Thanks, mate. I'll see you in the morgue. Sorry to be the bearer of such bad news.'

Slowly hanging up the phone, Jim blinked rapidly, rubbing his eyes before turning to face his family. 'That was Alan. Shocking news I'm afraid. It looks like Mark could be dead. Alan wants me to go and identify the body.'

Anh's hands shot up to her mouth as she stared at her husband in disbelief then went to comfort him. Their teenage sons sat stunned.

CHAPTER THREE

Don't let it be Mark, don't let it be Mark, swirled around Jim's head as he drove towards Glebe. Once the nightmare of finding a parking space was over and after supplying his details and the reason for his visit, the lady at reception allowed him entry and he quickly made his way to the correct floor. Exiting the lift, he followed the signs. A constable standing at the door asked Jim for identification then pushed the door open.

Taking a deep breath, Jim entered the morgue. As in movies and television murder mysteries, the room was cold and clinical, lined with stainless steel cabinets. Other than grey, there was little colour except for the bright white sheet covering a long rectangular metal slab. The outline of a body was discernible and standing next to it was his old friend Detective Alan Stone, and a man wearing a white lab coat whom Jim assumed was something to do with forensics.

Stone strode over and shook Jim's hand. 'Thanks for coming so promptly. We really have to stop meeting like this.' Jim smiled weakly, acknowledging Stone's indirect reference to past events. Although he hoped the body wasn't Mark's, his gut told him it would be. He thought back to those months ago when he and the family had picked up the young man from the airport.

Sydney International Airport was bustling with friends and relatives waiting for the arrival of the British Airways flight from Manchester. The scene was one of excitement. Balloons and welcome signs were held aloft and children, inspired by the happy atmosphere, ran amongst the crowd. Expectant parties, intent on watching those who walked through Arrivals, ignored the activities of those around them.

Jim and Anh stood with their sons, watching for Mark Dunlop to emerge. They had no idea what he looked like as they'd agreed to his staying with them at the request of an old friend in England. As many of the passengers were young men, they found themselves moving forward in anticipation only to find the man walk straight past into the welcoming arms of one of the many groups waiting.

Suddenly, a tall, slim, solitary figure emerged dragging a suitcase. His scanning around the excited throng caused Jim to nudge Anh. 'That could be him. We should have brought a sign.'

'Mark?' Jim questioned cautiously.

'Mr Cameron?'

'Yes. Call me Jim. How are you? Good flight?'

'Long. But great to be here. Cheers. Thanks for meeting me.'

'No problem. Let me take your bag. Come and meet the family.' Jim took the suitcase and led Mark to Anh and his sons who were staring at the new arrival with undisguised curiosity.

'Hello Mark. Lovely to meet you,' Anh greeted, reaching up to give him a hug.

'Alright?' Mark asked, looking at Josh and Daniel.

Not sure how to reply, they answered that they were alright."

Jim could tell his sons found the man's strong accent puzzling. Although he'd warned them their visitor may speak differently to Aussies, he realised Mark wasn't going to be easy to understand.

While making their way to the terminal exit, Josh whispered to his father asking if Mark had to learn English to come to Australia? 'No. Mark just has an accent, Liverpudlian,' Jim explained and how he sounded like The Beatles and that people from different parts of England and the rest of Britain, had accents which weren't like the Australian one.

Josh and Daniel nodded. This was all new to them.

The forensic technician reached over to pull back the sheet. Jim swallowed. He knew what was coming but was filled with despair. During the Vietnam War he'd seen enough dead bodies to last a lifetime, but Mark wasn't a soldier. He was a great bloke and they'd enjoyed his stay and were sorry when he moved out into his own place after a few short months. He'd fitted in, was helpful, tidy and considerate. He and Anh had developed a warm, chatty relationship and once the boys had become accustomed to his way of speaking, they loved his company.

Despite the age difference, Mark had treated Josh and Daniel as if they were equals. Like a loving uncle, he'd taken them to the movies, to the beach and listened to their tales of school friendships and activities with non-patronising interest.

Jim closed his eyes, then forced himself to open them when Stone asked formally, 'Is this Mark Dunlop?'

Mark's face was colourless, passive. Tears pricked Jim's eyes. 'Yes. Yes it is. It's Mark Dunlop.'

'Thank you, Jim,' Stone said, indicating for the sheet to be returned to its original position. He patted Jim on the back. 'Never easy.'

'What happens now?' Jim asked, straightening his shoulders.

Seeing the forensic technician glance at Jim, Stone said, 'Neil, you can say whatever in front of Mr Cameron. We've worked together before.'

The technician nodded. 'It's early days but it looks like he died by drowning as there's water in the lungs. We're waiting for the results of blood tests as there are no signs of an attack. No blows to the head or the body, and we're checking for drugs.'

Jim frowned. 'Drugs?'

Procedure was the reply.

'What was he wearing?' Jim asked.

'Normal clothes. Jeans. The usual.'

Jim and Stone stared at each other. 'Surely not suicide?' Jim queried.

Neil shrugged. 'Have to wait till we get the results. Will let you know a.s.a.p.'

'Time of death?' Stone asked.

'Somewhere between six and ten p.m. last night.'

'Well, if that's it, we'll leave you to it,' Detective Stone said, signalling for Jim to follow.

Informing the constable guarding the door that he'd meet him back at the car, Stone walked with Jim down the corridor towards the lift. 'Sorry, Jim, but it's looking a bit complicated. It might be suicide, or he could have been pushed into the water. Or maybe it was just an accident after too many drinks. Too early to tell till we get the results of the blood tests.'

'Jesus, Alan. I don't believe Mark would commit suicide. Why the hell would he? And why would anyone want to hurt him?'

Stone shook his head. 'We'll just have to wait and see.'

Jim stared at Stone. 'How long will he be in here?' The thought of Mark lying alone in a bleak, cold room was unbearable.

'Hard to say. When a death is suspicious it can take a while before the body's released,' Stone explained as they neared the lift. 'We'll have to contact his parents and tell them the bad news.'

Jim grimaced. 'Don't envy you ... Do you want me to?' he offered. 'I don't actually know his parents. It was a friend who asked if he could stay with us but if it makes it easier for you?'

Stone sighed. 'Thanks, but it's part of the job. I'll let you know when we've contacted them and then you can get in touch. Oh, do you happen to have Mark's address in Sydney?'

'We do. In fact he gave us a spare key in case something happened.' Jim thought for a few seconds. 'That was typical of Mark. He was careful. Organised. Got a job almost immediately. He didn't seem the type to take risks.'

'Maybe he'd just had a few too many and without thinking placed himself in a dangerous situation?'

'Possibly. But it still doesn't sound like him. And you said he didn't have his wallet. Again, that's out of character.'

Stone shrugged. Seeing the anguish on Jim's face, he reached out, placing a hand on his friend's shoulder. 'Don't worry, mate, we'll sort this out.'

CHAPTER FOUR

Waiting impatiently, Anh opened the front door the instant she heard Jim drive into the garage. The bleak expression on her face showed the fear that the dead man was Mark. As Jim neared the front door, he held out his arms. She clutched him tightly and burst into tears. He finally let go of the grief he felt, the two united in sadness. Mark arrived a stranger but had become a friend.

Jim led Anh into the kitchen, sat her down, and made them a cup of coffee. A whisky was what he really wanted but it was too early. He had more to do. He promised himself one later or even more than one to numb the sight of Mark's lifeless body on the slab.

Anh, her tears now under control, waited to hear about his visit to the morgue.

'He looked very peaceful. The forensic bloke said there were no signs of wounds to the head or body.'

'Is that good?'

Jim thought about her question. 'Yes and no. It seems he drowned but they still have to investigate his death. They're checking for drugs. Doing blood tests.'

'Drugs?'

'Yes.'

'Mark wouldn't do things like that,' Anh denied, her voice rising in protest.

'Well, we don't know. Who knows what he got up to after he left us? He was a young man and from what I've gathered, lots of young people take drugs.'

'How can you even think he did?'

'Anh. We have to accept what the police tell us,' Jim said, trying to pacify his wife.

She shook her head in disbelief. 'He was a lovely boy. I don't believe he'd be that stupid. He wouldn't want to risk his job, or his visa.'

Although he couldn't help but agree, Jim said, 'It's procedure apparently. We just have to wait and see. I told Alan we have a spare key to Mark's place. He wants me to drop it off to him at the station so they can check out his unit. Do you mind if I take it now?'

Anh shook her head. 'No. Of course not. You have to do whatever you can to support Mark. Josh and Daniel can entertain themselves today.'

'Oooooh, you're a hard woman,' Jim said lightly, attempting to lift the mood. 'Where's the key?'

With a sigh, Anh walked to the sideboard, retrieved a key with a security fob attached, and handed it to Jim.

'Thank you, darling. I won't be long.'

Avoiding the Bondi Junction shopping centre, Jim was relieved to find a parking space close to Waverley Police Station, and after informing the desk sergeant who he was, was shown to Stone's office.

'Sorry to keep you, Alan, but Anh wanted to hear the news and of course was pretty upset when I told her it *was* Mark. They'd become quite close.'

'No problem. Thanks,' Stone said, accepting the key set from Jim. 'I know it's not protocol, but do you fancy coming with us when we go to check out Mark's unit?'

'You sure?'

'You can help us identify anything of interest. Maybe spot something unusual.'

Jim reluctantly agreed.

Mark Dunlop's unit was in a newish building on Oxford Street, Bondi Junction. Jim, following Stone and Sergeant Ridge, was surprised to see a small gym on one side of the long, glassed entrance with a swimming pool on the other. It crossed his mind how Mark must have been doing well to rent in such a block.

The unit was situated on the ground floor past two lifts in the foyer. The front door opened into a short hall which led to a spacious lounge. Outside was a large terrace surrounded by plants. The kitchen was modern and the two bedrooms with their own ensuites, had sliding doors onto another terrace at the back of the unit.

'Not bad,' Stone muttered. 'Wish I lived here.'

'Yes! Not what I expected,' Jim replied.

'Haven't you been here before?'

'No. We usually met out or he came to our place.'

'What was his job?'

'He didn't talk about it much. Said it was a boring office job.'

Stone turned to Sergeant Ridge. 'We'd better start looking for anything of interest. Anything connected to his associates. Friends, photos, letters. Jim, you okay to stay?'

Jim pushed a hand through his hair, contemplating Stone's request. 'You seem to be treating Mark's death as if it's a crime. Is it?'

The detective pulled his head back in thought. 'We don't know yet. The fact that someone rang telling us about Mark's body, and the fact he was fully clothed indicates it may not be a simple case of suicide or even accidental drowning. We have to look at his death from every angle.'

Reluctantly, Jim followed the two policemen into Mark's bedroom. He looked at the bed with a white singlet neatly folded on top of the pillows and personal items placed around the room. It was too much information.

'I'd like to help you but to be honest I'd feel funny searching through Mark's private stuff. Too invasive. If you don't mind, I'd rather leave you to it,' Jim declared, struggling to explain his feelings.

'Fair enough,' Stone said, as he walked Jim down the hall, holding the door open. 'I'll give you a ring later and let you know what we find.'

Jim couldn't wait to leave the building and go home.

CHAPTER FIVE

To his relief, Sunday afternoon was nearly at a close. Jim parked the car, looking forward to seeing Anh and the boys, and having a whisky. He didn't want to think about what Stone and his colleague might find in Mark's unit.

'I'm home,' he called out. There was no answer to his greeting as he made his way into the kitchen. It was empty. Where was everybody?

After what seemed like hours, he heard the opening of the front door and Anh appeared carrying a beach bag and towels, followed by Daniel and Josh still wearing wet boardshorts. Their black hair damp and messy. Jim felt enormous relief upon seeing his family. Their presence was something he took for granted but Mark's death made him feel even more protective of their safety and without them he would be nothing.

'Wondered where you were. Been to the beach?'

'Yes. As it was a lovely day, I thought we might as well. But not Bondi. Went to Bronte instead. How was it?' Anh asked, taking the towels into the laundry, indicating for Jim to join her.

Reading Anh's signal for a little privacy, Jim followed. 'Went to Mark's unit with Alan and another police bloke. Quite a place. God knows how he could afford it.'

'Really?'

'Yes. Definitely not cheap. They were going to search through Mark's stuff, so I thought it better to leave.'

'What were they looking for?' Anh asked, frowning.

'Anything that might give them a clue as to why Mark died.'

Returning to the kitchen it was obvious their attempt at privacy had failed as Josh and Daniel wanted to know why the police were involved. 'Wasn't it an accident?'

'They don't know.'

'Shit. Really?' Daniel responded, glancing guiltily at his mother.

How much should he tell them? Jim wondered and while he was enlightening his sons with a few details, it occurred to him they might have found out something about Mark's life when he lived with them. 'Guys, did Mark ever tell you where he went? What he did in his spare time? Who he knew? And did he ever seem unhappy?'

The boys looked at each other, shrugging. 'He went to the Regent a fair bit. He told us lots of Poms drank there and there were guys from Liverpool.'

27

'Did he ever mention the Viceroy? It's much nearer to his home in Bondi Junction than the Regent.'

'The Viceroy?' Daniel questioned. 'No.'

'Well, what about girls? Did he have a girlfriend?'

'Dunno.' The boys thought for a few seconds. Daniel, looking at Josh for confirmation, asked, 'Didn't he say there was some girl called Shebon or some weird name like that?'

'Yeah, but she had a boyfriend. Some guy who hung around her all the time,' Josh added.

'A jealous boyfriend?' Jim asked eagerly.

'Dunno. Mark didn't tell us much. Just said there was an Irish girl he met in the pub, and they were friends.'

'Anything else?'

'Nah. Not really.'

'Hang on. Didn't he say the guy who hung 'round the Irish girl was a druggie?' Josh suggested.

'A drug dealer or someone who took drugs?' Jim prompted. His sons looked nonplussed. 'Guys, this is really important. Mark's death is a bit suspicious.' He didn't want to use the word suicide.

'Jesus,' Daniel exclaimed. 'Sorry Mum.'

'Mmmm. It's alright this time, darling, but you must not use that language in front of your teachers. I'll get the dinner on while you help your dad,' Anh excused.

Daniel glanced guiltily at his father.

'Was Mark murdered?' Josh asked, his voice rising in anguish.

'Calm down. We don't know what happened. And, you *must …
not …* tell anyone about this. It's only between us.' The boys
crossed their hearts. 'Can you remember if he told you whether the
guy who hung around the Irish girl was a drug dealer or a drug
taker? Do you remember his name?' Jim stared at both of them in
turn.

Daniel exclaimed suddenly, 'It was Trev something. Mark
thought his name was funny as it seemed so Aussie.'

Jim sat in silence, impressed by his older son's memory. 'Thank
you. You've both been very helpful.' The boys smiled proudly.

'Better get ready for dinner. But if you can think of anything
else … please let me know.'

They said they would.

Dinner over, Daniel and Josh were in the lounge watching
television, bickering over which channel to watch, when the phone
rang in the kitchen.

Jim picked up the receiver but before he had time to speak
Stone jumped in, 'Got some information for you.'

'That was quick.'

'Found an item in Mark's flat that's of interest,' Alan paused
theatrically, 'a mobile phone.'

29

'Good grief. A mobile phone? Who has one of those?' Jim asked. 'They cost a fortune.'

'Exactly. And this one was in Mark's bedroom. In his wardrobe to be precise. The question is, why did he have one? Did you ever see him with it?'

'Hell no. Would have remembered. Maybe he had it for work?'

'For an office job? Highly unlikely.'

Jim turned to Anh who shook her head. 'Anh's as puzzled as me. What else did you find?'

'We've bagged some photos and letters. The photos may be helpful if we can identify who's in them, and judging by the beach location, some were taken at Bondi. A couple of blokes appeared in different ones. There were letters but mainly from family in the UK. He did have a few pub coasters from the Regent and some other pubs, including the Viceroy, so it seems he could have been a regular at a few hotels. An odd thing to collect but perhaps he wanted a few souvenirs when he went back to England.'

'Were there any drugs?' Jim asked, hoping the answer would be negative.

'No. We'll check the mobile phone and see if we can find out who he spoke to or received calls from. It's like a bloody brick and God knows how it works. I know bugger all about this new technology.'

'Alan, do you think Mark was involved in drugs?'

30

'As I said, we have to look at everything. The blood tests will tell us if he was using drugs, or ... God knows what at this stage.'

'I just hope it wasn't suicide. Doesn't bear thinking about.'

'No.'

Jim hung up the phone. What a Sunday.

CHAPTER SIX

The working week began and for Jim it was a mixed blessing. Being busy kept his mind off Mark, but the running of a school had its own issues. The role of Deputy Headmaster at St Cuthbert's was demanding. The Head, Robert Pritchard, was nearing retirement and relied heavily on Jim to solve the problems with staff, students and parents.

Since the death of the gay teacher, Bentley Shute, back in the 1980s, the school had made an effort to be more inclusive of women teachers and to change its traditional culture. Although Jim was pleased the school was moving with the times, he knew many of the male staff, and some parents, still had old-fashioned values. The male teachers' jealousy of any woman's success continued, as did their subconscious view that women were inferior to men. He found it hard to deal with complaints from parents against female teachers when he knew if a male teacher had behaved in the same way, there wouldn't have been a problem.

His analysis of the dynamics of the school was interrupted when Daphne, Robert's secretary, popped her blonde head around the door to ask if he'd had a good weekend.

Jim winced. 'Bloody awful.'

Daphne frowned. 'Oh dear. Why?'

'Do you have a minute?'

'Anything for you, Jim.'

He couldn't resist smiling. Daphne had worked at the school for as long as he had. She'd survived the slings and arrows of the school's outrageous fortune over the years.

'Remember Mark, the chap from Liverpool who stayed with us?' Jim asked. She nodded. 'Well, he was found dead down at Bondi Beach on Saturday night.'

Daphne opened her mouth, closed it before finally saying, 'Oh my God, Jim. How awful. What happened?'

'The Bondi police said he'd drowned but forensics are still doing blood tests. Alan Stone contacted me.'

The look of sympathy on Daphne's face encouraged Jim to continue. 'Suicide has been suggested but I don't believe it.'

Daphne gasped. 'How did Alan know it was Mark? Had he met him before?'

'No, but I'd told him about Mark when he stayed with us. Alan said that the Bondi police received a phone call on Saturday night from a Pommie bloke telling them it was Mark.' Jim scowled in

33

disbelief at Daphne. 'Most unusual. Then the Bondi police contacted Alan. When we were watching telly on Saturday night there was a request for information about a body found at Bondi. For some reason it made me think of Mark and then when Alan rang yesterday, my premonition was correct.'

'My God. Did the man who rang the police give them his name?' Jim shook his head. 'Why on earth wouldn't he? At least I hope he tried to rescue Mark.'

'Yes. I hope so … I had to identify the body.'

'Oh, how awful. You poor thing.' Daphne reached out, rubbing her hand on Jim's arm.

'Identifying a body is certainly something I didn't think I'd be doing on a Sunday.'

'You liked him, didn't you?'

'I did. Mark was a great bloke. The kids loved him, and he and Anh got on like a house on fire.'

The two stood silently and Daphne was about to leave when she asked suddenly, 'How is Alan? Do you see much of him? Haven't seen him for ages. Still the same? Married?'

'Yes, the same but married, no. He's still the tall, dark, well brownish, and handsome Kiwi. Has had the odd relationship but nothing lasting. A shame. Just a bit older. Amazing to think I've known him since we met in Rarotonga. Bloody hell, that's about twenty years ago.'

'Well, I've been with Ray for nearly ten years. Where did the time go? Anyway, please give him my regards when you next catch up,' Daphne instructed. 'And if you need anything, please let me know.'

'Will do ... Actually, could you see what you can find out about the Regent? Apparently, it's a pub Mark went to a lot, mainly because of the British clientele, but I don't know much about it.'

'What are you trying to say, Jim?'

He grinned. 'Daphne, I know you have connections.'

'Ray by any chance? You could always ask him yourself.'

'I know but he seems so busy. Working in the Cross. That den of iniquity. Don't want to bother him.'

'Jim,' Daphne groaned. 'I'll talk to him and I'm sure he'll be happy to help. Especially as it's you. And Alan.'

'Thank you,' Jim said, as Daphne left his office.

CHAPTER SEVEN

'Gidday, Jim. Hope I'm not interrupting important school activities?' Stone enquired when the phone was answered.

'Nothing that won't keep. Any more news?'

'Some. Was wondering if we can have a quick drink after you finish work? Might seem a bit odd if I come to the school. Someone might recognise me from my previous visits regarding Mr Shute and that could bring back bad memories,' Stone said with a murmur of a laugh.

'Ha, yes. Just told Daphne the news about Mark and she's going to do a little investigating for me. With Ray's help of course ... Here we go again.'

'You're not wrong. What was that quote? The past is a foreign country, and we certainly don't want to go back there.'

'Quite. On another note, which is totally irrelevant to all this; Daphne was curious about your private life as she hasn't seen you for a while. She's as bad as Anh, hoping you've met someone. Have you?' asked Jim.

'I wish. Maybe I should join a dating service but it all looks too hard. Getting set in my ways.'

'That's bullshit, Alan.'

'Anyway, moving right along,' the detective deflected.

'Where shall we meet?' Jim asked, but before Alan could answer, he suggested, 'Why not come to my place? I know Anh would love to see you.'

'Sounds good. I won't stay long but can give you an update about what I've heard so far. What time suits?'

Jim was waiting impatiently for Alan to arrive. He couldn't sit still. A drink would settle his nerves, but he should wait.

'Alan. So nice to see you,' Anh welcomed, tea towel in hand, when Jim led him into the kitchen.

'Great to see you too. Looking wonderful as usual.'

Anh blushed and ran her fingers through her long dark hair. 'We're so glad you're involved in the investigation. It's such a tragedy. Mark was a lovely young man. But what about you, Alan?' Anh asked, cocking her head to one side.

'What about me?' Stone asked, feigning innocence.

'Have you met someone?'

'Too busy.'

'No one is too busy for love,' Anh chided. 'You should have someone nice to go home to.'

37

'One day. Think you've been talking to Jim. I don't seem to have much luck when it comes to women. Not easy with the hours I keep.'

'I don't believe you. I know you've had girlfriends so why not now? You're still young and handsome,' she persisted.

'Don't know about young or handsome, but thanks anyway,' Alan responded.

'Leave the poor man alone,' Jim insisted, sensing Alan was becoming uncomfortable. 'Let's have a drink and sit down.'

Accepting a beer, Stone followed them into the lounge, sitting opposite his hosts who leaned forward in anticipation of the information he might have.

Looking from Anh to Jim, he began, 'It appears Mark was a regular at the Regent. Nothing wrong with that, but it's got a reputation as a place to score drugs.'

'What's that got to do with Mark?' Jim butted in.

'At the moment, nothing, but we have to look into every possibility. Maybe taking or selling drugs?'

Anh glanced anxiously at Jim.

The three sat thinking about Mark until Jim said, 'This may not be relevant but we had a chat with Daniel and Josh about Mark, and they remembered he'd mentioned some chap called Trev. And, according to the boys, Mark was friendly with an Irish girl, Siobhan who's a mate of this Trev and he might be a drug dealer.'

'They'll make detectives yet,' Alan said, smiling at Anh. 'Anything else?'

Jim shook his head then asked, 'Have you got the results of the blood tests?'

Stone glanced at the lounge door in case Daniel and Josh were within earshot. 'Yes. Well, this is why I wanted to talk to you ... Forensics said Mark *did* have drugs in his system. A large amount of amphetamines.'

A stunned silence radiated around the room. 'Was there a suggestion of suicide?' Jim asked finally.

'Mark would never have committed suicide,' Anh interjected, glaring at Jim. 'He was happy.'

The two men stared at her. Jim leant forward, placing his hand on her arm. 'Darling, we never really know how people feel.'

Anh shrugged off his hand. 'How can you say that? He told me he was enjoying living in Sydney. He felt much freer here than in Liverpool. Why would he kill himself?'

Jim's glance at Alan indicated she must know a lot more about Mark's life than he did.

Neither spoke. Jim stood up to get Alan and himself another beer, giving Anh time to calm down.

Sensing the tension, Alan asked, 'Anh, do you mind telling me what Mark told you about his private life? The more we learn

39

about him, the more chance we have of solving the reason for his death.'

Jim returning, handed a beer to Alan and was about to sit down when it occurred to him he hadn't offered Anh a drink. He was too busy thinking about Mark or was he being a chauvinistic pig as feminists labelled old-fashioned men?

'Darling, I'm sorry. Would you like a drink?'

'A red wine, please,' Anh said, giving Jim an admonishing look.

He hurried back to the kitchen quickly returning with Anh's Merlot, and the tension in the living room eased slightly. Anh raised her glass and the men tapped it with their beer.

'So, can you tell me more about Mark and what he told you when he lived here?' Alan asked.

She took a sip of wine before raising her head and saying, 'Mark was gay, as they say. He met a man here and they had a relationship. They didn't live together as Mark wasn't ready to go that far, especially if he couldn't stay in Australia.' She drank more of her wine. 'He said his family wouldn't like it. He told me people in Liverpool don't like homosexuals.'

Alan nodded. 'Do you think that's why he had a two-bedroom unit? Put his parents off the scent if they came out?'

'I don't know.'

'Why didn't you tell me all this before?' Jim questioned, unable to keep the irritation and hurt out of his voice.

'Because you and most men don't accept men who are gay. I knew if I told you, you wouldn't like him as much.'

Jim rubbed his forehead. She had a point. He prided himself on being tolerant and understanding but there was something about gay sex which he couldn't come to terms with and judging by the conversations he'd overheard in the staffroom or at the pub, many men felt the same. And the whole AIDS epidemic hadn't helped the prejudice.

Putting down his beer, Jim looked at Anh. 'Darling, I'm sorry to say, you're right. I don't mean to be prejudiced. It's just after years of hearing negative comments about homosexuals by colleagues and society in general, I must've absorbed the prejudice.' He took a swig from his stubbie. 'I feel ashamed … Mark could talk to you but not to me.'

'You're not the only one, Jim,' Alan sympathised. He looked at Anh. 'Lots of men find homosexuality threatening. Some are frightened they're gay and they know how prejudiced society is. Some want to prove they're macho so join in the slagging off. It's as if they think by sympathising with gays everyone will think *they* are gay. It's rubbish, but that's the way a lot of men react.'

Anh's face softened slightly. 'I'm sorry I sound angry. I feel very sad for Mark. He's dead. Alone. In a strange country.'

41

Jim was about to say Australia wasn't a strange country but thought better of it. He didn't want to upset Anh any further. Perhaps he'd taken her assimilation into Australian society for granted. She seemed to have adapted quickly to her new life, but maybe she hadn't. Was she always missing her home in Vietnam? He'd assumed she was happy in her new country after all those years of war.

'You want me to tell you what I know about Mark?' Anh prompted.

'Yes. Please,' both men answered.

'Well, *Detective Stone,* as a policeman, you ask the questions and I will do my best to answer them,' Anh instructed with a sneaky grin.

'Righty ho.' Stone pretended to lick his biro as he pulled out a notebook. 'Mrs Cameron, when did you find out Mark was gay?'

'Soon after he arrived and stayed with us.'

'How did the topic come up?'

'He told me how much he liked my dress.' Anh turned to Jim. 'When I wore my national dress to the party. Remember? The one I brought with me when I came to Australia.'

Jim nodded, thinking of her journey to Australia in a small boat all those years ago, bringing with her a few precious possessions, including that special dress.

'We talked about clothes, and he said how some men like wearing women's clothes, but he didn't. I asked him why not and he said he was a straight gay man. He laughed then told me not to tell anyone.'

'I wish you'd told me,' Jim repeated, only to receive a withering look.

'Okay. He didn't want anyone to know. Did he say why?' Stone continued.

'He didn't want his family to find out. They'd disown him. He liked being here because there's a gay community in Sydney and for first time he felt he belonged. But it was still hard for him to admit he was gay.'

Stone nodded sympathetically. 'You mentioned he had a partner. Did he tell you his name?'

Anh thought carefully. 'I never met him, but he's older than Mark. His name is Darcy and he's an Aussie.'

Jim and Stone couldn't resist raising their eyebrows at the man's name but quickly lowered them. 'His job?' Stone asked, lighting a cigarette.

'Hairdresser or a coiffeur as Mark said he liked to be called.'

Jim knew Alan would be thinking the same. Such a cliché job for a gay man. Mentally, Jim slapped himself. He was doing exactly what Anh had said.

'Do you know where he worked?'

'Somewhere in Kings Cross.'

Stone made a note. 'Shouldn't be too hard to find him. I'll get Sergeant Ridge onto it. Sorry Anh, you've been most helpful … but can I ask one more question?'

'Of course.'

'Did Mark say anything to you about going to the Regent? Did he mention anyone in particular?'

Sipping her wine, Anh thought about her answer. 'I think he went there because of the other English people. He felt at home, but he didn't want to tell the men he was a homosexual because he was worried about what they might think.'

'It's 1995, not the 1970s,' Jim interrupted, scowling.

Alan glanced at Jim before repeating his question.

'There was the girl with the funny name and her boyfriend.' She turned to Jim. 'The girl Daniel and Josh told us about, and her friend, Trev? I can't think of anyone else.'

Stone stood up, placing his empty beer bottle on the coffee table. 'Anh. Thank you. You've been very helpful. I'm sorry we men are not as accepting as we should be, but if you do think of anything else, please contact me or tell Jim and he can get in touch. I'm very grateful for your assistance. We really do want to find out what happened to your friend.'

Jumping up, Anh hurried over to Alan and gave him a hug. 'So good to see you. Why not stay for dinner?'

'I'd love to but I can't.'

'That's a shame, but I will let you know if I think of anything.' She stepped back. 'Next time I see you, it will be with a nice girl. I don't like to think you're lonely.'

'Don't have enough time to be lonely,' Stone replied, before heading for the front door.

Dinner was a stilted affair. Jim and their sons glanced occasionally in Anh's direction. There had been no chance for Jim to explain to Daniel and Josh why their mother was in a strange mood. As soon as dinner was finished and the dishwasher loaded, both boys made a hasty retreat to their bedrooms, supposedly to do their homework. Anh sat with Jim watching television for a while, then took herself off to bed.

Jim remained in the lounge thinking how Anh's behaviour was out of character. They rarely had an argument. She was usually accommodating and accepting. He was aware he may have sounded homophobic, which he hadn't meant to, but she'd never gone to bed before him without saying goodnight.

He felt nervous as he walked into their bedroom. Perhaps she wanted a divorce? No. That wasn't possible. Surely? He knew he was overreacting but …?

Anh was in bed pretending to be asleep. Jim sat on her side of their bed and took her hand. 'What's the matter, darling? What have I done?'

His wife shook her head as much as it were possible being buried in the pillows. She squeezed his hand, raising her head. 'I just feel angry about Mark. The way society talks about gay men makes me angry. Mark was a human being and now he's dead. It's not your fault but the prejudice is very upsetting.'

She was right. 'I'm so sorry. I didn't realise. It's good that you've made me aware.'

'Darling, you are a wonderful man. It's because of what's happened to Mark. I'm being intolerant too.' Anh held out her arms and Jim snuggled into her body, awash with relief.

CHAPTER EIGHT

Excluding how upset Anh had been, the conversation between Alan and her the previous evening had given Jim an idea. From what little he knew of the Regent and its young crowd it would look odd if he and Anh hung around trying to eavesdrop or join in a conversation so he needed to find a young Pom who could do that for him, and he had just the man in mind.

Julian Butterworth was currently working at St Cuthbert's as an exchange teacher from England. He'd recently finished his teaching qualifications and had come to Sydney for work experience before returning to London to accept a fulltime position at a private, or public school as the Brits called them. His age and attitude were ideal as he could mingle with the Pommie drinkers in the pub without drawing attention to himself. There had been an enormous influx of British backpackers in the last year or so. Of course, Julian would have to agree to his suggestion of going to the pub and the reason why. He would inform Alan later, assuming Julian was willing to be involved.

The bell rang for morning break and Jim made his way down the noisy corridor to the staffroom. Teachers were making morning tea, huddled together for a quick chat about painful students, the sport results, and pending exams. Julian was in conversation with a couple of the younger teachers but seeing Jim give him a nod, excused himself.

'Do you mind coming to my office?' Jim asked quietly.

'Not at all, Mr Cameron. Hope I'm not in trouble?' Julian asked, grinning.

'Far from it. Just want to have a private chat.'

Julian followed Jim and sat down as instructed while Jim closed the door. 'Sorry, this seems a bit mysterious, but I want to ask for your help.'

'I'm all ears,' Julian responded.

'You have to keep this to yourself. This is nothing to do with the school. It's a private matter and I need your assistance. But *only* if you're willing.'

'Good lord. I'm intrigued. How can I help?'

'I'll be quick as I have a meeting shortly, but it's about a young English friend of ours, Mark Dunlop. He stayed with us when he first arrived. He was found dead, supposedly drowned, down at Bondi Beach on Saturday night.'

Julian stared at Jim, his long fringe flopping over his eyes. 'Jesus. Not an accident?'

'That's what we want to find out. Mark was over here for a new experience. He was from Liverpool.'

'Ah. A Scouser. No doubt selling drugs. Probably done in by the competition.' Julian laughed knowingly.

The scowl on Jim's face caused Julian to backtrack. 'Sorry. It's just that Scousers have a bit of a bad reputation in Blighty. I'm sure it doesn't apply to all of them.'

'Putting your prejudice aside, do you think you can help me find out what happened to Mark by going to the pub he used to frequent? You seem to be the right man for the job as you're young and English.' Jim knew he was taking a risk involving a member of staff but the distress and futility he felt meant he had to do something.

'Happy to be of assistance. Sorry if I was out of order regarding Liverpudlians.'

'It's okay. It's been an incredibly stressful and upsetting couple of days, so my sense of humour is a bit stretched. However, I have to stress that this must go no further. To put it bluntly, I'd be in deep shit if you say anything to anyone. But I have to assist Mark in any way possible.'

Julian smiled sympathetically. 'I'm flattered that you trust me.' He crossed his heart. 'Won't say a word.'

Jim's eyes wandered around his office while fidgeting with the items on his desk. 'I'd like you to go to the Regent Hotel down at Bondi and see if you can overhear anything which may give us a clue as to what was behind Mark's death …' He stopped. 'I've just found out … and I want you to keep this to yourself … Mark was gay.'

Julian opened his mouth to ask a question then closed it. Jim could see he wasn't sure how to react to the information. Perhaps Julian thought the inference was that *he* was a queer. It was hard to tell these days especially with the foppish hairstyles and pretty boy looks so many actors and singers cultivated.

'It shouldn't make any difference to anything, but many men are prejudiced against gays. There was a period in Sydney, not that long ago, when a lot of gays were murdered, and the AIDS epidemic hasn't helped their reputation,' Jim explained. 'The thing is Mark may have merely drowned, but perhaps he was attacked, or God forbid, he committed suicide.'

Julian listened to Jim's reasoning before asking, 'Aren't the police investigating his death?'

Jim thought for a moment. 'Yes. The police *are* involved but there's a difference between interviewing those who might lie or distort the truth rather than just chatting to the blokes in the pub who could let something slip. Your info can be a tip off for my detective mate, Alan Stone who's involved in the investigation. My wife and I don't believe Mark would have committed suicide which is what the police originally implied.

'Poor bugger. Where is this pub and what approach do you want me to take?'

'It's just back from Bondi Beach. Glenayr Avenue, but not exactly sure. The thing is, if Anh my wife and I went to the pub, we'd stand out. I want you to listen for any gossip about Mark's death. Who he mixed with. Friends, acquaintances.' Jim stood up with his hands splayed on the desk. 'To be honest, I have no idea what Mark got up to in his spare time, but having someone on the ground, so to speak, may … well you know what I mean.'

'I do,' Julian agreed.

'But of course, only do this if you feel comfortable. I'd totally understand if you say no.'

'And the school doesn't need to know?'

The guilty look on Jim's face answered the question. 'As I said, Mark stayed with us when he first came out from England and I feel I've let him down. He was a decent young chap but perhaps he got caught up with the wrong crowd. He was meant to go back to England and go to uni.' Jim scratched at his face. 'I just wish he'd told us if he was unhappy.'

Julian's silence caused Jim to wonder if he'd made a mistake asking for his help. 'I understand if you don't want to be involved …'

Julian held up his hand. 'More than happy to help. You want me to go to this pub and worm my way in so I can pick up any info regarding your nephew?'

'He wasn't my nephew. Just a friend who stayed with us. But yes, that's the idea.'

'And I don't mention I'm working at St Cuthbert's?'

'Yes. Just over here on holiday. Or have a temporary job.'

Julian nodded. 'Do I ask about scoring drugs?'

'No. Don't,' Jim stressed. 'Too dangerous. But if you could get chatting to the regulars and learn the names of those who knew Mark, that would be enough. And no mention of suicide! Are you sure you're happy to be involved?'

'Bit of espionage sounds good to me. Can I ask why you chose me?'

Jim pursed his lips. 'As I said, you're English, young, so won't look out of place and you seem pretty worldly to me, coming from London. I know I shouldn't take matters into my own hands, but I've worked with Alan before,' Jim said, wiggling his fingers around the word worked, 'and I think he'll understand. He knows what I'm like. I can't sit by and do nothing.'

'You've worked with him before?' Julian asked in surprise. 'How? When?'

'Let's put it this way. I've known him for a long time and we've been involved in a couple of investigations.'

'Jesus, Mr Cameron. You're a man of mystery. When do I start?'

'As soon as possible. I've heard the Poms go to the pub every night of the week and most of them are tradies. Don't know how they manage to get up in the morning.'

'Steady on. Remember we need the support of my fellow countrymen,' Julian said, sensing Jim's judgemental attitude.

'I know. I know,' Jim agreed. 'If you could go soon after school finishes that's when a lot of them should be at the pub. I'm happy to give you some cash to cover expenses.'

'Don't be daft,' Julian exclaimed. 'It'll be a nice change to go to a pub full of Brits who speak my language.'

Jim grinned. 'Well, let me know. Don't want you to be out of pocket.'

'She'll be right, mate,' Julian said in his best Aussie accent as he stood up to leave.

'If you change your mind, no hard feelings.'

The lunch bell rang but Jim stayed in his office as he wasn't in the mood to chat to the staff in the common room. He had so much on his mind and it wasn't all work related. He wondered if he should take leave, but Robert couldn't cope without him these days. Also, apart from Daphne and Julian, he didn't want anyone at the school to know about Mark's death.

Speak of the devil, Daphne peered around the door. 'Got a minute, Jim?'

'Of course. Of course.'

Daphne pulled up a chair and sat in front of Jim's desk smiling at him. 'Well. I've got a bit of news,' she pronounced, smoothing her skirt.

'Don't keep me in suspenders,' Jim encouraged, his mood lifted a little by Daphne's presence.

She suppressed a laugh. 'You must be feeling a little better if you can make a joke.'

'Just an act. Feel bloody awful ... and guilty.'

'Guilty? Why?'

'I wish I could have helped Mark more. Oh, to turn back the clock.'

'But you didn't know what was going to happen. I'm sure you and Anh took great care of him ... He was an adult after all.'

'As usual, wise words. Anyway, cheer me up with some useful information.'

'Well, Ray just rang to say the Regent has been on the radar for a while. It seems the pub is known to be the source of various drugs.'

'How does he know?' asked Jim.

'He didn't say, but it looks like Bondi is the place for ecstasy, speed and cocaine as well as marijuana. And, apparently Bondi is in competition with the Cross to be the centre of the drug trade.'

'But surely none of those drugs would kill a person. They're ... what are they called ...? Recreational drugs?'

'Yes, I think so. Perhaps Mark was selling, and he fell out with the suppliers?'

'Bloody hell, Daphne, I hope not,' Jim said, rubbing his eyes. 'If the police know about Bondi and drugs, why haven't they done anything about it?'

'I gather it's a work in progress. The Cross and its criminal activities probably take precedence.'

'Has Ray heard anything about a bloke called Trev? Trevor? He's been mentioned in relation to selling drugs at the Regent and is indirectly connected to Mark because he was friends with an Irish girl, Siobhan who is linked to Trevor.'

'Golly. Talk about a tangled web. Trevor?' Daphne grinned. 'I'll ask Ray. Do you know this man's surname?'

Jim shook his head. 'Anyway, please thank Ray for the information. It's good of him to get onto it so quickly.' Standing up, he asked, 'Does he prefer working at Kings Cross instead of Waverley?'

'A mixed bag. He liked working with Alan but felt he'd have more chance of promotion at the Cross.'

'An entertaining area to work,' Jim said, raising his eyebrows.

'Oh yes. Strippers, bikies, prostitutes, drug dealers. Lots of fun. On that note, I'd better get back to work.' Daphne rose from the chair as Jim walked around his desk to stand next to her. 'Thank you. You're a gem. So sorry if I seem a bit … out of sorts.'

'It's quite alright,' she reassured.

'And everything's alright with you?'

Daphne shook her head slightly. 'Don't see much of Ray at the moment. He seems terribly busy. But that's to be expected in his line of work.'

'No rest for the wicked.'

CHAPTER NINE

Julian decided to walk down to the Regent as it wasn't too far from the school and as it was a warm day he'd enjoy the view of the beach and its golden sand. It would give him time to work out his plan of action.

He'd dressed casually in Levi jeans, a Fred Perry T-shirt and Adidas Gazelle trainers in the hope the Brits would recognise him as English. Should he barge in and start chatting or hang back and look mysterious? He mocked himself for his thoughts. What would he do in a pub in London? Or, what would regulars do in Liverpool where he'd heard the crowd was friendlier? Despite their reputation for criminal activities, they were also known for a great sense of community and humour. But surely, not everyone at the Regent was going to be a Scouser?

He arrived at the pub by four-thirty, assuming the tradies would be present by then and he wasn't disappointed. The bar was full of navy blue and khaki work shirts, with logos of the construction companies on breast pockets and the occasional orange high-vis vest. The majority of the drinkers were young men, although there were a few women dotted amongst them.

Normally, Julian drank spirits but judging by the schooner glasses held in hardened hands, beer was the drink of choice. He doubted if the pub would sell Fullers London Pride so asked the barmaid for a recommendation. To his delight she too was from London, on a working holiday.

'The nearest thing to London Pride might be Reschs or Toohey's Old. I'm not really sure as most of the lads drink VB or New and I'm not a beer drinker.'

'No worries.' Julian grinned. 'I'll try a Reschs.' The barmaid smiled, pulling the schooner.

'Worked here long?' he asked.

'Couple of months. Heading home in a few weeks, but don't tell the boss.'

Julian drew a finger across his lips. 'I won't. Cheers.' He raised his glass at her before turning to face the crowd.

Where to position himself? Julian knew he couldn't immediately join a group. It just wasn't done, as his mother would have said. He wandered over to one of the large wooden pillars positioned around the public bar and nonchalantly leaned against one while listening to the various accents of the group nearest to him. There was a mixture of Scouse, Geordie and Scottish. Judging by their shirts and heavy work boots they were in the construction business and from their conversation it appeared they worked on the same building site in the CBD and the foreman was a fucking cunt.

'He's a fooken numpty,' a Scot pronounced. The others agreed, staring into their beer. What else could they add to such a true statement?

'Anoother?' the Scot suggested to his drinking partners.

While waiting for him to get the round, the others gazed at the growing crowd. One focused on Julian who was doing his best to seem content to be on his own.

Moving towards Julian, the man asked, 'Alright?'

Julian, recognising the Scouse accent, wasn't sure if the man was being friendly or antagonistic but he decided on friendly.

'Alright. You?'

'Fuck me. A bloody Southerner. What ya doin' here?' the man asked.

'Probably like you. On a working holiday. Julian,' he introduced.

'Steve. Been here long?'

'A few months. Arrived at the end of last year. First time I've spent Christmas on a beach. Bit different to home.'

The Scouser nodded and was about to ask another question when a few of his mates edged closer. Julian knew that they knew he wasn't one of them. His clothes alone indicated he wasn't a tradie. Let alone his accent.

'From the South? What's your graft?' a Geordie asked, stepping towards Julian.

Julian thought quickly. His answers would either alienate or make him acceptable.

'Yeah. London. But don't hold that against me. Managed to get a boring office job. Hoped to get a better one, but the Aussies don't seem too keen on Poms so had to take what I could get.'

His audience nodded in sympathy. The general consensus of opinion was most Aussies didn't like anyone from the UK, especially the English.

The Scot returned with a large tray of schooners. Everyone grabbed a glass.

'It's alright for them to go to England and take our jobs, but not the other way 'round,' the Geordie muttered. His comment was met with grunts of agreement.

Seeing Julian's nearly empty glass, Steve asked, 'What're you drinking?'

Julian hesitated. He knew if he took up the offer he'd be included in the rounds which were expensive, but it also meant he was accepted to some degree.

'A Reschs would be great. My round next.'

His response satisfied his new acquaintance and the tradie hurried off to buy Julian a beer.

After a few questions about what Julian was doing in Sydney, the chat returned to their wanker of a foreman. Once they'd vented their spleen, the conversation changed direction. Julian dropped his pretended interest in their work issues, because now the chat had become relevant.

'Hear about Mark?' one of the men asked.

'No. What 'appened?' asked the Geordie, glancing around the group.

''Aven't you 'eard?' another asked, smugly.

'Drowned down at Bondi. Sat'day night,' added another.

'Shit. Drowned? … 'E was a poofter,' the Geordie stated.

Julian noticed a couple of the men nudge each other.

'Carl, ya fuck knuckle, what the fuck's that's got to do with anything?'

'Fuck all,' Carl replied sheepishly. 'But he did have a queer friend.'

This gained a titter. 'Nowt so queer as folk,' was suggested to more laughs but when one said that Mark didn't deserve to die, the mood became subdued.

'Why would a homo come to a pub like this? It's not a fuckin' gay bar,' Carl whined. 'Probably heard it's full of Scousers. Love a bit of arse.'

'Shut yer gob, Morgo, ya Welsh twat.'

'Settle down, ya bellends,' commanded the Scouser who'd bought Julian a drink.

There was instant quiet. Julian was amazed by the power Steve had. He'd make a good teacher.

'What's up your arse, Stevo?' Morgo asked.

'Nothing,' Steve sneered, 'except a fucking big turd and you ain't going up there to find it.'

Everyone laughed while Morgo looked suitably admonished.

'Mark was good mates with Shiv. She must be gutted,' another tradie stated.

There were mutterings of agreement.

Julian could wait no longer. 'Who's Shiv?'

The men turned to him. 'What's it to you?' Morgo asked, trying to regain favour.

Julian shrugged. He picked up his nearly empty glass. 'Must be my round.'

Checking what they drank, he was glad to have an excuse to leave although he was eager to hear more. He realised he shouldn't sound too interested. He didn't want to appear like an off-duty copper.

It took him two trips to the bar to complete the order but judging by the thanks he received, he hadn't totally blotted his copy book. He wished he'd taken up Jim's offer of refunding his expenses but bugger it. Gaining acceptance was more important.

Unfortunately, the conversation had moved on from the girl called Shiv to football. Liverpool FC's last game was discussed with much animation by some of the Scousers while the Geordies sang the praises of Newcastle. The Scot, unable to compete as Scotland was not involved in the Premier League, remained silent as did Julian.

'Follow Union myself,' Julian admitted to the Scot who stared at Julian as if he'd asked to borrow an enormous sum of money. 'Ya wha?'

'Not a rugby fan then?' Julian realised he'd cocked up. 'Celtic or Rangers?'

After another scathing look at Julian, the Scot replied that Hearts was his team as he was from Edinburgh, not Glasgow. Julian was about to give up. Trying to have a chat with this bloke was too hard but as he was turning away the Scotsman said, 'Where you from? You sound fooken posh.'

'Posh? Fuck off.' He was about to say he lived in Notting Hill but changed it to Hackney. 'Julian,' he said, holding out his hand.

'Jimmy,' the Scot informed, shaking Julian's hand.

'Been here long?' they asked in unison, causing each other to laugh. It was a typical opening question when someone from the UK encountered a fellow countryman overseas.

'You first,' Julian said.

'About six months. Got another six to go if I want to stay that long. Bit over Sydney so might head up to Queensland and go fruit picking. Makes a change from bricklaying. What do you do to pay the bills?'

'Nothing exciting. Not sure what I want to do in the future,' Julian lied. He wondered how he could get the conversation back to the Shiv girl and her connection to Mark. 'Certainly don't want to end up like that poor bugger. Who was he?'

'Mark. Bit of a regular but didn't really get to know him.'

Jimmy was about to move away when he nudged Julian, muttering, 'That's the hen. The Irish lass. Siobhan.'

Following the direction of Jimmy's gaze, Julian could see the object of his attention. The girl was with a tall, lanky man who looked a few years older than her. She was dressed in the way his mother would have said was 'common' but her long red hair and nice figure diminished his mother's judgement slightly.

As she waited for her companion to order drinks, Julian watched her glance around the large bar. When she saw the group he was part of she frowned, whispered something to the man and walked quickly to the beer garden. The lanky bloke, once served, took the drinks outside.

Finishing his beer, Julian told Jimmy he was doing the off and left the pub. He'd come back tomorrow and with luck he'd 'bump into' the Irish girl, Siobhan, now he knew what she looked like. Plus, he'd broken into the crowd from the North.

CHAPTER TEN

The next morning Jim and Julian passed in the corridor, giving each other a cursory nod. No words were exchanged but as soon as Julian had a free period, he went into Jim's office.

Jim stopped writing and lifted his head. 'Anything to report?'

'Yes, Jim, I do.' Julian couldn't resist sounding smug.

Jim waited and Julian did the same.

Giving in, Jim asked brusquely, 'Are you going to tell me? I'm a bit snowed under.'

'Of course I am. Just adding to the excitement.'

'Julian, this is not a game. The whole situation is bloody awful so please don't mess me around.'

'Sorry, old chap. Should know better.' Julian launched into his report. 'I had a few drinks with a group of Scousers, Geordies and a Scotsman. Sounds like a joke …' then seeing the look on Jim's face, he tried to look serious. 'Wasn't a cheap night. Bought them a few beers so they'd accept me.'

Jim scratched his thick greying hair impatiently. 'And?'

'They talked a bit about Mark, but some of them didn't really know him, although he *was* seen as a regular. Some didn't know that Mark had drowned down at Bondi Beach and one of them said something about his being a poofter.'

As Jim didn't respond, Julian continued. 'They mentioned an Irish girl, Shiv, Siobhan, who was friendly with Mark. And the best thing is she came into the pub so I now know what she looks like. Actually, she's jolly pretty and has long red hair, but she was with some dodgy bloke, bit older than her. When she saw the chaps I was with she made the guy go outside. Looked like she didn't want to talk to any of them, or maybe it was because she was with that fella.'

'I think I know of the girl you mean. What happened then?'

'I left.'

'Why?'

'Well, I thought that now I know who she is I'll innocently attempt to meet her and if she succumbs to my charms then I may find out more. She's obviously a regular. Plus, I didn't want to overstay my welcome with the lads. I don't really fit in as I'm from London and they're from the North, but hopefully over time I will. I'll have to find out a bit more about Liverpool or Newcastle.'

Seeing Jim's puzzled expression, Julian explained, 'Most of the Scousers support Liverpool or Everton and the Geordies support Newcastle. I know sod all about football as I'm a rugby man so I need to hone up on a few facts so I can contribute to the conversation.'

'Ah. Fair enough.' Jim nodded. 'Thanks very much for doing this, Julian. You've certainly got your finger on the pulse. But don't go taking any risks ... Before I forget, the bloke with the Irish girl is probably Trevor. Our boys told us Mark had mentioned a 'Trev' and he's linked to Siobhan.'

'That was probably him!'

'Apparently, this Trev has something to do with drugs, maybe a dealer, so keep that in mind,' Jim warned.

'Will do. He didn't look particularly savoury. I thought I'd pop back to the Regent tonight, and with luck our little Irish lass will be there.'

'One more thing before you go, if I haven't told you already, a Pommie bloke rang the police on Saturday night to tell them about Mark and where they could find his body … so if you hear anything about him that would be really useful.'

'They don't know who he was?'

Jim shook his head. 'Well, as I keep saying, take care. And don't do anything I wouldn't do.'

'Yes, sir,' Julian replied, saluting.

While Julian was chatting to Jim, Alan Stone made his way to Kings Cross to meet up with his ex-colleague, the now Detective Ray O'Shea.

'Gidday Ray, it's been a while. Thanks for meeting me. How are you?' Stone greeted with an enthusiastic handshake. 'Looks like you've lost a bit of weight. Not that you needed to.'

Ray grinned. 'Blame Daphne. She watches me like a hawk. The days of eating rubbish are well and truly over.'

Laughing, Stone asked. 'Have you got a few minutes for a quick chat?' He looked around the reception area of Kings Cross Police Station. It was empty except for the desk sergeant. He assumed it wouldn't be this quiet later in the evening.

'Mate, of course. Let's go and grab a coffee. Plenty of places around here. Not like Waverley.'

The two sat outside at a café near the police station, opposite the El Alamein Fountain. Kings Cross was empty at this time of the day. The strip joints were closed and the pubs hadn't yet opened.

'Think I know why you're here,' Ray said, eyeing Stone's muffin over his coffee cup.

'Thought you might. Word travels quickly.'

'Sure does. Daphne told me she'd heard the news about Mark Dunlop from Jim. Drowned down at Bondi, although I gather it's not clear cut.'

'Yup. It may not be a simple case of skinny dipping after too many drinks.' Stone thoughtfully took a sip of his coffee. 'Jim's filled me in about Dunlop. You know he stayed at their place when he first arrived in Sydney?'

'Yeah. Daphne said Jim is really upset. Bit of a different reaction to the death of that bloke at St Cuthbert's.'

Stone nodded remembering the teacher who had been murdered in one of the school's boarding houses.

'It must be at least ten years ago, but no-one seemed upset by his death if my memory serves me right.' Ray grinned at the memory.

'A nasty piece of work. A little bit of power went a long way.' Stone put down his cup. 'According to one of the bouncers at the Regent, Dunlop was last seen leaving the pub with some chap but as there were lots of people coming and going he couldn't describe him except he might have been wearing work clothes. Oh, and when we checked out Dunlop's unit he had one of the latest mobile phones. Who the hell can afford one of those? We're trying to find out who he called and who called him but it's a bloody slow process.'

'So *how* did he die?' Ray asked, lowering his voice.

'Amphetamines.'

'Shit.'

'It may just be a simple case of drowning by misadventure, or suicide, but that seems unlikely from what Anh and Jim have said.'

Watching Stone take a bite of his muffin, Ray asked, 'Have you talked to the Bondi guys? They must have some idea who's involved.'

'Do you want some?' Stone asked, noting Ray's interest in the muffin and lifting up the plate, offered what remained. Ray shook his head with a sigh.

'Well, if you change your mind. Anyway. Yeah. Bondi contacted me at the beginning and said they'd received a phone call on Saturday night from a Pommie bloke who told them where Dunlop's body was but he didn't give his name which makes it all harder.'

'A public phone?'

'Yup. Hard to trace.' Stone leant back in his chair stretching his arms.

'Why ring but not leave a name?'

'Guilty conscience or just stumbled across the body? Someone who didn't want to get involved? The usual reaction. The only thing we know is the caller had a Pommie accent ... Unless it was someone who could imitate one.'

'Jesus,' Ray groaned.

Stone sighed. 'As Mark had taken hard drugs, it's more likely they would have come from someone in your area. Bondi may sell weed and party drugs but for a bloke to die, it looks more like organised crime.' Stone stared at Ray. 'There's more heavy drugs in the Cross than in Bondi.'

Ray agreed, saying, 'I'll ask around.'

'That'd be great. Gangs, bikies or anyone who has a history of drug dealing and known to be violent. Is there an informer you use who might have inside knowledge?' Stone pursed his lips. 'There's one more thing. Anh, you know Jim's wife, told us Mark was a homosexual. It may have no bearing on the matter, but after all those gay murders in the Eastern suburbs over the last ten years or so, we should be aware of every angle.'

'Fuck, yeah. I'll get onto it straight away,' Ray reassured.

'Must be a bit more exciting here than Waverley,' Stone stated.

'It is, but I miss the old days working with you.'

'That'll do. You'll have me in tears.'

'Anyway, I'll get back to you as soon as I hear anything. Better get back to the office.'

They drained the last of their coffee, stood up and shook hands.

'Cheers, Ray. Good to see you.'

'You too.'

CHAPTER ELEVEN

Once dinner was finished and Daniel and Josh had put the plates and utensils into the dishwasher, Jim indicated for them to return to the dining table. A flash of worry crossed their faces.

'There's nothing wrong, I'm just hoping you've remembered more about Mark or the names of anyone he knew?'

'Dad, we didn't go to the pub with him,' Daniel protested.

'Of course you didn't, but is there someone he told you about?' The boys shrugged.

'Come on, guys. There must be something you can remember?'

'Darling, don't get cross. It's not *their* fault what happened to Mark,' Anh called out from the kitchen.

Jim leant his head into his hands. 'I know. I know. Sorry guys, just want to get some idea about what he got up to and who he knew.'

They waited until Anh joined them at the table. 'Your father is right. If Mark was harmed on purpose we need to try and help the police work out who it was.'

The boys muttered their understanding, although Jim was aware they were looking at him through different eyes. He was normally easy going but lately he must seem stressed and angry.

Daniel glanced at Josh. 'He said there were lots of people at the pub who were from Liverpool.'

'Yes, yes. You've told me that before. Anything elsc?' Jim said impatiently.

'Did he name any of them?' Anh asked gently, frowning at Jim.

'Not really. Um. I think he said some of them were um Scousers and some were … I don't remember the other place,' Daniel tried to explain. 'Something like castle, but dunno if that's right.'

Jim's face lit up. 'Newcastle?'

'Yeah. Think so. Daaad,' Daniel whined, 'Mark was hard to understand.'

Agreeing with his son, Jim turned to Anh, 'Julian told me he spoke to men from Liverpool and Newcastle at the pub last night.'

'Who's Julian?' Josh asked.

'Just a man I know,' Jim replied. 'Did Mark ever mention taking drugs?'

'No!' both replied defensively.

'He said he got *hammered*. Didn't know what he meant till we asked him ... it means getting drunk,' Josh explained authoritatively.

Jim nearly laughed and was about to stop pestering his sons when Josh stared at his brother, saying, 'Wasn't there some guy who pissed him off? Sorry Mum.' Josh looked sheepishly at his mother.

'It's alright, darling. Keep going,' Anh reassured.

'He called this bloke the 'c' word.'

'Yes, yes. We know what you mean. Did he say why he used that word? Who was he referring to?' Jim persevered. 'How come Mark told you all this?'

The boys thought about his questions and Jim could see they were weighing up how to answer. 'You guys were out and Mark had been to the pub. He was pretty drunk,' Daniel explained.

'And you were still up when he got home?'

'Yeah. It wasn't that late.'

Jim didn't bother to respond to Daniel's excuse, instead asked them to continue.

'Um … Mark didn't want to do something this guy wanted him to do,' Daniel began again.

'Did Mark say what it was?'

'Nah.' Daniel shrugged.

'And he didn't say who he was talking to?'

Both boys shook their heads.

'When was this?'

The boys grimaced, trying to remember, then Daniel explained that it wasn't long before Mark moved out of their place.

Changing tack, Jim asked, 'Apart from that conversation, did Mark ever seem unhappy? As if something was really wrong? Did he say he wanted to go home?'

They wriggled on their seats thinking. 'Mark said he felt homesick sometimes, but he didn't want to go home. He liked being with us and living in Sydney.' Daniel kept thinking. 'He said something about wanting more money,'

'He wanted more money?' Jim repeated.

'Yeah,' his sons replied.

'Did he say why?'

'Nuh.'

'Bugger ... Thank you. You've both been a tremendous help.'

CHAPTER TWELVE

The Regent was filling with tradies and a few older regulars were already settled at tables when Julian walked in. *Wannabe* was playing at a moderate volume. Nothing like a bit of Spice Girls to put him in a positive mood. He'd made a plan. Somehow, he was going to talk to the Irish girl. It had to be a subtle meeting, accidental. He would use their both being from the same part of the world as a talking point. If she were from Northern Ireland then they might have more in common. With luck, his charm would work. Of course, she had to be in the pub for him to put his plan into action. Ordering the obligatory beer, Julian noticed a couple of the Scousers from the previous evening, already with drinks in hand. Should he join them? They might find it odd if he presumed he was part of their circle, but if he didn't join them he'd look like a snob.

After his beer was poured by the same English barmaid from the night before, he turned to face the growing crowd. Suddenly, Jimmy the Scot appeared at his elbow. 'Back again. Can't resist our scintillating company?' he asked sarcastically.

'Absolutely. Love the sparkling wit and repartee,' Julian scoffed. 'Buy you a beer?'

'Och aye. Cheers.'

The beer bought; they wandered over to the others.

'Alright?' Julian asked. Their dismissive grunts were puzzling. Were they annoyed by his arrival or had something he'd said or done pissed them off? He knew he couldn't ask outright as he didn't know them well enough. They'd tell him to mind his own effing business.

He stood quietly with Jimmy, watching those who entered the public bar. So far there had been no sign of Siobhan or the chap she'd been with the previous night, but it was early doors and she or they might still appear.

A member of the Pommie group was complaining loudly to his audience how the police had raided their flat the night before, searching for overstayers. 'They came at fucking midnight, knocking to wake the dead.'

Jimmy asked if the police had found anything 'incriminating' but apparently the police hadn't, and the guys in the flat were okay with their visas.

'Fucken coppers, fucken scrotes,' one exclaimed angrily, the others nodding vigorously at the injustice of it all.

Julian couldn't resist. 'Did the police actually raid their flat?'

'Yeah, happens all the time.' The tradie stared dismissively at Julian. 'Mates been taken to Villawood for overstaying their visa. Then sent home like bloody criminals. Thought being a Pom would come in handy 'specially as we made the bloody country.'

Jimmy nudged Julian with a knowing grin. 'That's Brian. Typical whingeing Pom.'

Julian gave Brian a sympathetic look. He realised how lucky he was with his situation at the school. He was about to commiserate when he saw the Irish girl enter the pub on her own and make her way to the bar.

'Just going for a tinkle,' Julian excused himself to no-one in particular and walked towards the bar. He waited till she'd received her drink and as she turned, nudged her with his elbow.

'Oh. I beg your pardon. Hope I didn't spill your drink?' Julian apologised with a concerned smile. He was struck by her beautiful skin. Not a blemish nor wrinkle and so pale. Quite different to the tanned Aussie girls.

The Irish girl looked up at him. 'No, I'm grand.'

'You certainly are,' Julian agreed. 'Are you sure I didn't spill your drink?' he repeated. 'Can I buy you another?'

She refused.

'You must be Irish.' Julian stated the obvious with a grin.

The girl paused. Julian could tell she was weighing him up, forcing him to think of his next move. 'This is a corny line, but do you come here often?'

She couldn't help but laugh. 'Oh, you smooth talker you.'

Julian gave her his most innocent look. 'You can't blame me for trying. The name's Julian but don't hold that against me.' He was nearly going to sing, "If I said you had a beautiful body would you hold it against me?", but decided he'd sound like a complete twat.

'Siobhan.' Her smile gave him hope but then her forehead crinkled into a frown. The tall, lanky man was standing next to her.

'What's going on?' he asked aggressively.

'Nothing,' she replied angrily. 'He offered to buy me a drink as he was after bumping into me.'

The man pulled himself up, equalling Julian's height. 'She doesn't need your drink. I get hers.'

Julian stared at him. 'Of course you do. You're a lucky man.'

The man didn't respond but grabbed Siobhan by the arm and led her away mumbling belligerently. Although Julian had originally wanted to talk to her because of the connection to Mark, he was beginning to feel sorry for her. This bloke was a creep and acted as if he owned her. And judging by Siobhan's reaction, she didn't seem particularly enamoured by his possessive attitude.

CHAPTER THIRTEEN

Julian was waiting impatiently outside Jim's office, his face lighting up when Jim finally arrived carrying his briefcase, a newspaper tucked under his arm.

'Come on in. You look like you've got something to tell me.'

'I do,' Julian said keenly.

Once the door was closed, Julian couldn't wait to tell Jim his news. He'd met the Irish girl, Siobhan, he told Jim proudly, and thought he'd made a connection. He'd also met the tall, lanky bugger who might be her boyfriend. A nasty prick but she seemed to do what he wanted, although it didn't look as if she liked him.

Instead of being excited by Julian's information, Jim seemed dismissive.

'Come on, Jim. She *knew* Mark! I've made a connection with her, and her dodgy boyfriend looks like a drug dealer.'

Jim rolled his eyes. 'Lots of people look like drug dealers.'

'Jesus, Mr Cameron, what's the matter? Wrong side of the bed? Thought you'd be pleased.' Julian was tempted to add he was being a miserable sod but didn't think it wise.

'Sorry, Julian. Feeling out of sorts ever since Mark died ...' His face brightened a little. 'That bloke sounds like the man my sons mentioned. Trev? Acts as if he's Siobhan's boyfriend.' Julian opened his mouth to confirm the description but Jim continued, 'Sorry, I've never been someone who just watches on. I have to take action. I suppose I feel jealous because I can't do much. It's like during the Vietnam war.'

'Vietnam. Did you go?' Julian asked in surprise.

'Yes.'

'Fuck. You'll have to tell me what it was like.'

'Another time. Excuse my grumpy manner.'

'Yeah. It must be hard,' Julian sympathised. 'But we *are* making progress. I'll go back to the Regent this afternoon. In our world it's not odd to go to the pub every day. I can't seem too interested in what's going on, but I think they're starting to accept me.'

'Good-oh.' Jim confirmed before adding, 'Alan Stone is keeping me in the loop. He's a detective with the Waverley Police. We go back a long way. There was a murder in the mid '80s, at this school in fact, but I first met him years ago in Rarotonga, when a girl died. He was over there from New Zealand.'

'Jesus, Jim. A murder at St Cuthbert's? Bloody hell.'

'Yes, so make sure you take care of yourself and don't do anything stupid when you're in the pub.'

'I won't. We should have a beer one night and you can tell me all about those past events. And Vietnam.'

'When we have a free moment.' Jim sighed.

Jim knew he'd been hard on Julian. It wasn't his fault Mark was dead. He was doing what he could to help, but sometimes the Londoner's cavalier manner was irritating. It seemed like a game to him. The trouble was, he needed Julian's assistance.

The trill of the phone ringing refocused his thoughts. Wearily, he picked up the receiver. 'Cameron speaking.'

'Gidday, Jim. Alan.'

Although Stone had nothing substantial to tell Jim regarding Mark, he'd been in touch with Ray O'Shea at Kings Cross station, and the police at Bondi. Jim felt grateful. It was good to know the police were doing their best. He wondered if he should tell Alan he'd engaged Julian to assist in the investigation. He dithered. 'Um. Not sure if this is correct procedure, but there's a young Brit working at the school … and I asked him if he could go to the Regent and find out what he can. … He's already given me some information.'

Stone's silence urged Jim to explain his motive. 'I thought that as Julian's young and English, and most of the backpackers who drink there are too, he may get to know them and learn something about Mark.'

83

The continued silence at the other end of the phone confirmed his concern that Alan disapproved of his involving Julian. Finally, Stone responded. 'Not sure that's a good idea, Jim. Especially if he's asking questions.'

Jim groaned. 'I know, but I feel so powerless. No good my going to the pub. Who'd talk to me? Far too old for Julian's crowd. I have warned him to keep a low profile. Just listen to the gossip.'

'I understand your need to take action but perhaps it's better to leave it to the police. We know what we're doing.'

'I know. I know. I'm sorry. But I can't just sit back and do nothing.'

'That's what you said about Vietnam when we first met,' Stone reminded. 'And Vietnam didn't work out well.'

'Yeah, yeah. Alright. Shall I tell him to stop going?'

Instead, Stone asked, 'Do you think this bloke *can* take care of himself? If so, reinforce his keeping a low profile as I'd hate anything to happen to him. That's if Mark's death wasn't suicide ... and I suppose having someone in the pub could be useful.'

Relieved by Stone's change in attitude, Jim said, 'Quite. That was my thinking. Julian's from London so he's not from some naive backwater. I'll talk to him again and stress the possible dangers involved ... He's already met the Irish girl, Siobhan who

Daniel and Josh told Anh and me about. She was friends with Mark, and her bloke, Trev, is a possible drug dealer.'

'Great. Let me know if he finds out anything more.'

'Will do.'

'Right. Pity about the circumstances but it's good to have Ray back in the fold. Old times.'

The bell rang for recess and the majority of teachers rushed into the staffroom. Jim did the same but in search of Julian, rather than a cup of tea.

'A quick word?' Jim asked, nodding towards a gap in the crowd of teachers.

Julian followed. 'What's up?'

Jim peered around to see if anyone was listening before saying, 'I've just spoken to Alan Stone, the detective I've mentioned. Told him you're trying to find out information in the Regent and that you've met the Irish girl and her bloke. He's worried it's too dangerous ... however, he did concede it'd be handy to have an ear to the ground.'

The Londoner seemed relieved when he heard Jim's final statement. 'Mr Cameron, I think I can handle myself. To be honest, I want to be involved, risks and all.'

'That's really good of you.'

85

'*No worries, mate.*' Julian answered, attempting an Aussie accent. Jim gave a half-hearted grin. 'I promise I won't do anything stupid, and I'll let you know as soon as I learn anything new.'

Jim left Julian to make whatever it was he drank for morning tea.

CHAPTER FOURTEEN

Julian was excited. Siobhan was the focus of his visit to the pub and he was preoccupied with how he could get her by herself. The lanky prick was the problem.

He bought a beer, enjoying Pulp singing *Common People.* He could see Jimmy standing near the pool table with some of the Scousers and two chaps he didn't recognise but judging by their haircuts, clothes and pale complexions he assumed they were from home. *Just off the boat.*

'Alright?' Julian asked the Scotsman who gave a curt nod, not bothering to introduce him to the new arrivals. Miserable sod, Julian thought, but despite his irritation he maintained his aura of amiability and greeted the group.

Keeping half an ear on the conversation which revolved around the new arrivals' stories of their stop-over in Bangkok; the lady boys, the strip clubs, and the amazing feats the girls performed with their vaginas, Julian kept his eye on the growing group. The rapt audience nodded knowingly and interjected with similar tales of their time in Thailand.

More beers were consumed, but this time Julian kept to himself. He didn't want to look like he was currying favour by buying large rounds, especially as he wasn't a fully accepted member of this circle. They were Northerners while he was a Southerner. England had always been divided by regions, wealth and accents, but Maggie Thatcher had made the division even worse. He shook his head to remove her image. Julian could understand why the Scousers were against those from London as their once great city of Liverpool had been ruined by Tory policies which favoured the South.

The beer had its usual annoying effect on his bladder, causing him to make his way to the gents. As he neared the toilets, he saw Siobhan standing by herself next to the cigarette machine. He couldn't believe his luck as he hadn't seen her come in but here was his chance.

'Hello again,' Julian greeted, sidling up to her.

She jerked in surprise. 'Oh, hello. Trying to get this effing machine to work.'

'Let me help you.'

'Grand.' She stood aside to let Julian take control.

To his relief, a packet of Winfield Blue fell into the tray and with a flourish he handed it to her. Although he was eager to go to the loo this was too good an opportunity to give up. 'Would you like a drink?'

She hesitated, glancing quickly around the bar before answering that she would.

'Stay here and I'll be back in a jiffy.' Julian began to walk away then stopped, realising he didn't know what she drank. He mimicked drinking with a questioning look on his face. A beer was mouthed.

Please don't let there be a queue, he begged the gods and was soon back with their drinks. To his relief, Siobhan was still waiting for him next to the cigarette machine.

Now he had found her, Julian wasn't sure what he was going to say. Of course, he wanted to find out about her friendship with Mark but how to broach the subject?

'Shall we find a seat?' he asked hopefully and seeing a free table led her over to it, quickly placing the beers down, and pulling out a chair for her.

Once Siobhan was seated, Julian excused himself and dashed to the toilet. Sighing as he relieved himself, and double checking he'd done up his fly, he hurried back. He noticed how sad she looked. Was she about to cry?

'You alright?' he asked.

Quickly shaking her head, Siobhan looked up at him, forcing a smile.

'Been in Sydney long?' he asked, conscious of his lack of originality but he didn't want to appear to be prying.

'A couple of years. What about you?'

'Not long. Came out at the end of last year so I could teach at a school in Sydney.' Julian froze. He shouldn't have said he was a teacher and definitely shouldn't tell her where.

'Which school?' she asked.

'Oh, you wouldn't know it. Miles away. After a couple of days I decided it wasn't the place for me. Got a boring job in the city. Office work.'

'Where do you live?'

Bloody hell. He couldn't tell her he was in a flat in one of the school's boarding houses. A suburb, quick, a suburb? 'Kings Cross,' he blurted out.

'Oh. Know it well. Where abouts?'

'Just behind the station.'

'Why don't you drink in the Cross? Lots of pubs there.'

This was turning into a nightmare. Julian explained how he liked coming to Bondi as there were lots of his fellow countrymen. Made him feel at home. Smiling, he said, 'Anyway, enough about me. What's life been like for you living here?' He was desperate to change the focus onto her, especially as there were lots of Brits living in the Cross and his reason for drinking in the Regent didn't hold much water.

Siobhan didn't answer immediately, but seeing her unwrap the packet of cigarettes, he breathed easier. Offering him one, she lit it before taking out one for herself.

'I came here because I wanted to get away. I'm from Belfast and although things aren't as bad as they were, I wanted to go somewhere where there isn't all that religious crap. Neighbours against neighbours. The police watching your every move.'

'Understandable,' Julian sympathised, thinking how hard it must be living in such a small city and having The Troubles constantly in one's thoughts. 'But how do you like it here? After London, I find it a bit small. Parochial, if I'm being honest.'

Siobhan waggled her head. 'Know what you mean, but Australia doesn't seem to have the same religious rubbish and the people are friendly. More opportunities.'

'Doing what?' Julian asked, without thinking.

Her face clouded. 'Oh. I … Well, some of the people I've met through my job seem to have ways of making money.'

'Tell me how? I wouldn't mind earning a bit of extra cash.'

'That's for me to know and you to find out,' she answered with a sly grin.

He thought it better to change the subject and leaned forward. 'Do you have a boyfriend? I'd hate to be stepping on someone else's toes?'

Siobhan's brow wrinkled. 'No, I don't. There was a fella I was good friends with but …'

'But?'

'Don't really want to talk about it. He died recently.'

'I'm sorry. How awful. Are you alright?'

Siobhan's face drooped and her eyes filled with tears. She brushed them away with a clenched fist, smudging her mascara.

'I know I shouldn't ask, but how did he die?' Julian crossed his fingers, willing her to open up.

'He drowned down at Bondi Beach.'

Julian remained silent. He didn't want to interrupt her revelations. Would she mention Mark? Suddenly, Siobhan stood up. 'Sorry, I'd better go. Meeting someone.'

'Oh shit. Didn't mean to hold you up.' Julian rose from his chair. 'Be lovely to see you again. Can I call you?'

She hesitated then reached inside her bag, hastily pulling out a pen and paper. 'Here's my phone number,' she said, scrawling the digits. 'If I don't answer, try again. It can be hard sometimes. Leave a message.'

Julian took the piece of paper, placing it into his jean's pocket. As he watched her walk away, he could see the tall, lanky man at the bar following her movements with a scowl on his pasty face. Siobhan's reaction to him was not one of affection, more of reluctant acquiescence. It was clear this man had a hold over her.

CHAPTER FIFTEEN

Julian was in two minds. Should he head back to Churchill House or stay at the pub and maybe find out more? He found it odd that one of the boarding houses at St Cuthbert's was named after a British Prime Minister while all the others were named after previous Australian political leaders. No doubt something to do with World War II.

It was nice being amongst his own, and it *was* Friday night after all, except he had to supervise sport the next day. He'd found the English and Aussie humour quite different and there'd been times when joking with his Australian colleagues his levity had fallen flat. Even Jim Cameron whom he respected, had a serious side which made communication occasionally strained.

'No luck with our Siobhan?' Brian asked smugly, as Julian hovered at the periphery of his recently acquired group of mates.

'Luck? No. There's some bloke who's always in the way.' Julian sighed dramatically, nodding towards the lanky man standing possessively next to her.

The Scouser followed his gaze. 'That fuckin' twat. Treats her like shit. Thinks he's the dog's bollocks. But wouldn't want to get on his bad side. Got mates in all the wrong places.'

'Wrong places?' Julian asked neutrally.

'Yeah. He's in with all the drug dealers. The whole pub knows. That's why Siobhan, the lass you're trying to …' Brian laughed, 'does what he wants.'

Julian frowned, running his fingers across his long fringe. 'And there was me thinking she's a sweet and innocent flower.'

The only woman in the group of lads, and was clearly eavesdropping, joined in, 'My arse. She likes a bit of you know what, that's how he got her.'

Brian nodded. 'Twists her 'round his little finger. Or his little dick.'

'And you wish it was your little dick, don't you Mister Boylan?' she said, nudging Julian.

'Shut up, Shaz. What the fuck do you know? Just cos you're from Blackpool, you think *you're* the dog's bollocks.'

Shaz smirked knowingly at Julian who obliged her with a grin before he asked Brian, 'Who is this charmer? … Not you,' Julian said, looking apologetically at Shaz. 'Although I'm sure you *are* charming.' She beamed and fluffed up her hair.

'Fucken Trev. Thinks he's God's gift cos he supplies a bit of weed and coke,' Brian explained, clearly glad to return the conversation to the man in question.

Julian turned to look again at Siobhan's companion. 'Well, our Trev ain't the best-looking geezer.'

Steve who'd bought Julian a beer on his first night in the pub was listening with interest to the chat, stated, 'Fuck no. Only gets the girls cos of his gear.' Julian remembered how Steve had controlled the conversation that night.

The tradie stepped a little closer. 'Don't say I told you, wouldn't want to get meself bumped off, but word has it … because she got *chummy* with that Scouser, he ended up dead.'

'Which one?' Julian asked innocently.

'Mark.'

'Jesus. Because he was a Scouser?'

'No, ya bellend. Because of the Irish lass. Siobhan.'

'Fuck. Because he knew her he got himself killed?'

'I reckon.'

Julian was lost for words. It was as Jim had warned him. This whole situation was far more serious than he'd thought. Should he ask Steve if Siobhan was someone to avoid as she was associated with Trevor?

'This Trev guy looks older than Siobhan. Are they really going out?' Julian asked cautiously.

Steve thought for a moment. 'He makes out she's his girlfriend, but I doubt it … Imagine shaggin' 'im? He's got mates in the Cross. Own strip joints. Know what I mean?'

'Jesus. He owns strip joints?'

'Noooo. His connections.' Steve wiggled his fingers around the last word. 'He's got to get his drugs from somewhere. They're a pretty powerful bunch. Friends in high places from what I've heard.'

'Blimey,' Julian exclaimed. He began to doubt whether he should be helping Jim, but on the other hand, it was exciting. 'I'd better forget about my interest in the pretty Siobhan.'

'Yeah. Wouldn't go there. Too risky. As I said, look what happened to the woofter chappie, Mark.'

Before Julian dared ask for more information, the sound of glass breaking and raised voices could be heard. Everyone looked around for the source of the noise. Trev was holding a jagged schooner glass and using it to threaten one of the punters. Within seconds a couple of security guards dashed over. A heavily tattooed Māori bouncer grabbed Trev's wrist causing what was left of the glass to fall from his hand with a smash, while the other bouncer held back the subject of Trev's anger.

The bar had gone quiet, all clutching their drinks, fascinated by the unfolding events. Trev raised his hands in submission, and Julian could see that Siobhan had stepped away from the affray and was trying to appear as if she had no idea who Trev was. Unfortunately, her ploy didn't work and both she and Trev were escorted to the exit. The Māori bouncers, now accompanied by the manager, took them outside, but to Julian's surprise, within a couple of minutes Trev returned.

What the …? Julian couldn't believe he was allowed back in. What power did he have?

As Trev walked slowly back to the bar to buy another beer, every face was watching, some raising their eyebrows at each other as if to say, told you so. He downed his beer in a few gulps then sauntered out of the pub.

Steve grinned at Julian. 'See. Trev has friends in high places.'

'But where's Siobhan?'

'She'll have gone to work.'

Siobhan was waiting outside while Trev was giving his unsubtle middle finger to the pub and its occupants. Once he reappeared, he hailed a taxi and they both got in. Siobhan sat in the back, her arms folded tightly, a sullen look on her face. The driver soon gave up any attempt at conversation with Trev who was sitting in the passenger seat. His monosyllabic grunts warned the driver to shut his mouth.

Once the taxi had stopped outside an older block of units halfway between Bondi and Rose Bay, Trev thrust some cash at the driver while Siobhan got out of the car slamming the door then running to the entrance of the building. Trev ran after her, grabbing her arm before she had a chance to enter the foyer.

'What the fuck's wrong with you?' he yelled into her face.

'Nothing,' she yelled back.

'Whad'ya mean, nothing? You're acting like a bitch.'

'Me? You're the right eejit who loves glassing people. We're fucken lucky we didn't get barred.'

'Speak fuckin' English.'

'Oh, piss off.'

Her mind whirred. Trev was in a foul mood and the last thing she needed was a black eye, but deciding this would be the last time she ever spoke to the tosser she wanted to ask him about Mark. Through clenched teeth she enunciated, 'Let me ask you in English so you can understand. Did-you-have-anything-to do-with-Mark-Dunlop's-death?'

Trev stepped backwards. 'What the fuck? You think I killed him?'

'Everyone knows you hated him. You're jealous of anyone who talks to me. Wouldn't put it past you.'

'Jesus Christ! You're so up yourself you think I'd bump off some stupid gay Pommie idiot because …'

'Yes, ya gobshite,' Siobhan interrupted. 'Because we were friends, and you didn't like it.' Siobhan spat, her saliva hitting his cheek. Trev raised his arm, hesitated then dropped his fist. He wiped his face and flung the dribble back at her.

'You're not my fucken boss,' Siobhan snarled through gritted teeth, ignoring the spit hanging on her blouse. 'I can talk to whoever I want, and you can't do anything about it. I don't need you.' She turned away to open the door to the building, then swivelled around. 'I know stuff about you so don't you dare come near me again. Unless you want the police to be knocking at your door.'

Trev stood still. 'Don't you fuckin' threaten me. One phone call from me will see you out of the fuckin' country. Back to boring bloody Ireland.'

'Go ahead. But there'll still be time for me to tell the police all about your little secrets.' She could see his mind ticking over and his anger fading to worry. 'Why don't you just fuck off. Ya tool.'

'You're nothing but a fucking slut,' he shouted as he took one last look at her and stormed off back to the street, searching for a passing taxi.

Safe behind the glass door, she watched till she was sure he'd gone. It was now time for her to go to work.

CHAPTER SIXTEEN

Standing anxiously in front of the bedroom mirror, Jim asked Anh if he looked the part. Suggesting he twirl around, she stepped backwards to check his appearance. 'You look great, casual but not too casual. You'll fit in well.'

'So I won't be obvious?'

'No, but I'm still not sure why you and Alan are going to the Regent tonight when Julian is doing a great job of mixing with everyone and he's found out all sorts of things. You've been saying it's better if only goes as he's a similar age to Mark and the others.'

Looking at himself in the mirror, Jim contemplated his reply to Anh's logic. 'I know. It's just … it's just that I feel the need to be proactive. Julian has been amazing, getting to know the Pommie tradies and the Irish girl, but it's frustrating waiting for his news. You know what I'm like. I have to do something.'

Anh stepped towards her husband and put her arms around him. 'You're a good man. Just be careful.'

'I promise.'

Jim and Stone had decided to go to the Regent as it wouldn't seem odd if a couple of older guys turned up for a few drinks on a Saturday night; it was a night when lots of people went to the pub, although neither wanted to give away their profession nor draw attention to themselves. Julian had been informed that as they were attending the Regent, it would be better if he didn't and he was happy to oblige. He needed a breather from the intrigue for at least one night.

Arriving together, Jim and Alan scanned the large, crowded public bar, deciding on a suitable place to stand. The pool tables offered a neutral territory and with drinks in hand, they waited till one of the tables became free and quickly deposited a coin on the timber edge to secure their place in the line.

'Fancy a foursome?'

Alan and Jim twisted around. 'What?'

A bearded man stood nearby grinning. It quickly dawned on them he was taking the piss. Yes. They would be delighted to have a foursome.

After introducing himself as Terry or Tel or Tezza or Tex, he said, 'Call me anything but don't call me late for a schooner.' Terry guffawed at his own joke while his mate stared blankly and shrugged at Jim and Alan. Terry, explaining he was from Bristol, introduced his offsider, 'This is Scotty. He's a bloody Aussie, so you'll understand him.'

They all laughed and shook hands.

Terry handed out the cues and the game began but not before complaining how he wished there were more snooker rooms in Sydney. Jim and Alan could only shrug, while Scott groaned as if he'd heard this whinge many times before.

A few shots later, the conversation switched to what Jim and Alan did for a crust. Both glanced surreptitiously at each other. 'Computers,' Jim replied, and Alan muttered in agreement.

'Jeez,' Scotty said. 'No bloody idea how they work.'

'Neither do we,' Alan agreed, theatrically.

To their relief, the talk about jobs ended as the game required concentration. Jim was lining up his cue hoping to sink a tricky ball when a bloke suddenly stood next to the pool table. Distracted by the intruder, Jim looked up, delaying his shot. Shocked, he remembered Julian's description of the Irish girl's companion. This bloke could be the same man. Skinny, tall and definitely not handsome.

'Help you?' Jim asked, frowning.

'How long you gonna be?' the man asked.

'Shouldn't be too long,' Jim responded. 'We'll let you know when we've finished.' He took his shot, missing the pocket.

The lanky man didn't move away.

Terry scowled at the intruder before sinking his ball. He failed at the next shot and handed his cue to Scott. 'Trev, bugger off. Can't concentrate with you hanging 'round.'

'Haven't seen you in here before,' Trev accused, staring at Jim then at Stone.

'It's a free country,' Stone said, walking around the pool table to take aim from the other side.

Trev cocked his head as he watched Stone line up his cue. 'You a cop?' he asked.

Alan Stone paused, lifting up his head. 'Trying to put me off my game, mate?'

'Well, are you?'

'No. I'm fucking not. What's your problem? We came in for a quiet game but it's a bit hard with you asking stupid questions. Why don't you piss off? And as my friend here said, we'll let you know when we've finished.' Alan lined up his shot again.

Terry and Scott were standing back, watching the interaction with interest. Terry's expression showed he was pleased by Stone's attitude to Trev and Jim observed Scott giving Terry a subtle elbow.

Trev thought for a few seconds then swaggered off, his body language indicating they could all get fucked.

'Jesus, who was that prick?' Alan asked their new acquaintances. The two men glanced at each other. 'Trev. Trevor

Pearce. Thinks he owns the bloody pub.' Scott stopped, and Jim could see his reluctance to say anything more. This Trev bloke obviously had power.

'Let's finish the game before we're interrupted again,' Jim suggested, beckoning to Terry and Scott. He was relieved when they repositioned themselves around the table.

The game continued with Terry and Scott the winners. No-one wanted to tell Trev the game was over. They all knew he had no interest in playing pool.

'Can we buy you guys a beer?' Jim asked, before their pool companions had the chance to leave.

'Wouldn't say no,' Terry replied, and Scott nodded. Once served, each man stood with their beer, aimlessly peering around the bar. Jim wanted to ask their two guests what they knew about Trev but felt he should leave the questioning to Alan. He trusted his friend's investigative ability and was happy to let Alan take the lead.

'Sorry about that,' Stone apologised. 'Don't know what it is about me, but I often get asked if I'm a cop. Maybe 'cos I'm tall and ugly.'

Scott laughed. 'But you're a Kiwi so why would anyone think you're a cop?'

'Didn't think I still had an accent,' Stone uttered in surprise. 'And ... *excuse me* ... why shouldn't Kiwis have jobs with the police?'

'Sorry, mate. Just 'round here, most Kiwis are dealing drugs.'

'Really? Is Trev a Kiwi?'

'No. He's an Aussie. Just having you on.'

Jim and Alan forced a grin, both hoping Scott would reveal something useful but Terry interrupted, asking if anyone wanted another beer.

'Good idea,' Alan agreed. 'Fancy another, Jimbo? Or do you have to get home to the ball and chain?'

'Careful, mate. I'm me own boss,' Jim stated, grinning at Scott in an attempt to appear macho.

'Yeah, right. My round next,' Alan promised. 'This bloke, Trev, seems a real pain in the arse,' he complained to Scott once Terry had gone to the bar.

Scott peered around to see if anyone was listening. 'Yeah. He's a real hard case. Cos he's in with some of the dealers, thinks he's above the law. And, he thinks he owns the Irish chick, Siobhan. Never lets anyone near her. Don't know how she can stand him. He's a fucking prick.'

'Why on earth does she go out with him?' Jim couldn't resist asking.

Scott rubbed the side of his nose with one finger and winked.

Jim nodded his understanding.

'She was friends with that English guy. The one who drowned down at Bondi,' Scott continued.

'Oh, the one on the news the other day?' Jim's heart began to race. Scott must be referring to Mark. 'Did you know him?'

'Nah. Not really. Just another Pom in the pub. Seemed okay, although some blokes thought he was a poof.' Scott paused, before admitting, 'Wouldn't mind Siobhan meself but means getting past bloody Trev.'

The revelations came to a stop with Terry's return.

CHAPTER SEVENTEEN

As arranged after leaving the Regent on Saturday night, Detective Stone walked down the familiar corridor to Jim's office first thing on Monday morning. Memories flooded back; the teacher lying in his bed, dead. He wondered if any of the other teachers present at the time were still working at St Cuthbert's?

Jim was waiting in the doorway to his office and standing next to him was Daphne. Stone flushed with pleasure at seeing the headmaster's assistant again. His occasional contact with Ray O'Shea, and of course with Jim, had kept him in the loop to some degree but it had been ages since he'd actually seen her.

Forgetting he was in a school corridor with students and teachers passing, Stone rushed up to her holding out his arms. 'Daphne! So great to see you again. It's been too long. You look wonderful.'

'Alan. So good to see you too. You look just the same. Handsome as ever,' Daphne complimented, throwing her arms around him. They separated, beaming at each other.

'Come in, come in,' Jim urged, as he'd noticed the glances they were getting from students, and especially from the teachers who walked past. Stone realised how quickly the gossip would start.

Jim shut the door firmly and the three sat down. Although it was great to see Daphne again, Stone inwardly questioned her presence.

'It's just like the old days,' she said, smiling at him.

'Alan, you're probably wondering why I've asked Daphne to join us?'

'I'm sure there's a good reason. It's great to see you even without one,' Stone gushed.

Jim turned to Daphne. 'I'll let you explain.'

'Thanks, Jim. Well … I know you've caught up with Ray, but this is about the backpacker who's staying with us at the moment, and he's from the UK and has been to the Regent a few times as it's reasonably near to our place. Turns out Sean vaguely knew Mark. I only found out yesterday when I got talking to him about Mark's death. I feel a bit remiss that I didn't ask him before. He told me about Mark's drowning.' Daphne looked apologetically at both men.

'It's okay. Is he a relative?' Stone asked.

'No. It's a bit like Jim and Anh putting up Mark. I got a call from a friend I met years ago when I lived in London, and she asked if we could have Sean for a little while till he sorted himself out. He hasn't been with us for long. Sydney seems to be the flavour of the month these days for young Poms.'

'How's Ray taken to having a lodger?' Stone enquired.

'He's fine but so busy we hardly see him. To be honest, it's nice to have the company now the kids have moved out.

'I can imagine,' Stone sympathised, glancing at Jim before returning his eyes to Daphne. 'Jim and I did a recce at the Regent on Saturday night and got chatting to a couple of the regulars. Gathered a little bit of info.' Stone paused, unsure how much to share with Daphne. 'Ray may have told you I asked him if he knows about anyone in the Cross who has connections with the Regent. Drug dealers in particular.'

Jim, listening closely, joined in. 'We now know Mark was friends with an Irish girl called Siobhan and she's associated with a dodgy character, Trevor Pearce who we believe is a drug dealer in the Regent. Do you think you could ask your guest … um, Sean, if he's ever met Trevor, Trev, and if he's heard anything which connects him to Mark?'

Daphne agreed then asked, 'I thought Mark drowned but you seem to be implying drugs are involved?' Their silence caused Daphne to shake her head. 'So not just a simple case of drowning?'

'No. Mark had a large amount of drugs in his body,' Stone explained, realising he was wrong in assuming Ray would have

109

told Daphne about their catch up. The fact that Ray hadn't mentioned it to her seemed odd. Out of character.

Stone was about to stress how Sean shouldn't take any risks, when there was a knock and a young man put his head around the door. Was this guy old enough to be a teacher? Stone wondered as the man entered the office.

'Come in, come in,' Jim welcomed, introducing Julian Butterworth to Detective Alan Stone. Daphne who was about to leave, watched the two shake hands.

'Hello Julian,' she greeted.

He grinned in surprise, clearly unsure what to say in the presence of the Headmaster's assistant.

Sensing the awkward situation, Jim briefly explained Julian's involvement and how Daphne too was connected to the investigation. He stressed the need to keep this to themselves.

With a benign smile, Daphne took her leave.

'It's good to meet you, Julian,' Stone said. 'Thanks for your assistance. Jim's been keeping me in the loop as to what you've been doing. Why don't we fill you in on *our* attempt to learn about the goings on at the Regent?'

'Please do. From what Jim's told me about Mark, we need to do him justice.'

Julian's rather obsequious manner caused Stone to question the man's sincerity but as Jim had asked him to assist, he had to trust his mate's judgement

'It was an interesting evening,' Jim began, relating the conversation he and Alan had had with a couple of the locals and the surprising arrival of Trevor Pearce at the pool table.

'My God. This really is a whodunit,' Julian enthused, then seeing the expression on Jim's face, muttered a quick sorry.

'It's alright, mate. It appears that Mark's friendship with Siobhan put him at odds with this Pearce bloke. Very possessive. Seems he *is* a dealer and rumour has it Siobhan is partial to a bit of cocaine which could be why she's under his thumb.'

Julian's raised eyebrows showed he understood Jim's theory. 'And because Siobhan was close to Mark, her dealer mate *done him in.*'

Jim shrugged. 'We don't really know, but it is a possibility.'

'Yeah. I think it could be,' Julian stated. 'What you've told me reinforces what I've heard. And from what I saw the other night, Trev is a bloody nasty piece of work. Even though Mark was gay, Trev didn't like anyone getting close to her. Certainly wouldn't like to be his girlfriend.' Julian pushed fingers through his dark wavy hair exposing his forehead. 'As I've had a night or two off, how about I go back to the pub tonight and see if Siobhan is there?' He grinned. 'I got the impression she rather fancies me.'

'Julian, you have to take this seriously. These people are deadly,' Jim warned.

Stone, who'd been listening closely to the conversation, butted in. 'People have been killed for a lot less than drugs and money.'

'I don't think you should go to the pub again,' Jim said firmly.

Julian's demeanour changed. 'I know. I know. But I'll be fine. Remember I grew up in London. Won't do anything stupid. I'll keep an eye out for our Irish lass and with luck pick up more info from the regulars. Have managed to build up a bit of rapport, despite my being from the South of England.'

'What's that got to do with anything?' Stone asked.

'The infamous divide in Britain. North and South. Most of the guys in the pub are from the North. Liverpool, Newcastle, Manchester and a couple from Scotland.'

'Bit like the divide in New Zealand, North Island and South Island,' Stone compared.

'Probably,' Julian doubted. 'You a Kiwi? Thought you sounded different. Been here long?'

'Quite a while. You know Jim and I met years ago in Rarotonga when I was working with the New Zealand Police?'

'Ah yes. Jim told me. Sounds like the two of you have quite a history together.'

'We do.' Stone paused, looking at Jim. 'Julian, if you do go back to the pub you have to be bloody careful.'

Cross my heart,' Julian said as he got up and bade them goodbye.

CHAPTER EIGHTEEN

Silly old farts, Julian thought as he walked into the Regent later that afternoon. Jim and his police mate should realise that this is Sydney, not London or even Liverpool. But of more concern was whether Siobhan would turn up. He couldn't deny she was growing on him. She had an appeal he couldn't put his finger on.

As he'd had sport duty after school, he was later than usual and the pub was already busy. The English barmaid poured a beer without his having to ask. Neither Siobhan nor Trevor were in sight, but he could see lots of the Pommie lads and a few others he hadn't met. He made his way through the crowd to join them, lit a cigarette and waited to be included.

Stone Roses were singing *Love Spreads* and the song instantly took him back to London. His ex-girlfriend, Beth, had loved this song and she'd often put it on the juke box in their local. He wondered what she would have made of Sydney? His coming out here had been the main reason for their split as Beth had no desire to leave London and her family.

He moved closer to the large group, most still in heavy boots and work clothes. The Premier League was the topic of an animated conversation with the majority of the Scousers boasting about Liverpool's recent win. Julian, knowing or caring little about football, had no desire to join in the discussion about Liverpool's success. The few Everton supporters amongst the crowd were clearly not enjoying the gloating and one turned to Julian groaning, 'Fuckin' Reds and their fuckin' wanker supporters.' Julian, aware of the rivalry between the two teams, shrugged. 'You must support Everton?'

Hearing Julian's London accent, the tradie held out his hand. 'Alright? Paddy.' Julian shook the man's hand. 'Julian.'

'Cheers. Arsenal? Chelsea?' Paddy asked.

Julian thought quickly. He'd realised his saying he was a rugby union player wouldn't win him any favours with this crowd. 'Spurs,' he said emphatically. Paddy appeared to approve.

'Been here long?' Julian asked, keen to change the subject.

'Few months. You?'

'Since the end of last year.'

Both drank their beer.

'Good boozer,' Julian praised.

Paddy shook his head. 'Mmm. Not bad. Too many fuckin' rules here. No lock-ins.'

Julian felt it more diplomatic to agree rather than ask why Paddy bothered to stay in Sydney if he didn't like it. Everywhere was different and it always took a while to adjust. He was about to head to the bar when Paddy said suddenly, 'Heard about the geezer who got done in the other night?'

'Fuck. Murdered? Who?'

'Fella about our age. One of ours, a Scouser. Heard he got caught up in the drug scene and they done him in. Got on the wrong side of the dealers.'

'Jesus.' Julian peered around the room. 'Dealers, here in the pub?'

''Course there are. Fancy a bit of gear?' Paddy suggested smugly, rubbing the side of his nose. 'Prefer weed meself but give me the nod if you want any coke.'

Julian thanked him, although he wasn't sure if Paddy was big noting himself or just being helpful. 'Don't want to end up dead like that poor sod.'

'Yeah. Shame. Think he stood on someone's toes. If you get my drift?'

'You don't know whose toes?'

'Rather not say.' Paddy winked, tapping his nose again.

'Understandable. Can you point out the connection for some of *you know what*?'

Paddy looked nonchalantly around the bar then nudged Julian. 'See that guy over there in the AC/DC T-shirt? He's your man. He's a nob'ead but his gear's okay. Better than fuckin' Trev's.'

Julian gulped. He hadn't seen this bloke before. 'Cheers. You don't want anything?'

Paddy shook his head. 'Nah. Working six days a week on a building site in the city. Up at the crack of ...'

'Shit. No wonder. Good to meet you,' Julian said, and thinking on the fly in order to fit in, quickly added he needed a Geoff Hirst in his best Cockney accent.

Julian stood watching the interaction between the AC/DC man and a group of drinkers. Was that big bloke with him a minder? A few minutes later a couple of punters went with AC/DC man and his 'friend' towards the toilets. Not exactly subtle. Surely the bouncers and bar staff must see what's going on? Were they on the payroll?

He dithered. Should he make his move? Seize the day, he decided and nonchalantly walked in the same direction. After all, he was only asking for what the others wanted. If AC/DC man got the shits then so be it.

As he was about to push open the door to the toilets, a large hairy hand reached in front of him. 'Sorry, mate. No go.'

Julian stared at the big man. 'What do you mean, no go? I'm busting for the loo … toilet.'

'Tough. It's occupied.' The big man grinned. Julian could barely hide his surprise that such a man with his shaved head and

117

tattoos would know what a pun was. His question about how long he'd have to wait was met with a burly shrug. Should he go or should he stay? Maybe if he told the heavy what he wanted then he might be permitted entry.

Julian stepped towards the man who now stood with folded arms. 'I was, um, hoping to buy a little something. Know what I mean?'

'No.'

'Something beginning with C.' Julian smiled.

'Look matey, I don't know you. You could be the Prime Minister for all I care so why don't you just fuck off and find somewhere else to have a slash.'

'Will do, but if you could tell your boss I'm a willing customer, I'd be very grateful.'

The tattooed man shook his head ambivalently, before removing his gaze from Julian's eager face.

CHAPTER NINETEEN

While keeping an eye out for anyone to emerge from the gents, Julian considered his next move. It had been at least fifteen minutes since he'd tried to gain entry. Finally, one of the men who'd followed AC/DC man reappeared, but as Julian didn't know him he couldn't just go up and ask what was going on.

A minute later, the door to the gents was pushed open and to his amazement, Jimmy appeared. Julian felt a surge of excitement. They'd got on reasonably well when they'd last chatted and as Jimmy was Scottish, he too was slightly on the outer.

Watching Jimmy make his way back to the group and judging by the innocent look on the Scot's face, Julian doubted if any drugs had been taken in the toilets but having them on his person required an aura of nonchalance. Abandoning his own attempt at entry into this particular gents, Julian made his way to a different part of the pub to relieve himself.

'Think I owe you a beer,' Julian suggested to Jimmy once he'd rejoined the circle.

The Scotsman frowned. 'Aye?'

'I'm heading off shortly so thought I'd repay the favour.'

Jimmy still looked doubtful but to Julian's satisfaction he accepted. Of course he did. The Scots were renowned for being tight with money.

Julian hoped Jimmy would stay put as he hurried over to the bar. His plan was to tell the Scot he'd wanted to buy some cocaine as well, but the 'minder' had stopped him.

He handed the beer to Jimmy. 'Was going to buy a little something but couldn't get in.'

'Get in where?' Jimmy asked.

'The gents. Fancied some coke for the weekend but that fucking bloke wouldn't let me in.'

Jimmy stared at Julian. 'You dunnae look the type.'

'Love a bit of coke especially if I'm lucky enough to pick up.' Julian raised an eyebrow. He could see Jimmy was agreeing with the idea of sex and cocaine.

'You canna tell anyone I told you, but you need to speak to that bloke, Trevor. He knows who to introduce you to when he hasn't got what you're after. But you didnae hear this from me.'

'Lips are sealed. But how come there are two dealers in the same pub?' Julian asked. 'Never seen that before.'

'Prob'ly have the same supplier.' Jimmy shrugged, lighting a cigarette and offering the open pack to Julian.

'Ours is not to reason why,' Julian quoted, plucking a cigarette from the packet. He wondered if Jimmy's interpretation of the pub having two dealers was reliable. A lot of guys liked to look as if they were in the know. 'Trevor here tonight?'

'Haven't seen him. Bit odd as he's always fuckin' here. Maybe he's 'round at Siobhan's,' Jimmy replied with scorn in his voice.

'Is she his girlfriend?' Julian asked as casually as he could.

Jimmy shrugged. 'Wants her to be.'

'Can see why. She's fucking hot.'

The Scotsman grimaced. 'Bit of a tart if you ask me.' He stared at Julian. 'Wouldn't have thought she'd be your type. More Brian and Steve's. No taste.'

Julian didn't respond. If in doubt say nothing, his mother had told him.

'Speak of the devil. On her tod,' Jimmy exclaimed, inclining his head towards the entrance.

There was Siobhan walking in by herself, her head lowered as if she didn't want to make eye contact with anyone.

Jimmy nudged him. 'Laddie, here's your chance.'

'Don't want to look too eager. Give her a few minutes. She may have a date with some other handsome fellow.'

'Well, that certainly doesn't include your man, *Trev*,' Jimmy said, imitating the Aussie accent. 'Or yourself.'

Julian gave him a mock punch on the arm before moving off to mingle with the rest of the group who were standing in the centre of the room. He could observe her easily from a distance and it was obvious how Siobhan's arrival had caused a few ripples amongst the tradies.

'Siobhan seems to be copping a lot of flak. What's the problem?' Julian asked Steve who was also watching her progress through the bar.

'Looks like she's bin-bagged Trev.'

Julian's brow wrinkled.

'Dumped him,' Steve translated.

'Oh, right. Why?'

'Probably had enough of the bellend.'

'I thought she tolerated him because he could supply her needs?'

'Oh yeah. But sometimes even coke can't turn an old shoe into a prince.'

'Think you're mixing your metaphors,' Julian said with a chuckle.

'Yeah whatever, but ya know what I mean. She used him. Kept him dangling, thinking he'd get his leg over.'

'Ghastly thought.'

'Fuck yeah. He should have known he was out of his depth ... But our Trev has mates in high places. You don't want to get on the wrong side of your supplier.'

'I'm confused. Who's *he*? What's this got to do with Siobhan?'

122

Steve sighed. 'Her and *Mark. He* had no fucken idea. Should've been careful when it came to Trev.'

'Hang on. Mark? What's Trev got to do with Mark?'

The Scouser shrugged. 'Connections.'

Julian began to wonder if he was taking on more than he could chew as he was hearing such a mixture of gossip. He didn't know what to take seriously, but having Siobhan so close, and alone, was too good an opportunity to miss.

Giving Steve a nod, Julian excused himself and made his way over to Siobhan. 'Hello. Didn't expect to see you tonight,' he greeted. She looked at him doubtfully. 'Remember, we had a chat the other night?'

Siobhan squinted at him. 'Oh yeah. You're the posh Pom from London.'

'That's right. Not the posh part but yes, I'm from London. Can I buy you a drink?'

She thought about his offer. 'Gin and tonic.'

Manners, crossed Julian's mind, as he dutifully went to the bar. Once served, he turned around. Siobhan had gone. Fuck. He scanned the room. There was no sign of her. Feeling like a rejected fool holding two drinks, a waving hand caught his eye. She had found a table.

Resisting the urge to tell her he thought she'd gone, Julian put the drinks on the table and sat down. He was starting to question

123

the worth of going through the humiliation of dealing with this girl when she looked at him and smiled. 'Thank you.'

CHAPTER TWENTY

Despite it being a Monday night, the volume of the music had gone up a few decibels causing some of the punters to shuffle and sway in time to *Blister in the Sun*. Julian was finding it hard to hear Siobhan and judging by her request to go outside, she too was having difficulty. He followed her to the beer garden where they both agreed it was less noisy, although it crossed his mind that maybe Siobhan was worried Trevor might arrive and see them together, hence hiding outside. However, when she chose a table open to public view, he realised he may have misjudged her. Perhaps Steve was correct when he'd said she'd given Trev the boot.

As they chatted, he found he was enjoying her company and it certainly didn't hurt that she was attractive. Although there was a toughness about her, her tales of growing up in Belfast were entertaining and she seemed genuinely interested in what he had to say. However, despite the ease of the conversation, Julian couldn't find a way to casually mention Mark.

The small bar in the beer garden had closed and as the beer had gone straight to his bladder, Julian made his excuses and dashed back into the public to buy more drinks and have a jimmy. He hoped he didn't sound too eager by stressing she should wait for him. She'd lit another cigarette so he took it to mean she wasn't going anywhere.

The bladder relieved, and with drinks in hand, he hurried back and sat down lighting a cigarette in what he hoped was a composed manner. He was about to ask what Siobhan did for a living when they heard yelling and screaming from the public bar. 'Jesus. What the hell's going on?' Julian asked anxiously, leaping to his feet, but from where they were seated it was impossible to see inside the pub.

Siobhan stared at Julian, waggling her hands for him to sit down. 'Leave it. If there's trouble we don't want to get involved.'

'What if someone's hurt?'

'The bouncers and the manager will take care of it. It's happened before.'

'You sure? … It sounds serious.'

'Probably some lad jealous over a cailín. Happens all the time.'

'You'll have to translate. No idea what you mean.'

'Men fighting over girls.'

Julian shrugged in reply. It made sense, especially as many of the tradies started to drink from around three-thirty in the afternoon plus Siobhan knew the pub better than he did. This might be the opportunity to bring up Mark's supposed drowning. Just another drama at the pub.

'Is this what happened on the night the Scouse bloke died?'

Siobhan frowned suspiciously. 'What Scouse bloke?'

'The guy who drowned down at the beach about a week ago. Was there a fight then? Over a girl?'

'Mark wasn't interested in girls,' Siobhan snapped, her face both sullen and sad.

'Sorry. Didn't mean to upset you.' Whoops, thought Julian. Shouldn't have mentioned Mark but … 'You mean he was gay?'

Siobhan nodded, her eyes glassy. Julian could see she was contemplating how to reply, but before she could speak he admitted he had nothing against gays. He was just curious about what had happened as a number of the blokes had mentioned Mark and he'd assumed from what he'd heard that she and Mark were friends.

Clutching her glass, she took a large swallow before lifting her head to stare at Julian. 'Are you after information? Don't know if I can trust you. You could be a copper for all I know.'

'I'm just a bloke you met in the pub.' He leaned across the table. 'How about I tell you something I haven't told anyone in here. You will have my secret to show I trust you.'

'Jesus, Mary and Joseph. You sound like James Bond.'

'Which one?' Julian asked, relieved the tension had eased slightly.

'Sean Connery. The first and the best.'

'I'll take that as a compliment. Well? Do you want to hear my secret or not?'

'To be sure,' Siobhan said, grinning weakly at her use of the Irish cliché. He noticed the high colour of her face had returned to normal.

'I don't work in an office doing boring admin as I've told the guys here in the pub. I actually teach at a private school nearby and I've made a connection with a man who works there. Mark lived with his family when he first arrived.' Julian stopped abruptly, shocked at how easy it had been to tell her the truth. But had he been stupid? She was connected to Trevor the drug dealer and God knows who else.

His negative thoughts were interrupted by a hand placed on his. 'It's good you told me,' Siobhan consoled. 'You don't seem like the other lads. You're trying to find out what happened to Mark. Am I right or am I right?'

'Yes. You are.'

'How do you know I know … knew, Mark?'

'You mentioned him briefly when I first met you. At least I think you were referring to him. And I've heard you and he were mates. Some of the blokes think you had a relationship with him, but others think you're on with Trevor.'

The scowl on Siobhan's face revealed her irritation with the pub gossip. 'Fucken Trev thinks he owns me, but he fucken doesn't. I like the odd bit of charlie, but it doesn't mean I belong to him. He uses that to try and control me.'

'Are you addicted?' Julian asked, without thinking.

'No!' she answered. 'Lots of people like it now and then.'

'True. Me too. So, you and Mark were friends?'

'We were. Good ones. I didn't see him outside of the Regent, but he could talk to me. Liverpool and Northern Ireland have a strong connection. We're sort of related.'

Julian understood. 'But he wasn't openly gay?'

'Mark did his best to hide it in the pub, but I knew. That's why he liked talking to me. The lads are so old fashioned … but I didn't give a shit.'

'Do you think his being gay might be a reason for his death?'

Siobhan pulled her head back in shock. 'You think one of the lads killed him?'

'Do you?'

Siobhan frowned, staring at Julian. 'The lads may be old-fashioned tools, but they wouldn't hurt him. There must be another reason why he died. The Regent wasn't his only world, not like the lads in here.'

129

Julian remained silent, his arms folded, hoping for more revelations.

'You won't tell me what you know and yet you want me to tell you if someone killed Mark because I have drug connections? You must think me a right eejit?' Siobhan said angrily.

'Hold on. I've been honest with you why I'm interested in Mark, and I've told you something about me,' Julian justified. 'And I don't think you're an idiot. If anything, I really like you.'

'Oh yeah? For sure. You fucken men are all the same. You pretend you like me because you want something. You're no better than fucken Trevor. I'm off to work. *Thanks* for the drinks.' She shoved her chair back with her bottom and as she began to stand, Julian reached out and grabbed her arm.

'You're right. I did want to talk to you about Mark but since I've got to know you, I like you. Please believe me.'

'I *don't* believe you. You buy me drinks to loosen my tongue. Act all smooth. You're full of shite. Don't even think about ringing me.'

Julian remained in the beer garden to give Siobhan enough time to leave the pub. He knew she was right. He *was* using her for information, but she was wrong about one thing, he did like her. The couple of times they'd met had proved to be valuable in many ways and now he wished they could meet as friends and see what happened between them. He'd screwed up.

There was no point in following her. She was tough, and angry. He doubted she'd be won back easily. Plus, and this was a worrying thought, she now knew a lot more about him than he'd wanted to admit. The beer and being with her had made him lower his guard. Would Siobhan use her knowledge against him? If the English crowd behaved differently towards him or referred to him as a teacher, then he'd know she'd betrayed his confidence. He really hoped that wouldn't be the case.

Slowly finishing his beer, Julian stood up to leave. Socialising was the last thing he wanted now. There was no longer any yelling from the main bar. He'd heard sirens but according to Siobhan that was normal. He made his way back inside to leave by the front entrance where hopefully he'd find a taxi waiting.

The scene in the main bar was not what Julian expected. A large number of police were mingling with the patrons while ambulance servicemen attended to someone lying on the floor. The music had been turned off and the atmosphere was one of suspense.

Julian wended his way through the crowd surrounding the body. Being tall, he was able to peer over some of the onlookers and he could see blood on the floor and the legs of a person on a stretcher. Judging by the jeans and trainers, it was probably a man.

131

The police called for attention, asking their stunned audience to move to a different section of the pub where they must give proof of their identity and contact details to the waiting constables. Once they had given these details they were free to leave the premises.

Julian looked around for Siobhan, but as expected there was no sign of her, although most of the British contingent were standing in shocked silence. He made his way over to Steve who was standing in a huddle with Jimmy, Brian, and Paddy. 'What the hell happened?' he asked.

Steve shook his head. 'Fucked if I know. It was all so bloody quick.'

Jimmy eagerly joined in. 'Trev was talking to some guy and next minute he was on the floor. Looks like he was stabbed.'

'Trev? Jesus! In front of everyone?' Julian lowered his voice. 'What about the guy selling in the toilets? Is he still here?'

'Doubt it. It was only after Trev fell down we realised something had happened. That's when all the yelling started,'

'Is he still alive?' Julian asked.

'Dunno but there was a fuck load of blood.' Steve looked to Brian for confirmation. Brian grimaced.

'And no one saw who did it?' Julian asked.

'You sound like a bloody copper,' Steve stated with a snarl. 'Where were *you*?'

'I was outside having a drink with Siobhan. Didn't see a thing. Heard the yelling but didn't think anything of it.'

'Siobhan, eh? You won't be popular with Trev or his mates.'

Jimmy drew back stating sarcastically, 'Not if Trev's brown bread.'

Steve glared at Julian. 'Fuck. You're a hard man.'

'Just facing facts.'

They stood in awkward silence waiting for the queue to diminish so they could give their details to the police and leave.

CHAPTER TWENTY-ONE

Assembly had ended and the bell rang signalling for first period to begin. The chatter and footsteps of the boys stopped suddenly as they entered their classrooms and doors were closed. Fortuitously, Julian had a free period and made his way to Jim's office.

'Bad news?' Jim asked, seeing the grim expression on Julian's face. 'Grab a seat.'

Slumping on to the chair in front of Jim's desk, Julian sighed. 'What a night.'

Jim waited till curiosity got the better of him. 'Come on, mate. Out with it.'

'Where to begin?'

'At the beginning?'

'Alright, alright. You're a bloody taskmaster. I'll start at the end. You know the bloke, Trevor, Siobhan's mate and supposed drug dealer?' Seeing Jim nod, Julian continued, 'I'd been outside in the beer garden with Siobhan trying to charm her into confiding in me, but it didn't quite go to plan and she buggered off. I went to leave but when I walked back into the public bar a bloke was being attended to by the police and the ambulance guys. It was

Trevor.' Julian looked for Jim's reaction. There was none. 'Anyway, he was taken away by ambulance. Not sure if he was dead, but there was lots of blood. We all had to give ID, addresses and phone numbers to the police.'

'Did your *girlfriend* attack him?' Jim asked, his tone ambivalent.

'No! Of course not. We heard the commotion, but we were outside and didn't think anything of it. Siobhan said fights were common in the Regent. Par for the course.'

Jim raised his eyebrows. 'Really? … Any idea who did it?'

'No. Far too many people around.'

'Do you think this has any connection to Mark's death?' asked Jim.

'God knows.'

'Did Siobhan give her details to the police?'

'I don't know. By the time I went inside she'd gone.'

Jim pursed his lips. 'Doesn't that seem odd?'

Julian stretched his arms, yawning. 'Well, we'd been outside so perhaps she thought she didn't need to talk to the police. She was definitely with me when it all happened.'

'Mmmm ... Did she have anything of interest to tell you?'

Julian thought for a few seconds. 'She said Mark wasn't interested in girls, and they were just friends. Then she got the hump when she thought I was only with her for info about him.'

135

'Well, that *was* why you were with her, wasn't it?'

'To be blunt, Jim. I actually enjoy her company, and … I stupidly told her I'm a teacher at a private school nearby. I was trying to win her confidence.'

Jim blinked rapidly. 'If she spreads that around then there is no way anyone in the pub will trust you again.'

Scratching his scalp through his thick hair, Julian considered Jim's supposition. 'I had to make a snap decision and I told her about me so she'd trust me. I may be wrong, but I think she does.'

'What part of your anatomy are you thinking with? Are you compromising yourself for the chance of some sex?'

The young man's face fell as he realised Jim had touched on the truth. 'How about I go to the pub one more time and if I get the cold shoulder from the other chaps then I'll know she's blabbed? Oh, and I did assure her I have nothing against gays.'

'Jesus Julian,' Jim groaned. 'You have to take this seriously. It looks like we're dealing with some serious criminals. I'll get on to Alan Stone and see if he's heard anything about Trevor. It might just be a dissatisfied customer, but it seems jolly strange the two deaths have occurred so close together. Assuming Trevor has died.'

'I had to give my details to the police so I'll be interviewed.' Julian screwed up his face. 'You don't really think this is connected to Mark, do you? I've heard there've been a number of gay murders in Sydney, but Trev wasn't gay.'

Jim thought about Julian's question. 'Not sure … There were a lot of gay attacks back in the 1970s and '80s. I thought the prejudice had lessened of late, but apparently not and from what I've heard the anti-gay sentiment has increased because of the AIDS epidemic. Some are even saying it's God's punishment for being queer.' He sighed. 'What a load of tripe.'

'Well, I'll leave you to it,' Julian stated, standing up. 'I'll go back tonight and see what reaction I get and if it's not good then I won't go there again. Sorry if I've messed things up for you. I really did want to help.'

'It's alright, mate. You already have. Given us a good idea about the goings on at the Regent and its cast of characters. I'll call Alan and let you know what I find out about Trevor.'

'Thanks Jim. Maybe he's pulled through, although it didn't look likely.'

'I'm sorry but Detective Stone isn't here at present,' a constable informed Jim when he rang the station.

'Any idea when he'll be back?'

'No, but if you leave your name and phone number, I'll let him know you called.'

Once he'd given his details, Jim hung up wondering if Alan would be pissed off if he knew Julian had confessed to Siobhan what he really did for a job. It suddenly occurred to him that as she was connected to Trevor, she probably knew other drug dealers. Would this put Julian, and maybe even the school in jeopardy because of his connections to her? *Bloody hell.* He'd let his concern for Mark influence his thinking. He should let the police do their job and mind his own business.

A knock saved him from his disturbing thoughts. It was Daphne. She popped her head around the door checking if Jim was alone then walked in, shutting the door quickly.

'I've got some news,' she said, obviously excited.

'Yes?'

'Ray probably shouldn't have told me, but there was a murder last night at the Regent. A man was attacked and died later in hospital from his injuries.' Her face dropped slightly when she saw he wasn't surprised. 'Do you know this already?'

'I knew someone had been injured but I wasn't a hundred percent sure if he'd died. You've answered my question so thank you. I've just rung Alan to ask for confirmation, but he's not in his office.'

'How did you know this had happened?' Daphne asked. 'Julian Butterworth by any chance?'

138

Jim hesitated. 'Yes. Our young Pom went to the Regent last night and caught the tail end of the action. He recognised the man who'd been attacked. It was Trevor Pearce. The bloke who's connected to the Irish girl, and he's a drug dealer.'

'Oh my God. How come Julian knew who he was?'

'He's become friendly with a few of the locals, and they pointed him out. Trevor was well known for selling drugs but also because of his supposed relationship with Siobhan, the Irish girl. However, it turns out she wasn't a fan.'

Daphne sighed. 'Good grief. Is all this connected to Mark?'

'Don't know, but it seems odd that Mark died and now Pearce. There's no obvious connection except both were known to Siobhan.' Jim rubbed his chin.

'Do you really think she could have killed them?' Daphne asked.

'No. But she's the only one who knew both of them well.'

'Oh Jim. Really? If anyone regularly goes to the same pub, they're likely to know lots of the same people.'

All he could do was agree.

'Do you think Julian should stop going to the Regent? He could be in danger if he's asking questions,' Daphne suggested.

Jim walked over to the window and stared out at the large oval at the front of the school contemplating Daphne's words. 'You're right,' he said with a sigh. 'I've already said that to Julian but he's keen to go again.'

Daphne thought for a moment then shook her head. 'Well, I'd better get back to work.'

Jim slumped into his chair, head in hands. The phone rang and he wearily picked it up.

'Jim. You rang?' Alan said immediately.

'Yes.'

'You okay?'

A sigh was the answer.

'Okay … Well, I have some news. Trevor Pearce was killed last night. He was attacked in the Regent.'

'I know.'

'My God news travels fast. How did you find out?' Alan asked.

'Julian was there,' Jim said bluntly, 'although he was outside with Siobhan when it happened.'

'Did he see anything?' Stone asked.

'No. He went inside after Trev was attacked. Do you know who did it?'

'Nah. So many punters in the pub. It's going to take bloody ages to talk to everybody but hopefully someone will have seen something, or the person owns up.' Stone laughed bitterly. 'Actually, it'd be a good idea to talk to Julian on his own.'

'Why on his own?'

'From what you've told me about him, he might have learned something useful. A neutral atmosphere can produce better results. The other punters will probably be on the defensive, clamp up, especially if they've bought any drugs from Pearce.'

'Ah, yes … The trouble is I'm feeling guilty I got Julian involved in all this. He could be in danger, especially as he's become ... ah ... *fond* of Siobhan.'

Stone breathed out. 'Shit. Didn't see that coming. Perhaps tell him to stop going ... but can you give me his phone number?'

Jim flicked through his address book and read it out.

'Thanks, mate. I'll ring him once school is over. You finish at three, don't you?'

Sarcastically, Jim responded, 'Yes. Of course. Teachers only work from nine to three. My arse.'

'In that case it's better if you ask Julian to ring me. Tell him I'm waiting for his call.'

'Will do.'

After he'd hung up, Jim realised he hadn't informed Alan about Julian's telling Siobhan he was a teacher at St Cuthbert's and how he was going back to the Regent to talk to the tradies that evening.

CHAPTER TWENTY-TWO

To his surprise, Julian's stomach was churning as he stood in the staffroom phone box waiting for Detective Stone to answer his call. He felt guilty even though he'd done nothing wrong. Surely, after the meeting in Jim's office, the detective would know he was trying to help.

The ring tone seemed to go on forever and Julian was about to hang up when Stone finally responded. 'Waverley Police. Detective Stone.'

'Hello. It's Julian Butterworth. Mr Cameron asked me to ring you.'

'Ah. Yes. Julian. Thanks for calling. I gather you may have some more information for me.'

'Well, I hope it's of use.'

'Every little bit helps,' Stone replied. 'How about we meet for a coffee in Bondi Junction this afternoon? Once you finish work.'

Julian paused, then explained he didn't finish till five as he had to take sport.

'That's okay. How about 5.30 in the mall? Or, if you'd prefer, we could meet in the Viceroy for a beer instead.'

'A beer would be great,' Julian enthused. 'Be needing one after today.'

'Good oh. See you in the Viceroy. Public bar. I'll be wearing a suit.'

Julian laughed. 'And I'll have a rose in my lapel.'

The Viceroy was busy and like the Regent, there was a crowd of Irish and English tradies. Julian made sure he got there on time and checked out the bar. He grabbed a high table towards the back of the large, tiled room, claiming it with his jacket before he went to buy a beer. He wasn't used to dealing with the police but as Stone had suggested this venue, he assumed the detective would like a drink and he'd buy him one once he arrived.

He was standing at the bar when Stone walked in. He smiled seeing him in a suit when no-one else was. It wasn't that type of pub.

Julian waved him over. 'What'll you have?'

The schooners poured, Julian led Stone to his table. He was relieved to see his jacket was still there, but this was the Eastern suburbs of Sydney, not some rough part of London.

They sat sipping their beer in silence. Julian hadn't taken much notice of the detective at their brief meeting in Jim's office, but now observing him more closely, Stone was definitely not what he'd originally imagined when Jim first mentioned him. He'd

143

envisaged an overweight, grumpy character like Robbie Coltrane in *Cracker,* while Stone looked like he was in his late 40s or early 50s, tall, attractive and definitely not fat.

'Thanks for meeting me. Thought it'd be better here than at the station as we've already met, and you're not under serious contention as the murder suspect,' Stone explained to Julian who puffed out his cheeks with relief. 'Plus I needed a drink!' Stone added.

Julian grinned sympathetically. 'Ah. Did wonder why you wanted to meet me here. Not worried about being seen with me?'

'Nuh. Most people have no idea who the police are unless they're in uniform.' Stone winked at Julian. 'We just happened to meet here.'

Surprised by Stone's casual attitude, Julian asked, 'You must be interviewing a lot of people?'

'We are.'

A cheer emanating around the pub caused the two to look at the large screens which were showing a replay of a rugby league game. The Roosters had scored a try.

'Into the league?' Julian asked.

'Not really. Although I keep up with it so I can make conversation with my colleagues.'

'Being a Kiwi you must be a union fan?'

'Is the Pope a Catholic?'

144

Julian held out his hand. 'Good to meet a fellow rugger bugger. It seems only the public, whoops, *private* schools who play rugby union here. All the Brits I've met in the pub are football fanatics. Soccer, as the Aussies call it, is not my passion. Makes it a bit hard to have a blokey chat.'

Stone, still gripping Julian's hand, said, 'Totally understand. And the Aussies hate it when the All Blacks win. Which is most of the time.' He grinned, finally letting go of the younger man's hand. 'Anyway, don't want to hold you up so we'd better get down to business.'

Each took a gulp of their beer. 'Can I ask why you're so keen to assist with finding out what happened to Mark?' Stone began.

Julian cocked his head. 'I know it seems odd, considering I didn't know Mark, but I admire Jim and when he put it to me to go to the pub and see what I could find out, I thought, why not? He's been really supportive of me and of course, Mark. Stranger in a strange land and all that.'

'Yeah. He's a great bloke. You know he and I go back a long way?'

'I've gathered. So, what do you want to know?'

Stone rolled his shoulders. 'Anything you've learned about Mark Dunlop from your visits to the pub.'

Julian pulled at his lips. 'The main thing I found out was that Mark was queer. And, I've met the Irish girl, Siobhan, who told

145

me Mark wasn't interested in girls, but they became good friends. The other info was about Trevor Pearce, the chap who was attacked the other night. A drug dealer and from what I've heard, he was keen on Siobhan and very possessive.'

'Did the other blokes know Mark was gay?' Stone asked, seemingly ignoring the comments about Trevor.

'There was the odd joke, but I got the feeling most of the Poms didn't give a toss if he was. Some might be a bit homophobic, 'specially a couple of them from Liverpool, but I didn't get the impression Mark's being gay was an issue for any of them. If anything, it was Trevor who had it in for him. Don't think he liked Siobhan's friendship with Mark.'

'But if Mark was gay, why would he care?'

Julian shrugged. 'God knows. Some men are jealous of their girlfriends' friends, male or female. Maybe Mark was careful who he came out to, and perhaps Siobhan didn't tell Trev that Mark was gay.'

Stone, listening intently, said, 'And then Mr Pearce is attacked. Where were you when that happened?'

'I was outside with Siobhan. She didn't want to sit inside so I went out with her to the beer garden. Got the impression she might have been worried Trevor would see her with me and kick things off.'

'What exactly is your relationship with … Siobhan?'

'To be honest, I talked to her in the beginning because I'd heard she was friendly with Mark and might be a useful source of information but the more I've spoken to her … She's not normally my type but there's something about her. Bit of a sucker for red hair.'

Stone grinned. 'Putting your romantic desires aside, do you think she had anything to do with his death?'

'Whose? Mark's or Trevor's?'

'Well, either, but let's stick to Trevor.'

Julian sat up straighter. 'No. She was with me when it happened. There was no way she could have attacked him. We heard the shouting and the sirens but didn't think anything of it as we were still in the beer garden. She said it was normal and she left not long after. He was already on the floor when I went back inside. Didn't know it was Trev till later. The police and ambulance guys were there. All I saw were his jeans and trainers as he was carried out to the ambulance, so I presumed whoever it was, was still alive Then the police took everyone's details, including mine.' He leant back crossing his arms.

Stone stared at Julian. 'You're not protecting her?'

'Shit no. She's tough. She can protect herself. We *were* outside when it happened. She couldn't have done it.'

'Do you have her phone number?' asked Stone.

'I do. I got it from her on a previous occasion. We didn't part on the best of terms last night.'

'Why was that?'

'She realised my initial interest in her was because of Mark. I tried to explain it was no longer the only reason I wanted to see her, but it fell on deaf ears.'

'Oh dear.' Stone chuckled. He downed the dregs of his beer. 'Another?'

'Why not. Give me time to think of anything else I can tell you.'

Stone walked back to the bar while Julian thought about Trevor.

A couple beers later, the conversation returned to rugby union and how brilliant the All Blacks were. Julian stressed his amazement at how a small country like New Zealand could produce such a great team.

'Yeah, well, it's a religion. Whenever the Blacks lose, the whole country goes into mourning. Of course, as I said, the Aussies hate it when we win. Their little brother better than them syndrome.'

'I suppose it's like the Welsh or Scots if they beat England,' Julian confirmed.

148

'Absolutely. And of course, when a Kiwi band or an actor does well, the Aussies claim ownership, Crowded House, Russell Crowe, Sam Neil, but if it's the reverse then they're Kiwis.'

'Didn't know Russell Crowe was a Kiwi.'

'Left New Zealand when he was young, so maybe the Aussies can claim him,' Stone admitted. 'Returning to the investigation, is there anything else you can think of?'

Tightening his lips, Julian thought for a few moments, then as if a light bulb had been switched on said, 'The AC/DC bloke.'

'What?'

'The guy in the pub selling drugs. He was wearing a T-shirt with AC/DC on the front and he was there when Trev was attacked.'

'Thought Trevor Pearce was the drug dealer in the Regent?'

'Yes, but that night there was this other man selling in the toilets. His minder wouldn't let me go in. I'd told him I wanted to buy some coke but he barred me.'

'You were going to buy drugs?'

'Yes. That way I'd find out more.'

Stone's eyebrows rose. 'Bit risky. Did you find out who he was?'

'Not really. He seemed to know a lot of the people in the pub. His minder knew about puns.'

'Good grief. An educated minder.'

149

Julian laughed. 'A better class of heavy.'

'What did this bloke look like? The AC/DC man?'

'Nothing like Trev. Big chap, good looking. Maybe Greek or Italian. Thick head of black hair.'

'You say the minder wouldn't let you into the toilets?'

'Yeah.'

'That indicates the management at the Regent could have known what the dealer was up to.' Before Stone could continue, Julian blurted out, 'Yes. And Pearce nearly glassed some bloke the other night when he was with Siobhan. I thought he'd been kicked out but next minute he was back in the pub buying another beer. Maybe management are in his pocket or the bouncers are his henchmen?'

'More questions than answers,' pondered Stone. 'Thanks for the info, Julian. Very useful.'

'No problem. Another beer?'

CHAPTER TWENTY-THREE

The news of Trevor's death had travelled fast. Even though Siobhan had managed to sneak out of the pub while the police were taking names, she knew she'd be interviewed eventually. There were enough of her drinking mates to tell the police she was a friend of Trevor's and was in the pub when he was attacked. She hadn't told the pub crowd that she *wasn't* his girlfriend, but she'd certainly given Trev the message that she wanted nothing more to do with him. She doubted if he'd said anything to anyone as most of the crowd were only his mates because he sold them drugs. What to do now that Trev was dead? Jesus … dead.

Not going to the Regent before work was a strange feeling, but it seemed wise to leave the place alone for a while. She wondered if Julian had turned up again after all the drama? Had she overreacted? Perhaps he did like her but most men just said what they thought you wanted to hear as they were after a ride.

The afternoon dragged on. A shower and hair wash only took a short time and the couple of dishes in the sink took even less. She sorted out the few clothes she needed for work then flopped onto the couch but the TV offered nothing to distract her. A beer might subdue her feeling of anxiety. She strolled over to the nearly empty fridge and saw there were a couple of stubbies remaining.

Slowly sipping the beer, she thought about the first night she'd met Julian. He wasn't the type who'd normally chat her up and looking back she knew he'd only spoken to her to find out about Mark. His interest in Mark's death seemed a bit odd, even though he'd told her why. Yet, she was sure he wasn't the police. Maybe he was queer and they'd been lovers? But then Mark had told her about Darcy, and they were meant to be in love. Nothing made sense.

She lit another cigarette, ruminating over the events of the last week. Poor Mark dead down at Bondi and then Trev attacked in the pub. What was the connection between the two of them? There was no way Trev was gay. It couldn't be that, so *was* it about drugs? She and Mark had chatted about enjoying coke and a joint, but she'd got the impression he wasn't a real user. Why would anyone want him dead? Did he know something that put him in danger? And why was Trevor attacked in such an open place? Whoever did it must have known his routine. Shit. If they were watching Trev then they might be watching her as well!

A second beer was needed to settle her nerves, and another fag. This was scary. Was Julian the informant? But he hadn't been coming to the pub for long. Only a few nights. She'd seen him with the Scousers and the rest of the Poms. Were they giving him information? Some of them had bought gear from Trev so why would they want to risk losing their supply? Cutting off their nose …

Feck. Julian had only appeared at the pub after Mark died, and now Trev was dead as well. Siobhan banged her beer down on the cheap coffee table. She'd go back to the pub to see if she could meet him again. It'd be easy to pretend she'd forgiven him. She'd apologise for not trusting him and even if it meant she had to shag him she'd find out what he was up to. He'd told her he liked her and despite her suspicions, she nearly believed him. A good actor. Bloody Londoners. Think they're God's gift.

Stubbing out her cigarette, she was ready to go to work.

CHAPTER TWENTY-FOUR

It had been a long day and would be even longer as tonight was late-night closing. He'd listened to the clients' problems about partners, friends, jobs, and cleaners, and there'd be more to come. He'd built up a large number of clients over the years and his being gay was of no account to his customers. Darcy knew most assumed a male hairdresser was a homosexual. Did it matter that he supplied his regulars with a bit of weed? The owner of the salon had no idea, but he was pleased with the increase in customers. Connections in the Cross made it easy to buy dope and when a client walked out happy with their hair and a small bag of Mary Jane to enjoy at the weekend, it was win-win.

Putting his dabbling in drug dealing to one side, his real concern was Mark. Mark hadn't turned up to meet him in Oxford Street on Saturday night, hadn't answered his many phone calls and hanging around in The Albury like a spare part, hoping Mark would turn up, was extremely annoying. It made him look like he was waiting to be picked up and he certainly wasn't! Where the hell was Mark? He must have met someone else. Dirty boy. That must be the reason why he hadn't been in touch or answered the phone.

Darcy's anguish was interrupted when a tall, rather attractive middle-aged man who reminded him a little of Brad Pitt, entered the salon followed by a younger man in a police uniform. 'How can I help you?' he asked.

'Does Mr Darcy Bright work here?' the attractive man asked.

'I certainly do,' Darcy answered, puzzled. Judging from the man's tone, he didn't sound as if he wanted a wash, cut, and blow-dry. And what was the policeman doing here as well? Had they heard about his little sideline?

'Mr Bright. I'm Detective Alan Stone from Waverley Police and this is Sergeant Ridge.' Stone pulled out his identification, holding it for Darcy to see. 'Do you have a minute?'

'Yes of course.'

'I'm here in regards to Mark Dunlop. I gather you may know him.'

'Yeees?' Darcy answered, unable to keep the suspicion out of his voice.

'Can you tell me the nature of your relationship with Mr Dunlop?'

Darcy frowned. 'That's very personal. Why do you want to know?'

'Were you in a relationship with Mr Dunlop?' Stone persisted.

155

'Yes, but what does that have to do with anything?'

Darcy could see from the detective's expression he had bad news. 'I'm sorry to inform you Mr Dunlop is deceased.'

'Oh my God. What? How?' Darcy asked, clutching at his face.

'Unfortunately, Mr Dunlop died on Saturday night. We'd like you to come to Waverley Police Station. I know this will be difficult for you but we're talking to everyone who was connected to Mr Dunlop.'

'Why?'

'His death was unexpected, so if you could come to the station with us we'd really appreciate it.'

'Unexpected?'

'I'm afraid so. He was found dead on Bondi Beach.'

'And you want me to go with you, now? The salon doesn't close till nine.'

Stone and Ridge waited silently.

Darcy stood immobilised. This was unbelievable. Mark, dead on the beach? Pulling himself together, he called out to his assistant. 'Susie, I've got to leave. Ring my bookings and tell them we have to change their appointments. Make sure you lock up.'

The police car was parked nearby in a narrow street parallel to the main drag in Kings Cross and Darcy sat in the back feeling like a criminal. At least he wasn't in handcuffs. He hoped no-one he knew had seen him get into the car, but at the same time he was desperate to find out what had happened to Mark. He couldn't be dead? It was like a bad, bad dream. Surely he hadn't committed suicide? Whoa. He was getting ahead of himself. Perhaps it was an accident. Or did the police think he'd killed Mark? Was this why they were taking him to the police station? Oh my God.

The car stopped in front of the station and Detective Stone accompanied him into the building. Darcy watched grimly as Stone had a quick word with the desk sergeant before leaving him in the reception area. The sergeant instructed him to take a seat.

Darcy strutted towards a grubby plastic chair, thinking how the police needed to improve their PR. He made a point of looking at his watch to see how long he was to be kept waiting, ignoring the sergeant roll his eyes.

Stone finally reappeared, apologising for keeping Darcy waiting. 'We won't keep you long. Just a few questions.' He indicated for Darcy to follow him and once seated in his office, he was about to begin the questioning when Darcy asked, 'How did you know where I work?'

Stone delayed before answering, 'It wasn't hard to find out.'

Darcy, annoyed with Stone's explanation, asked, 'Did you search his home?'

'Yes. It's police procedure.'

All Darcy could do was shake his head.

157

'Can you tell me about your relationship with Mr Dunlop?' Stone persisted.

'What do you mean by *relationship*?' Darcy asked suspiciously.

Rubbing his forehead, Stone said, 'Perhaps that's the wrong word. Were you friends with Mr Dunlop? Knew him well?'

'If you're trying to ask if he was my *boyfriend* or partner, then the answer is yes. Homosexuality is no longer illegal, you know.'

'I'm aware of that, Mr Bright. What you do in the privacy of your own home is of no concern to me. I just want to clarify how well you knew Mark.

Darcy stared at Stone wondering if he had the same prejudice against queers as most of the police. They'd done very little over the years when gays were bashed or murdered. However, there was something about the detective which made Darcy think he was more tolerant and understanding than the average cop.

With tears welling, Darcy stated, 'We met soon after he came to Sydney, and it was love at first sight.'

Stone nodded and made a note. 'When was the last time you saw him?'

'Friday night. He stayed with me, and we were meant to meet again on Saturday night at The Albury but he didn't arrive. I work on Saturdays so there was no point in him hanging around all day at my place.'

'Was he normally reliable?'

'Yes, he was a man of his word. But sometimes when he went to the Regent and met up with his Pommie mates, he could be a little late.'

Stone nodded again. 'Weren't you worried, as it's been a few days?'

'Yes. Well not at first, although I was annoyed. As I said, I knew if he'd met up with his fellow ex-pats he might be late, but I have to admit not hearing from him over the last few days and when he didn't answer his phone, I questioned whether we were still a couple … I assumed he'd met someone else.' Darcy paused. 'Or he wanted to break up with me.'

Stone looked up. 'Why do you think he wanted to break up with you?'

Darcy sighed. 'I'm quite a bit older than Mark and from what he told me he couldn't exactly spread his wings in Liverpool, so I assumed he may have wanted to sample other wares. If you get my meaning?'

Stone did.

'Also he told me his parents would never understand or accept him being in a gay relationship so perhaps he wanted to be single.'

'Do you know if Mark was a drug user?' Stone asked suddenly.

'No!! Not at all. Unless you count the odd joint or ecstasy. He never took anything heavy.'

Stone made a note. 'Did you ever meet any of his friends?'

159

'Not really, unless you count the crowd in the gay bars. We got to know a number of the regulars but with my hours we either went to Oxford Street for a couple of drinks or stayed home.'

'Did you ever get the impression he was unhappy, depressed?'

'Are you implying he committed suicide?' Darcy questioned, his voice quivering at the implication.

'I'm sorry, but I have to ask.'

'Oh my god. I suppose you have to cover every angle … No, he'd never commit suicide. He was happy. We were happy. Well, *I* thought we were happy.'

Stone waited till Darcy composed himself before stating, 'As you say, we're covering every angle.'

'Of course.' Darcy stood up, assuming the interview was over, but Detective Stone continued to stare at him and asked abruptly, 'Can you think of anyone who'd want to hurt him?'

Sitting down again, Darcy glared at the detective who certainly didn't seem as attractive as he had previously. 'Absolutely not!' he rebuked.

'You don't seem particularly surprised by the news of Mr Dunlop's death. Were you expecting it?' Stone continued.

Darcy's jaw dropped. 'No! Of course not. I'm extremely upset. He was my partner. We were in love. How can you suggest otherwise?'

'I'm sorry, Mr Bright, but if my partner didn't show up when expected, I'd be very worried … and would try to find him.'

'But you're the police and you're meant to be worried, suspicious. I knew Mark was with his Pommie friends before he was meant to join me, so I assumed he was still with them … Or he'd met someone.' Darcy's voice rose in defiance.

Stone tightened his lips. 'I appreciate this is difficult for you, but if you *can* think of anyone Mark may have mentioned, who he'd had dealings with, fallen out with, it would be very helpful,' Stone repeated, his tone softened.

Darcy pouted, pulling his shoulders back. 'He hadn't been in Sydney all that long, so he didn't have close friends. There was the family he stayed with when he first arrived, and there were the guys he met at the pub. A lot were Liverpudlians, but I didn't meet them. I don't think he told them he was gay. From what he said, Liverpool wasn't exactly the gay capital of England.' Darcy became silent, thinking, then said, 'Oh, and there was an Irish girl he mentioned a number of times.'

'Siobhan?'

'That's her. They were quite matey. They saw each other at the pub.'

'So I've gathered,' Stone acknowledged. 'Do you think Mark came to Sydney because it's more accepting? The Mardi Gras. Gay bars.'

161

'Definitely. He could be himself for a change. From what he told me his parents would have disowned him if they knew he liked men.'

'I thought attitudes had changed but obviously not.'

'My dear, some things never change.' Darcy smiled at the detective who was beginning to look attractive again. 'Do you think this is a hate crime?'

Shaking his head, Stone explained how hate crimes still occurred but this was possibly something to do with drugs. An overdose or suicide.

'But I've told you, Mark was happy and he wasn't a drug user. He liked a bit of marijuana, and we did enjoy ecstasy occasionally but that was only at the weekend.' Darcy laughed weakly, realising who he was talking to and held out his wrists.

'Don't worry. That's the least of our worries. So, you can't think of anyone who had it in for Mark?'

Darcy's face became serious again. 'No, honestly, I can't.'

CHAPTER TWENTY-FIVE

The Waverley and Bondi police had been busy ringing the list of witnesses to Trevor Pearce's attack. Waverley station had at least twenty people waiting to be questioned with more to come over the following days. There weren't enough chairs to seat everyone and the foyer took on a party atmosphere. Most of the witnesses knew each other and planned to meet at the Viceroy in Bondi Junction to compare notes once the interviews were over as it was closer than heading down to the Regent at Bondi Beach.

A sergeant stood with a folder reading out names. Each person was allocated a room where they were to be interviewed by a detective accompanied by a constable. They were told they were not under arrest and had attended voluntarily; they were there purely to answer questions about what they had observed in the Regent and as soon as the interview was over they were free to go. A couple of witnesses were tempted to clap.

Jimmy the Scot made his way to the allocated room and sat down facing Detective Sanderson, taking little notice of the lowly constable in attendance. Once the pleasantries and personal details were over, Sanderson asked Jimmy if he knew Trevor Pearce.

'Yes, but only in the pub. He was nae a mate,' Jimmy replied.

'Did you see him being attacked?'

Jimmy paused. 'There was lots of people so hard to see anyone do anything. One minute Trev was standing, then on the floor. Someone yelled out to call an ambulance and some of the lasses got upset. Typical.'

'Did you know the people standing around him?'

'Know them? They're lads in the boozer so of course I know them. Depends what you mean by know?'

Sanderson stifled a sigh. 'Okaaay. Did you *know* if any of the *lads* had a grudge against the deceased?'

'Depends what you mean by grudge. Trev was dafty. Annoying. Wouldn't let anyone near his bird. Most of the lads only tolerated him because he sold the odd bit of hooch.'

The detective made a quick note. 'Was Pearce a regular drug dealer?'

Jimmy chuckled. 'Aye. But nothing hard.'

'What do you mean by hard?'

'Heroin.'

Sanderson grimaced. 'You mentioned his 'bird'. Who was that?'

'Siobhan. Irish. He acted like he owned her.'

The detective made another note. 'Can you name the others who were in the bar when he was attacked?'

'There were the Liverpool lads and some others I know by sight but dunnae their names.'

'Well, can you name the men you do know?' Sanderson asked, trying to keep the impatience out of his voice.

'Aye. Steve, Morgo, Paddy … Harvey, Brian. ... Gazza. Tommy, Billy. Bottlo.'

'Bottlo?' Sanderson looked puzzled.

'Worked in a bottle shop when he first arrived.'

'Ah, okay. And you didn't see anyone go near Mr Pearce? Did you hear anything; an argument between Pearce and whoever attacked him? Anyone holding a weapon?'

'Nae.'

The detective, about to pass Jimmy his business card and thank him for his assistance, quickly retracted his hand. 'Did you know Mark Dunlop?'

'Mark?' Jimmy repeated.

'Yes. Mr Dunlop was found dead at Bondi Beach last Saturday night and we gather he was a regular at the Regent.'

Jimmy glumly stroked his stubbly chin. 'Is this connected to Trev?'

'We don't know yet, but as you were familiar with Mr Pearce, it seems likely you might have known Mr Dunlop.' The detective stared benignly at the Scotsman.

'Aye. I did know him. Nae well, but he was part of the Liverpool clan seeing he was from their neck of the woods. And I'm mates with them so met him over a drink. Seemed decent enough.'

'You weren't aware of anyone disliking him or him doing anything that would cause someone to hurt him?'

'Well, he had the mickey taken out of him cos some of the lads thought he was a poof, but it was only for a laugh.' The ensuing silence indicated the Scotsman appeared to have run out of information, until he said, 'He was good mates with Siobhan, Trev's other half. Her and him was really close.'

'Do you know her surname?'

Jimmy put his head back trying to remember. 'Could be Greene. With an e, Northern Irish. Spell things differently there.'

'Any chance you know where she lives?'

Jimmy shook his head. 'No. Prob'ly 'round here seeing how she comes to the pub all the time. Mark and Trevor would know, but they can't help you now.'

Detective Bourke and his offsider were waiting for Steve Bartlett.

'Alright?' Steve asked, as he walked into the interview room. He stood till Bourke indicated the chair.

'Good. How're you?' Bourke responded, watching the tradie as he sat down. He noted the shaved head, work boots, high vis vest plus the tattoos peeping out from under the rolled up blue shirt sleeves.

'Sound as, our kid,' Steve answered with a grin.

'Right.' Bourke doubted whether the two of them were speaking the same language. 'A lot has been going on. The fellow on the beach last weekend, and now this fellow, Mr Trevor Pearce. Two deaths and both connected in some way to the Regent.' Bourke hovered his pen over his notepad.

'How can I be of assistance?' Steve asked in a mock posh accent.

Bourke sighed inwardly. This guy was taking the proverbial. 'We're talking to everyone who was at the Regent the night Mr Pearce was attacked. You were a witness to the event?'

The young man nodded.

'Well. Do you mind telling me what you saw?'

Steve took a deep breath. 'Trev was standing with a group of lads and next minute he was on the floor.'

'And you didn't notice anything unusual? Someone with a knife? An argument? A fight?'

'No. Like I said, he was chatting one minute, then face down on the floor. No-one ran off or put their hand up.' Steve smirked at Bourke. 'Perhaps he sold a dodgy bag of weed to some headcase.'

'So, Mr Pearce was known as a drug dealer?'

167

'You must know that. The whole pub knew he was, including the bouncers. Trev got away with murder.' Steve laughed.

'Are you saying the pub protected him?'

'You'll have to ask them, but he seemed to have the run of the place. You must know the Regent is the centre of the drug dealing in Bondi.' Steve folded his arms and stared at the detective then at the constable who was trying to keep a straight face.

'What about Mark Dunlop? I'm assuming you knew him as well.'

Steve's face sagged slightly. 'He was a crackin' bloke. Real shame what happened.'

'What happened?' Bourke asked quickly.

'He snuffed it down the beach.'

'That's all you've heard?'

'What else could it be? He was well liked even if he was a shirt lifter.'

'A shirt lifter? Do you think that had anything to do with his death?'

'How the fuck would I know? I just had a few bevvies with him in the boozer. We weren't exactly close mates.'

'Even though you were both from Liverpool?'

'Are you mates with everyone from Sydney?'

Bourke couldn't help but agree and brought the interview to a close. Steve stood up and to Bourke's surprise held out his hand.

168

CHAPTER TWENTY-SIX

A few hours later Stone called his colleagues into his office. The last of the many interviewees had finally left the building. Cigarettes were lit, coffee cups filled and although they were tired, each man wanted to share his information.

'Thanks for staying on. Bloody incredible we got through so many interviews. Although there's still more to do. Al, let's start with you,' Stone instructed wearily.

Detective Sanderson lifted his shoulders and opened his notepad. 'I spoke to Jimmy Mackenzie first. Scottish bloke. Friends with the lot from Liverpool. He knew Pearce but said he didn't see anyone attack him. Too many people around. He also knew Mark Dunlop but other than saying he seemed a good bloke, had nothing to add. Oh, and Mackenzie thought he was a poof, but it was no big deal. The only thing of interest was Mackenzie mentioned an Irish girl, Siobhan. She was good mates with Dunlop, and Pearce was very possessive of her. She's definitely someone we need to talk to.'

Another agreed, saying her name had been mentioned to him as well. The others muttered the same.

169

'Did you find out her full name? Address? Phone number?' Stone asked, looking around at the circle of men.

Sanderson flicked through his notes. 'Greene with an e. Apparently something to do with being from Northern Ireland. Jimmy Mackenzie doesn't know where she lives but said as she's a regular at the Regent, he assumed she probably lives around the area.'

'Makes sense. Follow it up, Al. She's definitely connected to both men.'

Sanderson made a note while Stone turned his attention to Detective Bourke. 'Dave, what's your news?'

Bourke groaned. 'Fucking Poms. Bloody nightmare. Up their own arses.'

The others laughed. 'So, you don't like them?' one asked with a grin.

Bourke shook his head vigorously. 'That Steve Bartlett bloke was a real prick. But funnily enough he actually gave me quite a bit of information.' He looked at his notes. 'Mark Dunlop was gay. Pearce was the main drug dealer around the pub and from what Bartlett said, Pearce had the pub and the bouncers under control. He didn't see anyone attack Pearce. Too many people around him.'

Again, the rest of the group agreed. No-one in the bar had seen a thing.

Stone shook his head. 'That's hard to believe. Are they protecting someone? Or are they too afraid to say? If drugs are involved they could be protecting themselves or are too frightened to say in case they meet the same end. As well as talking to this Siobhan girl, a visit to the Regent and a chat to the manager, staff and bouncers is our next port of call. First thing tomorrow morning. Let's spoil their opening hour.'

Once the chuckles subsided, Stone continued, 'Thanks for your feedback but I've also heard something else of interest.' His colleagues stared at him. 'A young English chap told me yesterday that there was another drug dealer in the Regent the night Pearce was killed.'

Judging by the frowns and puzzled expressions, Stone realised he should have mentioned this fact before.

At nine o'clock the next morning Detectives Stone and Bourke were waiting at the front entrance to the Regent. Although the pub didn't open to the public until ten, they assumed the manager and some staff members would be present to set up.

Their knocks on the double doors went unanswered until finally one of the bar staff realised it wasn't an impatient customer. An attractive girl in barmaid attire opened the door, and after showing her their IDs she quickly invited them in.

'Is the manager here?' Stone asked.

171

'Jeff? Yeah, he's out the back. I'll get him for you,' she replied, watched by the two men as she walked away. Bourke raised his eyebrows. 'Bit of a sort.' Stone thought the same but said nothing. He had a flash-back to the New Zealand detective he'd fallen for in Rarotonga and her scathing comments about how men viewed women as sex objects only.

They stood in the entrance area gazing around the pub. Although Stone had been in the pub the other night, he now viewed it in a detached manner. It was divided into different sections, but all were linked in some way to the public bar. They'd been told how the area where Trevor Pearce had been attacked was slightly off to the right of the serving counter which was in the middle of the room so customers could be served from all sides. There were large screens on the walls to show sporting fixtures with a number of high tables and stools positioned around the room, as well as low tables and chairs in various places for more intimate conversations.

The barmaid reappeared with a youngish man dressed in a check shirt and chinos. He held out his hand. 'Jeff Carter. The manager. Assuming you're here about Trevor Pearce?'

'Got it in one,' Bourke replied, as he shook Jeff's hand and introduced himself and Detective Stone. 'And while we're here, about Mark Dunlop as well. Your establishment has certainly been a hive of activity lately.'

172

Jeff grimaced. 'Yes it has, unfortunately. Anyway, how can I help you? I've already spoken to the Bondi police.'

'Yes, we're aware of that but just want to go over a few details,' Stone explained politely. 'We've interviewed a large number of your patrons who were here on the evening Mr Pearce was attacked and there were common themes. It seems Mr Pearce was known to be the main supplier of drugs in this pub.' Stone stared at the manager.

His face reddening, Jeff turned to the barmaid. 'Anna, were you or any of the other staff aware Trevor sold drugs?'

'No. Not at all,' Anna denied, shaking her head. 'He was too busy with Siobhan.'

Still staring at the manager, Stone asked, 'You had no idea Mr Pearce was a dealer?'

'No, none.'

Stone smiled sceptically. 'Well, that brings me to another point. Siobhan Greene's name has been mentioned a lot. What was her relationship with Mr Pearce?'

Anna glanced at the manager as if wanting permission to speak. Jeff's silence encouraged her to do so. 'He really fancied her but I don't think it was mutual.' She pursed her lips. 'From what I saw, she seemed keen on Mark.'

'Mark Dunlop?'

'Yes. They were always chatting. Got on really well.'

173

'But wasn't Dunlop …' Bourke began when Stone interrupted. 'We've heard they were good friends. Was Mr Pearce aware of their friendship?'

Again, Jeff deferred to Anna. 'Yes,' she answered. 'They were often together. It gave Trev the shits. He didn't stand a chance with her, but he acted as if she was his girlfriend. Bit tragic really.'

'Do either of you think Mr Pearce was capable of attacking Mr Dunlop?' asked Stone.

Both shook their heads implying Trev didn't have it in him. Thought he was tough, but he wasn't, was the consensus.

'I would've thought you'd have to be pretty tough to be a drug dealer,' Bourke suggested. 'Yet you seem to say Mr Pearce was a bit of a wimp.'

Neither responded.

'And you've never seen or heard anything about Mr Pearce selling drugs?' Stone repeated. Faces were pulled in denial. 'When do the bouncers arrive? We'd like to talk to them as well.'

'They don't come in until three. The place only starts to fill up after the tradies arrive at around three-thirty. During the day it's mainly tourists and older regulars popping in for lunch,' Jeff explained.

Stone gave a quick nod. 'We'll be back,' he said, indicating to Bourke it was time to go. They began to walk away when Stone stopped and turned around. 'Oh. Just one more thing. I've heard there was another dealer here that night. A man wearing an AC/DC T-shirt. His minder guarded the gents' toilets so this bloke could do his business. Any idea who he was?'

Jeff and Anna protested that they had no idea who Stone was referring to.

'What do you think?' Stone asked Bourke as they made their way back to the car.

'I reckon they knew about Pearce and the other bloke but they're not going to admit it. Damage the pub and lose their jobs. Or they're too scared.'

'Yeah. Can you organise a couple of sergeants to go down and talk to the bouncers this arvo? Doubt they'll give much away but it's worth a try.'

'Will do.'

'It's interesting how many times the Irish girl has been mentioned. Did she set someone up to get rid of Pearce? Does she want to take over his business? Or maybe she was sick of the sight of him. He sounded like a control freak,' Stone mused aloud.

'Buggered if I know,' Bourke replied, as they got into the car.

CHAPTER TWENTY-SEVEN

It seemed to take forever for the bell to ring at three-thirty, signalling the end of the school day. Being a Friday there was no supervision of sports' practice and the majority of the teachers were heading down to the Yacht Club in Double Bay for drinks.

Julian was also going out for drinks but not to the Yacht Club. He decided to change into something less teacher-like before catching a taxi to the Regent. He felt a mixture of nerves and excitement. With luck Siobhan would be there, but, and it was a big but, would she speak to him again?

The Regent was already busy by the time he arrived. The Scousers and their mates were huddled together in animated conversation. He wondered if he should join them or had Siobhan already betrayed him? It troubled him that some of the blokes fancied Siobhan and they must have seen him go outside with her on the night Trevor was killed.

He bit the bullet and walked over. 'Alright?' he asked. A couple waggled their heads. Sipping his beer, he stood listening to the conversation. It was what he'd expected. It was all about the interviews at the police station. Who'd bumped off Trev? Was

Mark's death linked to Trev's? Maybe Mark was selling drugs as well? The police were a bunch of tossers and didn't like Poms. Where was Siobhan and why hadn't she been interviewed?

Suddenly, the conversation stopped. Siobhan had entered the pub. She looked over at the group and after ordering a drink, wandered towards them. 'Join you?' she asked.

No-one answered. Steve raised his glass to his mouth, staring at her over the rim. 'Didn't see you down the nick yesterday. We were all there … Not invited?'

Julian saw how a number of the men drew back in surprise at Steve's blunt question, but he, like Steve, waited for her response.

'Not pretty enough,' she joked, causing a couple of the lads to laugh. 'Good craic?'

Julian watched for Steve's reaction. He seemed angry but whether it was because he'd been interviewed by the police and Siobhan hadn't, he couldn't tell.

'You don't seem gutted by *your boyfriend's demise*,' Steve stated in his mock posh voice, causing a few to groan at his attempt to sound upper crust.

Siobhan glared at him then shook her head. 'He *wasn't* my fecken boyfriend.'

'No?'

'No! He was someone I knew in the pub. Just like you. Especially, when *you* wanted something.' She turned her back on Steve and greeted the lad standing nearest.

Julian felt like clapping. She'd put Steve in his place. She could certainly stand up for herself. He was deciding whether to say hello or not when Siobhan spun around facing him. 'Fancy seeing you.'

Aware he was blushing, Julian asked quickly if she wanted another drink. She agreed, ignoring the oohs and aahs from the observers and to add to his surprise she walked with him to the bar. 'Am I forgiven?' he asked, crossing his fingers.

'Of course,' Siobhan answered, smiling sweetly. Julian assumed she'd have more to say, but no. What to say next?

'Do you want to stay with the others or shall we go outside again?' he asked cautiously.

'Let's stay with your Pommie mates. Might be some good craic. Can't stay long as I have to go to work.'

'Work? At this time of day?'

'Thought you knew? What with all the slagging I get from our *mates*.'

Shaking his head, he waited for her to explain.

'I'm a dancer up at the Cross, or in other words, a stripper.' Siobhan's eyes narrowed as she watched for his reaction.

Julian grinned. 'No wonder you're so fit. Good on you.'

178

Her eyes lingered on his then she led him back to the group. Once again many went silent. It was obvious they'd been talking about her but she acted as if she hadn't noticed.

Facing Steve and those nearest, she asked, 'So, what did the bobbies ask yous?'

'The usual shite,' one said. 'If we knew *Mr Pearce* and did any of us see what happened?'

'And you answered yes and no,' Siobhan said.

'Got it in one,' was the answer. 'But *your* name came up a lot. You'll be getting a call from the po-lice soon.'

'Thanks for the warning.'

With a nod to Julian, she walked towards the exit to the beer garden. Once again, he followed.

'You alright?' Julian asked as they sat down. He could see she was struggling emotionally. Finally, Siobhan shrugged. She stared into her drink then raised her head to look straight at him. 'You men are all the same. You're always after something. Trev was, Brian, Paddy … Morgo. All after a ride. Be grand if someone just wants to be with me for me.'

'I do,' Julian said.

'No you don't. You want to find out about Mark.'

Julian opened his mouth to deny her accusation but she was right. Would she believe him if he told her again that he liked her and it wasn't just about Mark or getting his leg over? 'That was in the beginning. I know you don't believe me, but the more I've got to know you I think you're a bit of alright.'

Siobhan, whose eyes had not left Julian's face, gave a slight smile at his choice of expression. She leant forward and put her hand over his. 'Grand. I like a bit of you too.'

Julian looked doubtful. 'You sure?'

'Sure. Even though you're a Sasanach. Anyway, let's enjoy this drink as I have to leave soon.' She raised her glass and Julian tapped it with his.

Siobhan couldn't deny she was sorry to leave Julian but she had to earn a living and there was something she wanted to do before her first shift started at The Love Hut. Despite her previous misgivings about Julian, she was starting to believe what he said, especially as he'd told her what his real job was. An effing teacher! She hailed a taxi, directing the driver to take her to Les Girls in the Cross. The fare paid, she walked down a side street to a small café run by an Italian acquaintance. She'd become friendly with Riccardo while living in one of the many backpacker hostels in the area when she'd first arrived in Sydney and knew no-one.

The café always had an eclectic mix of customers. She recognised a few of them including Sunny a 'masseuse', another was a big black chap who was a hit with the ladies, and an older man who was a permanent fixture, always at the same table. Greetings were exchanged before she made her way to the counter to talk to the owner.

'Siobhan. Ciao. Come stai?' Riccardo greeted. 'Café? Vino?'

'Vino blanco,' Siobhan answered, stumbling over the pronunciation of grazie. They both laughed. 'You come here early,' Riccardo stated, as he poured her the glass of wine.

Siobhan glanced around. 'I know. Want to ask you something.' She picked up the glass and moved down to the end of the counter.

'Che cosa?' Riccardo asked quietly.

'Two of my friends have been killed in the last week. One was gay and the other was a dealer. Have you heard anything?'

'Who is dead?' Riccardo asked. Siobhan explained her friends were Mark Dunlop and Trevor Pearce who she knew from the Regent. Riccardo scratched his head but before he could answer a customer needed service. A coffee served, Riccardo returned. 'I heard of Trevor Pearce but not the other one.' He lowered his voice, causing her to lean over the counter. 'He maybe work for Jason Zervos. He controls most of dealing around the Cross. Your friend must have done something bad.'

Siobhan tightened her lips. 'I don't know. Trev was the main supplier at the Regent, but maybe someone else is trying to invade his territory?'

Riccardo didn't answer immediately. 'I heard there's new kid on the block. Maybe he want to take over Zervos's territory and your friend easy target. A warning.'

'Jesus. Whoever did it was effin' brilliant. No-one saw what happened even though Trev was surrounded by lots of the lads. Unless they're telling porkies. This sounds well serious. What's the name of the *new kid*?'

'You really want to know? Could be dangerous.'

'I'm already involved. The police probably think it's me who killed Trev. Everyone's told them I was his girlfriend but I fecken wasn't. He was an arse.'

'You no like him?' Riccardo grinned.

Siobhan gave him a tight-lipped smile. 'Come on. Tell me the fear's name.'

'Scusi?'

'The man. The man who's trying to take over from Jason Zervos.'

Riccardo raised his eyebrows. 'Dio mio, Irish are hard to understand.' Before he could answer, a customer waved at him. Siobhan waited impatiently; she needed to know who the potential enemy was, and she needed to know before she went to the Love Hut.

To add to her frustration, a couple of customers stood up to leave and Riccardo was caught up saying farewells. Finally, he returned. 'Sorry, but don't know name of new kid, but Zervos might. He will know competition. Words travel quick 'round here.'

Despite her disappointment at Ricardo's lack of information, Siobhan thanked him, kissing his cheeks Italian style. If Zervos turned up at the Love Hut before her first performance started, she'd ask him about the competition, otherwise she'd have to wait for him to turn up at his other clubs later that night.

'And you've heard nothing about Mark Dunlop?'

Riccardo shook his head. 'I put my ear to the ground, as they say, just for you.'

CHAPTER TWENTY-EIGHT

The First Fifteen were playing a home game and the pitch was surrounded by supporters of both teams. Jim stood amongst the noisy throng, making an attempt to appear interested in the match while surreptitiously peering around to catch a sight of Julian. Attending the First's games was an unwritten obligation of Jim's role as Deputy Head, although many of the teachers were present as well.

He wanted, no, he was desperate to catch up on any news that Julian may have. With the attack in the pub he felt the investigation into Mark's death had taken a back seat. To him it didn't seem surprising that a drug dealer was bumped off. They must make lots of enemies, especially from the competition or dissatisfied customers, but Mark's death wasn't normal.

'Afternoon, Mr Cameron,' a voice greeted, interrupting Jim's analysis. Thank Heavens! It was Julian.

'Hello. Been looking out for you,' welcomed Jim, as he stepped back from the crowd.

'Ditto.'

'Any news?'

'Yes.'

'And?'

'Lots of the regulars at the Regent have been interviewed by the police. Mainly about Trevor Pearce but some were asked about Mark. Unfortunately, nothing to report there and apparently no-one saw anyone stab Pearce. However, the best news is I'm friends again with Siobhan.' Julian paused theatrically.

'And?' Jim asked impatiently, thinking how Julian could be bloody annoying.

'Come on, Mr Cameron. She's a great source of information. And judging by the other night, before she went to work, she's willing to share with me what she knows about both men.'

Sighing, Jim apologised.

'It's okay. I know I can be a bit glib at times which probably doesn't help,' Julian excused.

'We all have our own way of coping,' Jim replied, thinking back to his time during the Vietnam War. Reaction to stress was shown in many different forms. Some diggers laughed away their worries, others became aggressive and argumentative while others became silent and withdrawn.

'Anyway, what's the story with Siobhan? How did you manage to win her over?'

Julian grinned. 'Charm, mate, charm. And my staggering good looks!'

'Of course.'

'She hasn't been interviewed by the police yet but expects to get the call.'

'Does she have any idea why Mark was killed? Does she think both deaths are linked?'

'Steady on. Didn't want to push her too hard. Only just won her back. Turns out she's a *dancer,* euphemism for stripper, so couldn't stay long.' Julian grinned. 'Must go to one of her shows. But she did say she was with Mark in the pub on the night he died. They had a few drinks and then he left.' Julian stopped to think. 'He was meant to go to Oxford Street to meet his boyfriend.'

A huge cheer from the spectators erupted and they both looked to see which team had scored a try. Distracted by the conversion to be kicked by St Cuthbert's, they watched the successful result then Jim asked, 'I'm a bit puzzled why Alan wanted to meet you at a pub rather than the police station. Did he say why?'

Hoping Jim hadn't felt left out, Julian brushed off the question by saying Stone felt like a beer.

'Did he ask you about Trevor?'

'Only if I'd seen anything of interest, or anyone who could have attacked him. But I hadn't. Outside with Siobhan.'

They stood thinking. 'It must have been someone who didn't stand out. Someone who was a regular so wasn't noticeable. If it'd been a stranger, he would have been identified. Regulars are usually aware of new arrivals. When you first went to the pub, did you stand out?' Jim asked.

'Yes, of course. The Scousers eyed me with suspicion, as well as everyone else in that crowd. I know I'm still not fully accepted.' Julian ran a hand through his hair. 'Oh, and I did tell Alan about the other dealer who was in the pub on the same night Trev was killed.'

'What? On the same night? Who was it?

'No idea, but he seemed big time. Had a minder who wouldn't let anyone into the toilets unless he recognised them. I told Stone he was wearing an AC/DC T-shirt and looked Greek or Italian.'

'Shit. Another dealer on the same night?' Jim shook his head in disbelief.

'I know. Seems very coincidental.'

Maybe it's best not to go back to the pub for a bit. We seem to be dealing with some very, how can I put it? Shady characters.'

Julian ignored Jim's comment and turned to watch the game.

CHAPTER TWENTY-NINE

The building site was in the centre of Sydney's CBD. A multi-storey building was replacing a demolished historical icon in George Street. History didn't seem to matter to the developers nor the politicians, and to the tradies, a job was a job.

Steve stood outside on the footpath sucking on a cigarette waiting for Paddy, Brian and Morgo to arrive. 'Alright?' Paddy asked, glancing slyly at the others once they neared their mate.

'Yeah, ya nob'ead,' Steve said, throwing his butt on to the pavement and vigorously stubbing it out with his work boot.

'Wrong side of the bed?' Morgo grinned. Steve's withering look stopped any further chit chat and the four made their way to the alimak. In silence and the early morning light, they watched the city emerge as the work lift slowly went higher.

'What did the police ask you?' Steve questioned, while the alimak cranked its way skywards.

'We've already told you. The usual shite. Did we know Trevor and that Mark lad? See anything when Trev was attacked?' Paddy answered.

Steve scratched his genitals through his work shorts. 'Nothing else?' They shook their heads. 'Looks like the bizzies think both deaths are connected. Bought anything from Trev lately?' he asked. Heads were shaken. 'Oh yeah. Right. If the police talk to you again, don't tell them anything about buying stuff. You'll lose your visa and be on the first ship home.'

'Ship?' Paddy asked.

'No, ya bellend. A fucking plane.'

'Aye. 'Course. Knew that.'

Steve shook his head in despair. 'If you want to stay, keep your mouth shut. They'll do anything to get us out of the country.'

The alimak jerked to a stop on level 35.

Watching Steve stride over the recently set concrete floor, his mates turned to each other. 'Fucken 'ell. What's up with 'im?' Paddy complained, as he stepped out of the cage.

'Fuck yeah. He's in a right state. Does he know something we don't? Maybe he's bought a lot of gear off Trev lately. Doesn't want to get busted,' Brian suggested.

'Lose his visa.' Paddy laughed, then his face turned serious. 'We've all brought stuff off Trev. What if we get done?'

Morgo bent down to pick up his tool bag. 'Just hope the fucken coppers aren't bothered about that. The whole fucken pub's bought stuff off Trev. They can't arrest everyone.'

'Jeez. Hope not. Probably Siobhan who done him in. She's a right cow. And, she was mates with that guy Mark as well. Sooner the bizzies get her the better,' Paddy added.

'What's she ever done to you?' Brian demanded.

'Eeeeew,' Morgo whined. 'Fancy the bint do ya?'

'No! Just sick of every bugger slagging her off. Just cos Trev, the tool, treated her like shit, you don't have to.'

Paddy and Morgo nudged each other. 'Sorry, mate. Didn't know you were her bessie mate,' Paddy accused.

'Get fucked.'

'Ooooh. What's up *your* arse?' Morgo continued. 'She's a slapper. Did anything Trev wanted so long as she could get her fix. And she's a fucken stripper. Prob'ly a prossie.' He grinned at Paddy.

Seeing Brian clench his fists, they stepped back. 'Jesus, mate. Settle down. Can't ya take a fuckin' joke?'

Slowly unclenching his hands, Brian grabbed his tool bag, striding off in the same direction as Steve. Paddy and Morgo waited, watching. What was up with him? Both took deep breaths and slowly followed. Thank God it was Saturday and they only had to work till lunchtime. Then they could go to the pub.

CHAPTER THIRTY

As the hours ticked by, Stone sat fidgeting at his desk feeling frustrated with the lack of progress into both deaths. Two men were dead. The second one was more prominent as it had occurred in the middle of a crowded pub plus Pearce was a dealer, but did he deserve any more attention than Mark Dunlop? Mark's death had no leads other than the call from the bloke with a Pommie accent and as the call had been from a phone box it made it hard to trace. No-one else had come forward with any information and Darcy had been no help other than saying he and Mark were meant to meet later that night. The deaths didn't seem connected in any way except for the Irish woman, Siobhan Greene.

He walked out of his office to ask one of the constables if he'd found out where Miss Greene lived. Yes he had. 'She lives near Rose Bay, just over the hill from Bondi.'

'Be good if you'd let me know,' Stone reprimanded.

'Sorry, sir. Only just managed to track her down. She's moved around a lot.' The constable hurriedly wrote down the address and phone number.

Stone suddenly remembered he already had her number as Julian had given it to him when they'd met in the Viceroy. Too many beers, he thought guiltily, and being distracted by their chat about rugby. Forcing himself to concentrate on the matter at hand, he wondered how she could afford to live in an expensive suburb like Rose Bay? Most British backpackers lived in Bondi, Kings Cross or Manly. What was her job? A call to Jim might answer some questions, that's if he'd had any updates from Julian.

His call to Jim resulted in an arrangement for them to meet at the Viceroy in Bondi Junction once Jim had finished his school duties that afternoon.

Stone arrived first to find the pub packed. He was finally able to order two schooners and quickly claimed a space at the bar. He only had time to light a cigarette before Jim hurried in. 'Sorry to keep you, Alan. That bloody meeting …'

'No problem. Hope you like Coopers Green?'

'After that meeting I'd drink arsenic.' Jim picked up his beer and took a long swig. 'Aaaah. That's better. Whoever invented bloody meetings deserves to be shot.'

Alan laughed. 'Remember those old John Cleese videos showing how useless most meetings were?'

'Oh my God, yes. Bloody brilliant.'

'Bad day?'

192

'Just the usual twaddle. Anyway, let's not talk about work. What's going on?'

'It's a mixed bag. There've been interviews with a large number of the punters who were in the Regent the night Pearce was killed, but surprise, surprise, nobody saw anything. No doubt Pearce supplied them with their drugs of choice. I spoke to your mate, Julian Butterworth but he saw nothing. Was outside the whole time with the elusive Siobhan Greene.' Stone lifted his beer. 'How do the boys react to Julian's name, Butterworth? Take the piss?'

'A little at first, but he can take care of himself so they soon gave up,' Jim answered.

Alan drank before continuing. 'Unfortunately, no-one could really enlighten us about Mark. Some knew who he was and his being gay seemed reasonably common knowledge, but their information was minimal. Although, many of them did mention he was friends with Miss Greene. She seems to be the link between both men. Most of those we interviewed thought she was Pearce's girlfriend, as well as being mates with Mark. Also, I got the feeling some of the chaps are keen on her.'

'Do you think she's behind it all?'

'No idea, but we'll be talking to her as soon as we can. She took a bit of tracking down, but now I have her address and phone number will be in touch. She seems well known but not known, if you get my drift?'

'Yes. That's typical of pubs. They're mates in the pub but not necessarily outside. Alcohol is the lynchpin.'

'Good point. But I did get the impression lots of the Poms are genuinely connected because they're strangers in a strange land … Who said that?' Stone asked.

Jim thought for a moment. 'Think it's from the Bible. Normally I give Shakespeare the credit for most quotes, but don't think so in this case.'

'I'll take your word for it.'

'So, there was no update regarding Mark?' Stone shook his head and Jim frowned in disappointment. 'Hang on a sec while I get us another Coopers.' Jim waved his hand to get attention from any member of the bar staff but they seemed to have been trained in how to avoid eye contact. He slid off his stool and leaned over the bar waggling his hand unable to contain his frustration. 'Bloody hell, Alan. What do you have to do to be served around here?' Stone's attempt to calm him down had little effect. 'Jesus Christ. Sorry mate. What with everything that's going on and all you want is a quiet beer ...'

'Yeah, feeling the same.' The two men looked at each other, then laughed. Suddenly, a barmaid appeared in front of them, 'What'll you have?'

'Where were we?' Alan asked, after they'd received the long-awaited drinks.

'Mark. Any updates?' Jim asked despondently.

'Not really. A couple of people said they saw him in the pub with Miss Greene and then he left. I've spoken to his boyfriend, Darcy. Ever heard such an appropriate name for a hairdresser? Or perhaps his parents were Jane Austen fans,' Stone presumed, with a shake of his head.

Jim chuckled, telling Alan about the strange spelling of some of the students' names at St Cuthbert's. 'Thank God I've got a simple name, and no-one ever has to ask me how to spell it. Anyway, what was Darcy like? Anything interesting to say?'

'Obviously older than Mark. An Aussie. Got the feeling he wasn't particularly upset or surprised by Mark's untimely demise.'

'Really?'

Alan pondered. 'Although he'd rung him a few times, he just assumed Mark had met someone else or had ended the relationship.'

'Gosh. That's odd.'

Alan shrugged. 'Different strokes?'

Jim's lips thinned. 'A good actor?'

'Hard to believe Darcy could be capable of murder. Doesn't seem the type. How's that for detective work? To coin a phrase, did Mark jump or was he pushed?'

'Jesus, mate. That sounds so pragmatic.'

195

'Sorry, but murder often is, especially when it comes to drugs. I know there's the common belief most murders are committed by someone the victim knows, but not in every case.'

The two sat drinking in thoughtful silence. 'My turn,' Alan offered, seeing their schooners were nearly empty. 'Just a midi,' Jim ordered, 'I'm driving.'

Not bothering to try to catch the eye of a barman or barmaid, Alan walked towards the end of the bar and soon returned. 'Have *you* got any news? Anything from Mr Butterworth?' he asked.

'Jesus, sorry Alan, my head is up my bum. I do have some information. Julian told me that Siobhan is a *stripper* up at the Cross.' Jim raised his eyebrows, as did Stone. 'And,' Jim continued, 'there was another dealer in the Regent on the night Pearce was attacked. Apparently, he wore an AC/DC T-shirt. That's the only identification Julian got. Bit strange another dealer being there at the same time.'

Alan was about to inform Jim that this was old news when a man who looked vaguely familiar stood behind them.

'Evening, gents. Your pool skills improving?'

Both stared at him, then it dawned, he was the bloke they'd played pool against in the Regent.

Stone laughed, replying that they hadn't.

'How's I.T. going?' the man asked, giving them a sly grin through his thick, greying beard.

'Terry! And your mate was Scott,' Stone exclaimed.

'Good memory,' Terry confirmed. 'Any luck with the *investigation*?'

Stone held up his hands. 'It's a fair cop, gov. Did our terrible pool playing give us away?'

'Yeah, no. Word gets around and I put two and two together.'

'So, what've you heard?' Stone asked. 'Seeing as you're a bit of a detective.'

Terry stopped smiling. 'Not a lot. There are various theories about who attacked Trev, but nothing definite. The general view is he was bumped off by a rival drug dealer but from what I've heard no-one saw anything.'

'Any idea who the other dealer is?'

Terry shook his head.

'Can you think of anyone else who had it in for Trevor?'

'Where do I start?' Terry joked. 'His *clients* seemed happy with his products, so haven't heard many complaints. Although, when it comes to money there's always someone who whinges.' He stroked his beard. 'And of course, there's the lovely Siobhan who Trev took a shine to, but now it seems she's rather taken by a young Englishman named Julian Butterworth.'

197

Stone waited, glancing at Jim. This guy certainly had his finger on the pulse. He reached inside his jacket to pull out a business card. 'Here's my number. Ring if you can think of anything that could be helpful,' Stone said, passing it to Terry. 'And, by any chance, do you know anything about Mark Dunlop?'

Terry frowned. 'Sorry, mate. Wish I could help you there.' He gave them a tip of his imaginary hat and wandered off into the crowd.

CHAPTER THIRTY-ONE

Siobhan woke to the sound of the telephone ringing. It was too effing early. She hadn't got to sleep till the sun came up. She had a good idea who it might be and sure enough it was the police. Would she go to the Waverley Police Station to answer some questions?

Hanging up the phone, she returned to her bed and thought about what was ahead. They'd ask her about Mark and Trev. She knew they'd find her the link between the two men. Trev was well known in the pub but Mark not so much. Some of the Scousers were aware of him and had the odd chat, 'specially as he was from Liverpool, but whether it was because Mark was queer, they weren't that interested in him. Trev, on the other hand, sold them drugs. Her main concern was if the police going to ask about her drug use.

Siobhan slowly got out of bed and headed to the shower. With luck the water would wake her up and clear her head. How should she dress? To tart up might look too confident but to dress down wasn't good either. Dress like going to work in an office?

The Waverley Police Station was reasonably quiet when she arrived and after telling the desk sergeant who she was, Siobhan sat in the waiting area till she was summoned. It didn't take long.

'Thanks for coming, Miss Greene. I'm Detective Alan Stone,' he welcomed. As she followed him, Stone called out to one of the constables to join them. 'Please take a seat,' he instructed and shut the door to the interview room. He sat down at the small table facing her with the constable sitting further away.

'This shouldn't take long, and I want to reassure you, you are not a suspect. I just want to ask you a few questions.'

'No worries,' she said with a grin. 'Isn't that what you Aussies say?'

Stone smiled. 'That's if you're an Aussie, I'm actually a Kiwi. Slightly different.'

'Ah, sorry. Met lots of Kiwis in Bondi. Should have picked it.'

'No worries,' Stone repeated with a grin. 'I gather you're Irish. Do you get mistaken for Scottish or English?'

'Mainly for a Scouser.'

'Oh yes. I gather there are lots of Irish in Liverpool … Anyway, better get down to business. I'm sure you're aware of the deaths of two men with whom you have a connection. We've spoken to a number of regulars at the Regent and your name was mentioned in relation to both Mark Dunlop and Trevor Pearce.' Stone opened his notebook and took a biro from his jacket pocket. 'I'd like you to describe your relationship with both men. We'll start with Mark Dunlop.'

Siobhan sat up straighter and crossed her legs. 'Mark was grand. I didn't know him long as he'd only been in Sydney for a few months, but we became good friends. You know he was gay?'

Stone said he did. 'Do you think his being a homosexual had anything to do with his death?'

'I heard he'd drowned,' Siobhan gasped, her shoulders jerking back in shock.

'At the moment we're treating his death as suspicious.'

'Why? He'd never hurt a soul.'

'Did Mark ever take drugs when you were with him?'

'No. If he did, it was never serious. He told me him and his partner took the occasional pill or the odd joint but nothing more than that. Why?'

'Unfortunately, I'm not at liberty to tell you. But can I ask if you think he ever took heavy drugs?'

'No! Never. He looked after himself, and Darcy did as well. Is that how Mark died? An overdose?'

Stone shook his head. 'As I said, I'm not at liberty to say.' He waited for a few seconds. 'Can you think of anyone who would want to harm Mr Dunlop?'

Siobhan contemplated the question. 'The only person I can think of is Trevor but he's dead too.'

201

'Mr Pearce? Why would he harm Mr Dunlop?'

'He was jealous of Mark. Didn't like us being friends. Trev thought he was my boyfriend, but he bloody wasn't,' she said emphatically. 'He couldn't understand how I could be friends with a man without sex. Stupid twat. I could talk to Mark. He told me about his life, and I talked about mine. But fecken Trev was a dinosaur. So effing possessive.'

'Why were you friends with Mr Pearce if you didn't like him?'

Rolling her eyes, she stated, 'The whole pub was friends with Trev.'

'Because he sold drugs?'

Siobhan pulled her lips together then shrugged her shoulders.

'As you and Mark were close, are you sure you can't think of anyone who'd want to hurt him? Did he ever tell you he was worried about someone who had a grudge against him?'

She leant her head back, thinking. 'He told me he felt safer in Sydney than in Liverpool. He knew his family didn't approve of anyone being queer, so he was glad to leave and come here.'

'Did they know he was … queer?'

'Don't think so. His ma was always after him to get married so maybe she didn't know or didn't want to.'

Stone made a note. 'And what about Mr Pearce? Did he have enemies?'

She laughed. 'His job might have made him unpopular with other dealers, but he never told me about enemies. And the others weren't going to bite the hand that fed them.'

'The others?'

'The regulars at the Regent.'

'But you seemed closer to him than the other patrons.'

Siobhan put her head to one side. Her mind was whirring. Should she tell him what she knew and keep schtum about Riccardo's information?

'Miss Greene. We just want to find out why Mark died and who attacked Pearce. We're not out to get you,' Stone stressed, looking into her eyes.

Siobhan blinked rapidly. 'I want to help you find out about Mark, but I don't give a, excuse the language, fuck about Trev. I'll tell you what I can as long as I'm not placing myself in any danger.'

'Don't worry. Whatever you tell me will be in the strictest confidence,' Stone reassured. He hoped he could keep his promise.

CHAPTER THIRTY-TWO

Siobhan wished she'd taken the night off. What with being woken up early, talking to Detective Stone and only catching up on a little sleep in the afternoon, made the thought of dancing exhausting. But, she needed the money and she needed to talk to Jason Zervos as soon as possible. He hadn't been at the Love Hut the previous night. Strange as he usually started there before moving onto his other clubs.

With fingers crossed she walked into the Love Hut, asking the doorman if the boss was in residence. He was. Feeling more awake, Siobhan made her way to the dressing room. After saying hello to the other girls who were busy adorning their faces with exotic makeup, she changed into her skimpy costume. She couldn't believe how nervous she felt and seeing her nearly naked image in the mirror made her question what the hell was she doing? She wanted to be taken seriously. Looking attractive to Zervos was part of her plan but to talk to him wearing very little was not appropriate. She grabbed a long cardigan, pulled it tightly around her body and went into the bar. Jason Zervos was there, sitting on a high stool with a couple of his minders.

Her aim was to tell her boss that she was *not* Trevor's girlfriend and she was *not* involved in his drug dealing, then to ask him if he had any idea who could have killed Trev. And more importantly if he knew anything about why Mark was dead.

Zervos glanced sideways as she stood next to him. 'Daniella. How are you?' he asked, eyeing her body in its revealing outfit. Realising her cardigan had fallen open, she was about to draw it around her but now she was standing next to Zervos, decided not to as a bit of temptation might make him more amenable to answering her questions.

Surprised he'd remembered her stage name, Siobhan confirmed she was grand. Zervos took sip of his drink.

'Mr Zervos, I'm sorry to bother you. I know how busy you are, but can I tell you something?'

The minders stared at her, and she sensed they were about to move her on when Zervos answered, 'Of course. Go right ahead.'

'It's a bit complicated.' She paused. 'You've probably heard of Trevor Pearce?' Seeing him give a flicker of recognition, she continued, 'Everyone thinks I was his girlfriend, but I wasn't. Not my cup of tea.' She smiled knowingly. 'He was attacked in the Regent a few nights ago … And a good friend of mine, Mark Dunlop, also died not long before. Went to the same pub.' Touching his arm, she asked, 'I'm wondering if you can help me?'

'How exactly can I help you?' Zervos asked, his eyes flicking over her breasts.

'I've heard *you* may know who was behind their deaths,' Siobhan stated, hoping her tone indicated that Zervos was a man of power and who knew what was going on. 'Trev was an easy target but I'm angry about Mark. I'd do *anything* to find out who killed him.' Her offer was not lost on Zervos. He grinned, delicately licking his top lip. Siobhan's stomach churned.

'Was this Mark bloke your boyfriend?' Zervos asked, looking into the distance at the empty stage.

'God no. He was queer. But he was a good friend … I can't think of any reason why anyone would kill him. Unless it was a nob'ead who hated gays.'

'Wouldn't know,' Zervos dismissed. 'How'd he die?'

'He drowned, but the police say his death is suspicious.'

Zervos's nostrils flared. 'What exactly do you want to know?'

'I know you're an important man in the Eastern suburbs so I'm hoping you may be able to tell me what you've heard. Is someone trying to take over Bondi, so they got rid of Trevor? And why my friend may have been killed?'

'How do I know you're not working for the police?'

Siobhan laughed coquettishly. 'Do I look or sound like the police? Don't think I'm big enough or strong enough to arrest anyone.'

206

Zervos smirked. 'No.' He leant back, his eyes grazing her body. 'If you're a good girl I might see what I can find out.' He grinned at his minders before saying, 'I think you've got a show to do.'

'Your wish is my command,' Siobhan flattered, then with a swing of her hips walked away.

The following afternoon, Siobhan caught the bus down to Bondi Beach. She'd had a decent sleep during the day and was pleased that Zervos had been willing to talk to her. It would be interesting to see if he came up with the answers to her questions.

The Regent was quiet as it was early doors. Siobhan ordered a schooner before going out to the beer garden to catch some sun. Lighting a cigarette, her thoughts returned to Trev. Why did someone want to kill him? It was hard to believe it could be one of the regulars. Why cut off their nose to spite their face? Logically, it came back to Zervos. He hadn't seem surprised by Trev's death and Trev had always implied that Zervos was his supplier. Her boss came across as a rich wanker, used to getting his own way, but why would he have Trev murdered if Trev worked for him?

Her beer finished, Siobhan returned to the main bar. It was still quiet, making her doubt whether it was worth staying. One more, she decided and stood waiting for the barmaid to finish collecting the few used glasses left on tables.

'Another beer?' the barmaid asked on her return, giving her a smile.

'Thanks, Anna. Haven't seen you for a bit.'

'Been off sick. The manager told me to come back when I was myself again.' Anna winked.

Siobhan laughed. 'Grand. Nice to have an understanding boss. Might be looking for a job meself.'

'Want me to have a word with Jeff?'

'Ah no. The regulars would expect free drinks.'

'Know what you mean.' They both laughed.

Siobhan raised her glass to the barmaid, sensing Anna's eyes following her as she walked back to the beer garden.

Making the schooner last as long as possible, the chatter and laughter emanating from the public bar told her more regulars had arrived and maybe one of them would be Julian. Should she stay in the beer garden or go inside? Deciding on inside, Siobhan peered around to see who'd arrived, but there was no sign of Julian. Her disappointment at his absence surprised her. Don't go soft, she reprimanded herself.

Anna was busy serving and when her turn came, Siobhan quickly asked for another beer, not wanting to engage in any more chat. Once served, she made her way over to join the Pommie crowd. 'Alright?' she asked.

Steve grinned. ''Ello, 'ello. Look who's 'ere. Thought you'd be in the big 'ouse by now. Who'd you bribe to get out?' The other Poms laughed, watching to see how Siobhan would react.

'Used my charm and beauty,' she responded. 'Had the po-lice eating out of my hand.'

''Course you did.' Steve's face became serious. 'What did *you* tell the bizzies?'

Siobhan stared at him. 'What did *you* tell them?'

'Nothing. Nothing to tell.' Steve glanced at his mates, shrugging his shoulders.

Lying twat, Siobhan thought, but kept quiet.

It was getting on for six o'clock when Julian finally entered the Regent. He'd had sport's practice after class and couldn't leave the school grounds until the teams had gone home or back to their boarding houses. Catching a taxi to save time, he hoped to talk to Siobhan, that's if she were in the pub, and he was keen to hear the news from his new 'mates'.

The pub was heaving, but he forced his way through to the bar. As it was later than usual, he decided to have something other than beer. Fuck it if the Scousers mocked him.

'A double scotch, please,' Julian ordered.

He paid, then as usual searched the venue for familiar faces. He saw a number of the English crew and was about to walk towards them when a hand prodded his back. Turning, he faced Siobhan. The tingle he felt shocked him.

'Hello. I was hoping you'd be here,' he said. Siobhan returned his smile and said the same. 'Shall we go outside? Get away from the masses?' he suggested and began to walk in the direction of the beer garden. He stopped. 'How are you for a drink? Sorry, I should have asked.'

'I'm grand,' Siobhan replied, holding up her glass.

The beer garden was nearly full, but they managed to find a couple of empty seats. They sat for a moment staring at each other. 'It's good to see you,' both began then laughed. Julian placed his hand over Siobhan's. 'I've missed you.'

Siobhan withdrew her hand and took a sip of her drink. 'I've got something to tell you.'

Seeing Julian's face droop, she continued quickly, 'I talked to Jason Zervos.'

'Who?'

'He's a bigwig in the Cross. A king pin … Owns lots of the clubs where I dance. Don't panic,' she reassured. 'I heard he was Trev's supplier, so I wanted to ask him some questions.'

'Jesus, Siobhan! What the hell are you doing? It's dangerous dealing with men like him.'

'I know. But I want to find out what happened to Mark. And you do too.'

Julian could only nod, amazed at her determination. 'Why do you care so much?'

'I'm sick of most men being total gobshites. Mark was a lovely man and he didn't deserve to die. Trev, on the other hand, was a waste of space. Total control freak.'

'And how did you get on with this Jason … whatever his name is?'

'Zervos. He's my boss so I asked him to help me find out about Mark and Trev. He seemed interested, so maybe there's someone who's treading on his territory. He didn't exactly say Trev worked for him, but it was obvious. Of course, he'll already have his spies investigating but I want him to help us find out why Mark died.'

'Siobhan, why would he tell *you*?'

She smiled knowingly, thrusting out her breasts.

'You didn't?'

'Not yet, but a girl's gotta do what a girl's gotta do.'

'For God's sake. Well, I'll have to come with you. I can't let you do this on your own.'

'Don't be an eejit. How on earth can you come with me?'

Julian gulped his scotch and looked around to see if the beer garden's small bar was still open. It was. He stood up without asking Siobhan if she wanted another and went straight to the servery. He should never have got her involved, he scolded himself. Why the hell was she messing around with this Jason bloke? Was she really so fond of Mark Dunlop to go to such lengths?

He picked up the schooners and returned to Siobhan. 'You can't do this,' he stressed, looking around to see if anyone had heard him. 'It's far too risky. Mark is dead and nothing you do can bring him back.'

Siobhan drew her glass across the table. 'I know that, but I'm not letting some arse-wipe get away with murder.'

Julian opened his mouth to argue but seeing the determination on her face, closed his lips. He watched her staring into her beer. He wanted to break the silence. This was not what he'd envisaged when he was hoping to see her again. 'Well, if I can't stop you I want to be with you when you talk to your boss again.'

'How can you? He'd be suspicious and I'd learn nothing,' Siobhan argued.

Julian gazed around at those seated at the nearby tables. 'I know, but I can be your gay brother or gay friend. Your protection. Don't dealers always have a 'heavy' to protect them?'

'You? Gay? A heavy? You are joking?' Siobhan choked on her mouthful of beer.

'Why not? He wouldn't be threatened by me, and I'd just need to dress a little differently. Most men can't tell who's gay or not, unless it's really obvious. Know what I mean?'

'But what if he's prejudiced against queers? Sydney's not as bad as home but the AIDS thing is a worry. Jason's probably the sort of eejit who thinks you catch it by having a chat.'

'Then I'll be the guy who stands in the background wearing dark sunglasses, looking mean.'

Siobhan sighed, but Julian could see she was considering his proposition. 'I'd have to tell him about you. Warn him. Hint you're no threat … sex and all that.' She gulped her drink. 'Can you defend yourself?'

''Course I can. I play union and did a bit of boxing at school,' he boasted.

'Not much use if someone has a gun.'

Julian shrugged. 'Well. What exactly is *your* plan?'

'I work for him and I want him to trust me, then in the throes of hot passion he'll tell me what happened to Mark and maybe Trevor. Someone had it in for Trev. There can't be that many dealers, so surely Jason must have some idea who wanted him dead, or it could be that Jason had Trev killed as he wanted more of the takings?' Siobhan took another swig of her beer.'

213

Reaching for Siobhan's hand, Julian queried if she really would have sex with Zervos to get the information? She'd done worse, she informed him, once again sliding her hand away from his.

CHAPTER THIRTY-THREE

'What the hell!' Jim yelled. 'You're both mad. She can't sleep with a drug lord, or whatever you call this bloke, so she can find out who killed Mark or that other guy. You'll both end up dead. Is that what you want?'

'Of course not. I tried to talk Siobhan out of it, but she wouldn't listen.'

'So, you're going to be her *gay* friend and protector. I've never heard such bullshit. I'll have to tell Alan Stone about this. God knows what he's going to say. Wish I'd never got you involved.'

'Mr Cameron! Calm down. Tell Alan and see what he says. He may think it's a good idea. Siobhan's tough. She is a stripper at Zervos's clubs.'

Groaning, Jim sat down behind his desk, head in hands. 'Julian, this is getting out of hand. We should have left everything to the police.'

'Too late. She's involved and so am I. I think you should contact Stone and arrange a meeting with him and us. If he tells Siobhan not to get involved then hopefully she won't do anything more or …'

Jim butted in. 'But this Jason Zervos bloke, *her boss*, knows what she's doing so he'll be putting out feelers to find out more about her. She's in danger no matter what.'

'Ring Alan now,' Julian commanded. 'We can meet him after school. I can contact Siobhan and tell her where to meet us.'

Jim rolled his head back, stared up at the ceiling then picked up the phone.

As expected, Stone was pissed off at the news, telling Jim he'd already interviewed Siobhan, but once he'd had time to mull over the details, agreed to meet in The Viceroy at four- thirty that afternoon. Julian rang Siobhan and insisted she join them. However, her argument about not wanting to be seen in public with the police was convincing. If word got back to Zervos that she'd been seen socialising with a detective then her plan would be buggered. Sydney wasn't the biggest city, especially not the Eastern suburbs.

'She's right,' Julian said to Jim. 'We need to meet in private. But where?'

Grumbling, Jim told him it would have to be at his place. Calls were made to rearrange the venue. He waited till Julian had left his office before ringing Anh. Rather than being annoyed, his wife was amenable, saying she looked forward to meeting Julian and

Siobhan. Jim heaved a sigh of relief. He wouldn't have been as accommodating.

Julian grabbed a lift with Jim. The atmosphere in the car was a tad stressed but once at the house, Anh's smiling face soothed the tension.

'Come in. Come in,' she welcomed. 'Jim's told me all about you.'

Julian couldn't resist asking, 'All good I hope?' To which she replied that it was.

While Anh took Julian through to the lounge, Jim answered a loud knock on the front door. He opened the door to find Stone and Siobhan standing together. Seeing Stone's car parked in the street and a taxi driving off hinted that she had not come with him. Too risky to be seen together. Apart from a quick hello they both acted as if they'd never met before.

Siobhan was not what Jim had expected. For some reason her long red hair reminded him of Little Red Riding Hood. She was petite although muscular which he put down to her occupation. They followed Jim down the hall, joining Julian and Anh in the lounge. 'Where are the boys?' Stone asked, after saying hello and introducing Siobhan to Anh and Jim.

'Not home yet. Footy practice,' Anh informed, indicating for them to sit down. 'What can I offer you? Tea, coffee? A beer?'

217

Noting their hesitation Jim suggested, 'Beer would be great, darling … Yes?' The consensus was a definite yes. Seeing an ashtray on the coffee table, Siobhan asked if she could smoke. Of course she could.

Each with a cigarette and a beer, the atmosphere became a little more relaxed. Stone leant forward to face Siobhan who sat on the couch opposite. 'We meet again. I gather you have a plan. Would you mind explaining it to me?'

Jim was surprised by Siobhan's aura of confidence. She showed no fear of Stone and the position he held, but before she could begin Anh walked back into the lounge holding a glass of wine. 'Do you mind if I join you?'

'Grand,' Siobhan confirmed as Anh sat down next to her husband.

Smiling at her, Siobhan began. 'Not sure if you know I'm a dancer and I perform in some of Jason Zervos's clubs.'

'How wonderful. No wonder you have such a good figure,' Anh enthused.

Jim was about to tell his wife *dancer* was another word for stripper but decided it wasn't the right time.

'Ah, thank you, Anh.' Siobhan smiled. 'It's an … *interesting* occupation. Because I work for Mr Zervos, I have access to him as he comes into his clubs most nights of the week. Likes to keep an eye on his customers. And staff. Anyway, I had a chat to him

218

about Mark and Trevor and he said he'd let me know if he heard anything.' She stopped. 'I tried to use my womanly charms and it may have worked.' She grinned at Anh who smiled back, but Jim could see his wife was worried by the possibility of Zervos taking up her offer.

'What do you hope to achieve by this?' Stone asked, 'Why would someone who owns clubs and virtually runs the Cross tell you anything?'

'Like us, Siobhan wants to find out about Mark … and Pearce,' Julian interrupted protectively.

The sudden noise from Daniel and Josh arriving home put a stop to the conversation. Anh went out to inform them that she and Dad were busy in the lounge with visitors and could they stay in the kitchen or their bedrooms till everyone had gone?

The sound of doors shutting and the distant noise of a video game assured the visitors the boys were not in earshot.

'Yes, but how would Zervos know anything about Mark?' Jim asked, satisfied his sons were elsewhere.

Siobhan frowned at Jim. 'Zervos seems to have his finger in lots of pies. He probably hears about everything. And he might know of someone who is trying to build up business in Bondi. A threat to his empire.'

Pursing his lips, Jim went silent.

219

Stone jumped in. 'I'm assuming from what you're saying, Zervos used Mr Pearce to sell his drugs in the pub? Did Pearce ever confirm that?'

'Not in so many words but he boasted his supplier was a big fish in the Cross. Trev liked being the big man with big connections,' Siobhan reasoned.

Leaning back on the couch, Stone thought for a minute then sat up straight. 'You may be right, but we can't assume it's Zervos who supplies the drugs or has anything to do with the two deaths. Word has it that Zervos is anti-drugs. Perhaps Mark got drugs from some other source and just overdosed.'

'Why?' Anh asked angrily.

Ignoring Anh's reaction, Julian suggested, 'Maybe Mark wanted to sell drugs to make money? It's not that far-fetched.'

Jim stared at Stone. 'Is that why he had the mobile phone?' Stone shrugged.

'But why would Mark want to sell drugs?' Anh asked. 'That's not like him at all.'

'As Julian said, maybe for the money,' Jim justified.

Anh's face fell. 'He could have asked us for money.'

'There may have been another reason,' Jim tried to soothe. Turning to Siobhan he asked, 'Was he being blackmailed?'

'Ah sure, I don't know. But he didn't like people knowing he was queer.'

'Yes,' Julian reinforced, 'but from what I've heard the prejudice isn't so bad in Sydney. Don't you have a Mardi Gras and gay clubs?'

'True, but don't forget the stigma of AIDS. Since the epidemic began lots of people have developed a very negative attitude towards anyone of that persuasion, so Mark being from Liverpool where you say they're not the most accepting, and then with AIDS, he may have felt very much on the outer,' Jim argued.

'Mark liked it here because he felt accepted,' Anh added emphatically, glaring at her husband. Her frustration was clear, then seeing the drinks were finished, she hurried out to the kitchen to get more. Jim looked apologetically at the visitors. This was not normally how Anh behaved.

'Anh's right. Mark *was* happy,' Siobhan reinforced, looking from man to man. They stared back at her in silence.

'So Siobhan, you spoke to Jason Zervos and did your best to win him over?' Stone reiterated, keen to change the subject.

'Yes. I wanted him to think of me as a potential ride, and as I know so many of the regulars in the Regent, he might see me as a possible supplier. That way he might give me information.'

'I don't like the idea,' Julian butted in, ignoring Siobhan's annoyed expression, 'but she won't be dissuaded so I've suggested I go to the clubs as her queer friend. If I'm *gay* I won't be seen as a threat if her boss fancies her.' Julian turned to Siobhan. 'Not that I want you to have sex with him, but I can be your protector.'

The frown on Alan Stone's face indicated his disbelief in Julian's theory. 'I don't think either of you realise how ruthless these drug kingpins can be. There is a huge amount of money and power involved and they'll do anything to protect their turf. If Zervos has the slightest inkling you're spying on him, he could easily have you both bumped off.'

Julian glanced knowingly at Siobhan. 'That's what I told her … but we both want to do something … And so does Jim. What do you suggest we do?'

The detective took a long swill of his beer. 'I need to think about this. We have to find out if Zervos did have any connection to Pearce's death. But why bump off his salesman? And if there was any connection between Mark and Zervos, which I doubt, I'd prefer it if the two of you did nothing till I talk to you again. Siobhan, if Zervos does talk to you again let me know immediately. Don't go rushing into anything. You've got my number.'

Jim interjected, 'What about Ray? Daphne's chap. Wouldn't he know more about Zervos and the whole scene in the Cross?'

'I've spoken to him already but will get onto him again. He's got his feelers out.'

Siobhan stood up. 'Sorry, gotta go. Work calls. Do you mind if I use your phone to ring a taxi?' Anh jumped to her feet to take her into the kitchen. The call made, Siobhan thanked her hosts and said goodbye.

Accompanying her to the door, Anh warned Siobhan to take care before giving her a hug. She stood watching the young woman walk down to the street and waited till Siobhan got into the cab before she returned to the lounge.

CHAPTER THIRTY-FOUR

As the hair salon where Darcy worked was on the main drag near to Kings Cross Station, Stone decided to take the train rather than drive. The salon was amongst the strip joints and pubs but being early there was no action except for the occasional delivery van. Stone bought a coffee and waited till the door to the salon opened at nine-thirty. He doubted anyone would want their hair cut this early.

He was greeted by the same young woman as on his previous visit, but she now had a different exotic hairstyle. She asked what he wanted doing to his hair, but Stone formally told her he was there to talk to Mr Bright. She informed him Darcy was not in yet but should arrive soon.

'I'll wait if you don't mind,' Stone said, and she led him to a chair. Stone looked at himself in the mirror wondering if he should have a cut while he was in the salon but decided against it. He flipped through a women's magazine, puzzling at such interest in celebrities' love lives, most of whom were completely unknown to him.

Suddenly, the door to the salon burst open and Darcy rushed in. 'Hello, darling,' he called out to the assistant, pulling off his jacket. He stopped when he saw Stone sitting in the chair. 'Hello Detective, need a trim?'

Stone grinned and stood up. 'Probably need one but not right now. Just want to have a quick word.'

'Give me a minute to make a coffee and I'll be with you. Would you like one?' Darcy asked.

Stone declined and sat down, watching him put the kettle on. He reverted his gaze to the magazine and soon Darcy sat in a salon chair next to him.

'How can I help you?' Darcy sipped his coffee loudly, grimacing at its heat. 'I never learn. Any developments?' he asked, speaking to the mirror and Stone found himself doing the same.

'Mr Bright, do you own a mobile phone?'

'Good heavens no. Why?' Darcy asked.

'I'm curious about why Mr Dunlop had a mobile phone in his unit. They're expensive and not very common. Do you know why he had one?'

'God no. I wasn't aware he did. As you say, not many people do. Mainly business types. Size of a bloody brick so can't see why anyone would want to cart the thing around.'

Stone nodded. 'Were you aware of his having any connections with drug dealers? We thought he may have used the phone to contact suppliers.'

'Absolutely not! Where on earth did you get that idea?' Darcy responded angrily. 'Mark hadn't been in Sydney long so how on earth could he make such connections? He showed very little interest in drugs other than the odd recreational imbibing.'

'He had an expensive apartment in Bondi Junction. Perhaps he didn't earn enough to pay the rent.'

'That's rubbish. He's no more a dealer than I'm a straight man.'

'The unit is a two bedder, did he share it with anyone? You, for instance?'

Darcy blinked quickly. 'We talked about living together but I'm happy where I am and he wanted two bedrooms in case any family and friends visited from England. Living together can dull the attraction,' he said, cocking his head to one side, staring knowingly at Stone's reflection.

Stone observed Darcy's expressions in the mirror, and decided he seemed genuine in his protestations. Changing his line of questioning, he asked, 'Do you happen to know a gentleman called Jason Zervos?' Darcy flinched slightly at the name, smoothing his hair with both hands. 'Never heard of him.'

'You sure? I thought he was a familiar character around the Cross.'

'Jason.? Jason Zervos you say?'

'Yes.'

'Do you know where he works?' Darcy asked, causing Stone to wonder if he was playing for time.

'I don't think he works in the normal sense of the word, but he owns strip clubs and other venues.'

Darcy shrugged his shoulders dramatically. 'I imagine there are many in this area who do the same. Is this Zervos bloke on the police radar or has someone said Mark knew him?'

Without answering the questions, Stone asked, 'How well do you know the Irish girl, Siobhan Greene?'

Catching Stone's eyes in the mirror, Darcy frowned. 'Siobhan? Is she involved with Zervos?'

'That's not what I meant. She's very upset about Mark's death and wants to do what she can to find out why he died. You must feel the same?'

'Of course, I do, but what can *I* do? He's dead. I loved him but he's gone. I have to accept that, or I won't survive.'

'Survive? … I understand what you mean in one way but are you being threatened by somebody? Is someone out to get you if you ask questions about Mark's death?'

Darcy looked again at his reflection and primped his hair. 'Let's just say, I want to remember Mark as my partner, not some nasty drug dealer with a target on his head.'

227

'So, you're saying he *was* a dealer?'

'No! I'm not! Look Detective, I've got customers booked so if you don't mind, I really need to get myself organised.' Darcy stood up and moved away from the mirror.

Stone did the same. 'Thanks for your time. If you do think of anything that may help us with the investigation, please get in touch. And, if you hear anything about Jason Zervos let me know,' he said, holding out his hand.

Darcy ignored Stone's outstretched hand and strutted to the back of the salon. Stone let himself out. His next port of call would be Kings Cross Police Station.

Darcy's huffy manner puzzled Stone. Was he trying to deflect attention away from Zervos and his possible connection to Mark? The interview hadn't revealed much except for his strange attitude to Mark's death and that he'd heard of Siobhan. And, why did Darcy pretend he didn't know who Zervos was? A visit to Kings Cross Police station might unearth something more useful.

At the reception desk Stone flashed his police ID and was informed Detective Ray O'Shea was not in the building. Was there anyone else he could speak to? The constable checked who was available and after a short wait, Detective Demetriou emerged, looking grumpy and tired.

228

Introductions over, Stone apologised for taking the detective away from his busy schedule. 'Won't keep you long, just need a bit of information.'

Checking his watch, Demetriou led Stone to his office. 'What do you want to know?'

'You've probably heard about Trevor Pearce being stabbed in the Regent, down at Bondi. Word has it he was a dealer for Jason Zervos. Is this correct?'

'Pearce. He's small fry,' Demetriou sneered. 'Trouble is, Zervos always maintains he's anti-drugs, but you can't trust a word the prick says. So far we haven't been able to connect him to selling or supplying.'

'Shit ... It seems odd Pearce wanted to link himself to Zervos if he was getting his supplies from another source. Is there someone else or a gang trying to break into the Bondi area? Or the Eastern suburbs generally? I've heard there was another bloke selling in the Regent the same night Pearce was killed.'

'The same night? That's bloody weird. Who was it?' Demetriou asked, peering again at his watch.

'All we know at the moment is he was wearing an AC/DC T-shirt and had a minder with him. Looked Greek or Italian or even Lebanese.'

'The minder?'

Stone shook his head. 'No. The AC/DC man. The dealer.'

'Greek you say?'

'Or maybe Italian.'

'Did he or his minder attack Pearce?'

'Doesn't look like it. In the toilets the whole time.' Stone raised an eyebrow.

'And no-one saw anything?' Demetriou asked sarcastically.

'Of course not.' Stone thought for a few seconds. 'The pub's full of Poms, but I think if they'd seen a stranger they'd say.'

'You've interviewed them?'

Stone nodded. 'If you have your doubts about the supplier being Zervos, is there anyone else you can think of?'

Demetriou swivelled around in his chair. 'Sounds bloody suss that this bloke and his minder were in the pub the same night Pearce was attacked. Don't usually have two dealers on the same turf.'

This last statement caused Stone to reflect on the information he'd received via Julian. AC/DC man had probably been selling in the pub on other occasions, but as Julian was new to the Regent, it wasn't surprising he hadn't seen him before. Julian had assumed AC/DC was a new arrival.

'There's always the possibility they were connected to the attack, but no-one's mentioned them and no-one else has stood out,' Stone surmised.

'Jesus, I wonder why?' Demetriou sniggered. 'Most of the pub probably bought stuff off both dealers so they're not likely to admit to anything.'

'Exactly. That's why if Zervos isn't the connection, we need to find out who is.'

'Doubt if it'd be the bikies. They only seem to hang around the Cross. And they'd stick out like dogs' balls in Bondi. Not exactly Eastern Suburbs types.' Demetriou ran a hand across his dark one-day growth. 'You say most of the clientele at the Regent are Poms?'

Concuring, Stone added there were also local Aussies and tourists who went to the pub, but the majority of regulars were backpackers.

'Haven't heard of any Pommie bastards getting into organised crime. Too busy screwing, overstaying their visas and taking our jobs,' Demetriou stated.

Stone feigned agreement and was about to call it a day when he remembered Mark. 'Speaking of Poms, there was also the death of a bloke, Mark Dunlop. Heard about him?'

Demetriou looked doubtful.

'A gay bloke, found drowned down at Bondi Beach. It's another death that looks suspicious.'

'Jesus. I thought the Cross was bad enough. Not a poofter hate crime?' Demetriou suggested.

231

'Who knows. Thing is, he and Pearce died within a few days of each other and the common denominator is the Regent. When we searched Dunlop's unit which was pretty flash, we found a mobile phone.' Stone noted Demetriou's reaction. 'Yeah. Who can afford one of those?'

'Do you think he was a dealer?'

'Dunno. Seems unlikely but then his death was unlikely.'

Seeing Demetriou look at his watch yet again, Stone asked quickly, 'Do you believe Zervos when he says he's not into selling drugs?'

Demetriou stared at the ceiling. 'Fucked if I know. I've talked to him a few times and he always maintains he's not. But his brother is. Now in prison and maybe that's put him off.'

'Not surprised.' Stone realised he was getting nowhere with Demetriou but had one more question. 'So you've never heard of this mysterious AC/DC man? ... I'm assuming you're of Greek background judging by your surname.'

The angry expression on the man's face caused Stone to wonder if he'd overstepped the mark. 'I just thought as Greeks are a tight-knit community you might have some idea who he could be.'

'Listen, *mate*,' Demetriou began, 'don't bring your preconceived racist ideas in here if you want help.'

'Sorry. I didn't mean to sound racist. I'm clutching at straws as we're not making much progress with the investigations into either death.'

Demetriou stood, indicating it was time for Stone to leave.

CHAPTER THIRTY-FIVE

Daphne, after receiving an unexpected call from Alan Stone, informed Jim that he wanted another meeting as soon as possible. She would inform Ray, Stone would contact Siobhan and Jim could tell Julian.

'What the … we met last night. Bloody hell, doesn't Alan know we have a life?' Jim complained. This situation was getting out of hand. Was Alan taking advantage of their friendship?

'He's obviously keen to find out what's going on and to keep you and others in the loop,' Daphne responded, trying to abate Jim's annoyance.

'Mmm? I'll ring Anh and see how she feels about another do at our place.'

He wearily returned to his office to ring Anh and tell her of Alan's request and as usual she was happy to oblige and suggested the following night, as they had nothing booked in. She seemed willing to do anything to help Mark.

What really annoyed Jim was not so much the meetings at his house but that everything was about Pearce. Sometimes he thought drugs should be legalised as that might stop the dealers making money, hence preventing the crime associated with the drug trade and, he was going to stress to Alan yet again, the need to find out more about Mark.

Jim knew Alan was totally reliable and would do all he could regarding Mark, but were the other police as concerned? There had been rumours in the 1970s and '80s that the police had brushed aside gay deaths as if they were of no account. He was also uncertain about Siobhan. She was a pretty girl, and he could see why Julian was attracted to her; the red hair and flawless skin, let alone her body, but Julian wasn't the first man to be blinded by good looks and the lure of sex. However, was she trustworthy? Plus, was her friendship with Mark genuine?

The boys had been given their instructions to make themselves scarce once the visitors arrived around six o'clock. Following Anh's instructions, Jim put crackers, cheese and dips on plates, found paper serviettes and suitable knives. He'd just finished his domestic chores when there was the first knock at the front door. It was Alan with Siobhan who was looking exceptionally lovely. No doubt ready to go to work.

'Hello. Come on in,' Jim welcomed and led them into the lounge.

While they settled themselves, he dashed to the kitchen to get them a beer and picked up the nibbles. 'You'd make someone a

235

good wife,' Alan joked, seeing Jim balance the various items in his hands and under his arms.

Alan, rescuing the stubbies, turned to Siobhan. 'Ray, a detective in the Cross is coming as well. Jim and I have known him for a number of years. He helped us solve a murder at Jim's school, and the lucky man ended up in a relationship with Daphne, the headmaster's secretary.'

Siobhan opened her mouth to ask a question when there was another knock. Jim leapt to his feet, returning with Julian and Ray. Ray had a six pack of beer and Julian was holding a bottle of wine. They looked ready to party.

'Ray, this is Siobhan, a friend of Mark's. Siobhan, this is Ray,' Jim introduced.

Siobhan smiling, held out her hand which Ray shook firmly.

'Nice to meet you,' he said, beaming back, slowly releasing her hand.

'You too.'

Jim, observing the exchange, glanced quickly at Julian. Luckily, he seemed oblivious to the spark between the two. Just as well Daphne isn't here, thought Jim. For Alan to include Ray didn't seem like such a good idea after all, even if he did have useful information.

'Can I get you guys a beer or a wine?' Jim asked, picking up their offerings. Preferences were stated and he went into the

236

kitchen, placing the bottles on the table. The boys had finished their dinner and were already in their bedrooms while Anh was tidying up. He put his arms around his wife and leaned his head on her shoulder.

'You okay?' she asked, with her hands holding dirty plates.

'I realise what a great hostess you are. It's bloody exhausting.'

Anh gently pulled herself away from him. 'What do they want to drink?'

'Beer for everyone except Julian who wants wine.'

'Leave it to me. I'll get them.' Anh smiled sympathetically at her husband who kissed her cheek and fled from the kitchen.

Soon all had the drink they wanted, the nibbles were being eaten, and everyone was ready to begin the meeting. Jim was conscious of how close Ray was sitting to Siobhan. He couldn't subdue the funny feeling in his stomach.

'Thanks for coming and thanks to Anh and Jim for having us again so soon,' Stone began.

Anh acknowledged his gratitude with a small bow of her head.

'Right,' said Stone, 'Let's get cracking. As Ray is with us, I'd like Siobhan to tell us again about her meeting with Jason Zervos.'

Julian jumped in. 'Does she have to?'

'Yes. That's one of the reasons why we're here,' Stone justified. 'Siobhan, you okay to tell us about your conversation with him?'

'Grand,' she began, smiling sweetly at her audience, but before she could continue, Julian put up his hand and waved it around, claiming attention.

'What's the matter now?' Stone asked.

'Sorry to interrupt, Alan, but unless you've told them already, I think it's better if I start and tell everyone about the other drug dealer who was in the Regent on the night Trevor was killed. Was it pure coincidence or planned? Seemed a much bigger fish than Trevor. Had his own minder and lots of the customers knew him.' Julian stared at Alan to see if he should continue. A slight tilt of his head told him to do so. 'Siobhan, this was after you'd gone.' Turning to the others he added, 'She was annoyed with me so left the pub. I deserved it of course.' There was a titter.

'Well, can you tell us who he was?' Ray asked.

Something in Ray's tone Jim found disturbing, but Julian, seemingly unaware of Ray's condescending attitude, carried on. 'The main thing I noticed was he was wearing an AC/DC T-shirt, and he looked of Mediterranean background but his minder looked Aussie. A big bloke. Had hairy hands.' More tittering. 'He wouldn't let me into the toilets but one of the chaps I've got to know went in and bought something. Management must know about this bloke and what's going on.'

'Were he and his *mate* still there when Trevor was attacked?' Jim asked.

'No idea. That happened while Siobhan and I were outside. Didn't go back inside until,' Julian glanced at Siobhan, 'you'd gone and then all the attention was on Pearce. Police, ambulance etcetera. I've already told Alan these details.'

'They probably buggered off at the first sign of trouble,' Stone added. 'As Julian is new to the Regent it was the first time he'd seen this particular dealer but according to a few of those interviewed, the dealer was well known to the regulars. It wasn't his first visit. However, Julian's right. It is coincidental for him to be there at the same time Pearce was attacked.'

'Do you think this bloke, AC/DC or whatever, attacked Trev?' asked Jim.

'Seems unlikely. On the other hand, *no-one* has recognised anybody who could've attacked Pearce.'

Ray joined in. 'Do you think this AC/DC bloke was making a statement that he was taking over the territory? Sticking it up Pearce? Showing his power? He's obviously an established dealer.'

'Like a warning?' Jim asked.

'Probably. And then the attack occurred.' Sliding closer to Siobhan, Ray asked, 'Do you have any idea who this bloke is?'

She shook her head. 'I've seen him around but never spoken to him and Trev avoided him like the plague.'

'I'll get everyone to look into it and Ray, it'd be good if you could too,' Stone suggested.

'Sure.'

'Thanks … Now back to Siobhan. Please carry on. Tell us about Mr Zervos.'

Siobhan sat upright and looking at Anh she began. 'I talked to him the other night at work. He owns the clubs where I dance. I told him I wasn't Trev's girlfriend and I wanted to find out what happened to Mark.' She glanced at Julian. 'I might have given him the impression I was up for a shag in return for information.'

'How did he respond?' Stone asked.

'Put it this way, he didn't say no.'

'I'm not surprised …' Ray muttered as Julian butted in again. 'I said to Siobhan we should talk to this Zervos bloke together and I'd be her gay brother or whatever so she'd be safe.'

Stone shook his head. 'Mate, you don't know who you're dealing with. Ray, can you explain what Zervos's like?'

There was silence as the group waited for Ray's revelation. It seemed to Jim that Ray wasn't sure how to answer. Did he actually know Zervos or was he being careful about what he was going to say? Finally Ray spoke, 'Put it this way, the Drug Squad have had him in their sights for a while. He's definitely in the drug business although he always denies it, and so far they haven't been able to pin anything on him.' Turning his attention to Siobhan, Ray warned. 'You need to be careful. Zervos is much more ruthless than someone like Pearce and look what happened to him.'

'But I have to do something,' Siobhan protested.

'Good on you,' Ray praised, gently tapping Siobhan on the knee, 'but we don't want you to be the next victim.'

Bloody hell, thought Jim, seeing Julian's frown at the physical contact. The last thing needed at the moment was any jealousy within the group. Everything was already complicated enough.

'Can I change the subject for a moment?' Jim asked rhetorically. 'All the attention seems to be on Zervos and his connection with Pearce, but what about Mark? Is there *anything* being done to find out who may've killed him? Siobhan and Julian seem to be the only ones who are taking action but even then it always comes back to Trevor Pearce. And now it's about Zervos and this other fellow in the toilet.'

Silence returned until Alan responded, 'Jim, I know it looks that way, but their deaths being so close together and drugs being a factor in both, we're following whichever lead we have. Finding out about one may lead to finding out about the other.'

241

'But what about the phone call from the bloke who told you Mark was dead? Has that been followed up?' Jim asked. 'You'd think with the police asking for information on TV, the guy would have the decency to contact the police again.'

Aware of Jim's frustration, Stone explained, 'The trouble is he rang from a public phone box down at Bondi and apart from his English accent we have no other leads.'

'Can't those calls be traced?'

'We're trying to do that. And Crime Stoppers will put out another request for information.'

Jim sighed deeply. 'Surely, as this bloke is English, someone must have an idea who he is? The regulars in the Regent? And what about the cc…tv thing that's being installed in public places?'

'Good point, but I wasn't aware of seeing any cameras when we went to the Regent,' Stone said. 'And we did ask the interviewees about Mark when we talked to everyone after Pearce was killed and some of them knew Mark a little, mainly because he was from Liverpool, but they had no idea who he was friendly with outside of the pub. The only person they mentioned was,' he stalled, then turned towards Siobhan, 'was you.'

Siobhan gasped. 'You think I killed him?' she wailed. 'Why the fuck would I do that? He was one of the few men I could talk to without being after a ride.'

It took a moment for Stone to decipher Siobhan's meaning. 'No. No. That's not what I meant. I was trying to say Mark wasn't well known at the pub and you seem to be the only one who did.'

'Sorry, I didn't mean to upset anyone, I just hope you,' Jim said, jumping in and looking at Alan then Ray, 'and the rest of the police are giving the same time to solving Mark's death as they are to Pearce's. It seems that a drug dealer's death is more important than a gay man's.'

The small gathering listened but the atmosphere had soured.

To break the tension, Anh asked if anyone needed another drink. All quickly responded in the affirmative and once she returned with wine and beer, the mood lightened a little.

'Let's get back to business,' Jim suggested, as he wriggled his bottom closer to the coffee table and cut a piece of cheese, placing it on a cracker. 'What's our next move?'

Stone crossed his arms. 'It's too dangerous for Siobhan to act on her own with Zervos. Sorry Julian, but I don't think you'd come across as gay or as her brother so let's forget that plan. The police would be held responsible if anything happened to the two of you. We need to think of another way of dealing with him.' His face crinkled as he analysed the situation. 'If Siobhan is willing, we could put a wire on her. We'd be listening to what's being said and there'd be support nearby to react immediately if she was in danger … No, forget that idea. It's too dangerous and with your job, where on earth could you hide a wire?'

'I can talk to him before I start my shift and if my female charms work then I might meet him in private with more clothes on. A few drinks and then who knows what he'll tell me.'

Julian scowled. 'For fuck's sake, Siobhan. This isn't a bloody Yank movie or *Z Cars*. What if he realises what you're doing and attacks you before the police have time to arrive?'

'Well, what do *you* suggest?' Siobhan demanded.

Before Julian could answer, Stone cut in. 'Ray, do you have any ideas? We don't want to put anyone at risk but we're not getting anywhere. Obviously, someone must have seen something, but for whatever reason they're not saying. Offer a reward for information?'

'Yes, to all of the above. Regarding Pearce, we have to find out why no one is admitting to seeing who did it, and rather than Siobhan putting herself at risk with Zervos, why doesn't she,' Ray turned to smile at her, 'and some of the younger police go to the pub and try to find out what happened?'

'Won't it be obvious if she's with a bunch of strangers and they're asking questions?' Julian huffed.

Ignoring Julian, Jim stated, 'Alan and I went to the Regent the other night and there were a couple of blokes who were quite useful.' Jim looked to Stone. 'Remember that chap, Terry, and his mate, Scott? And we saw Terry again in the Viceroy a couple of nights later.'

Stone nodded vigorously. 'Yes. Is it worth asking Terry if he could keep his ear to the ground? Trouble is, he's a Pom so probably doesn't like helping the police.'

Jim sighed in agreement. 'Yes, from what I've heard, particularly the Poms from the North of England, are anti the police because of Margaret Thatcher, and from what Mark told us Liverpudlians can't stand her because she destroyed Liverpool.' He looked at Julian to confirm his theory. He did. 'Although judging by his accent, Terry's not a Scouser.'

'So you think they're not saying anything because they don't like the police?' Ray doubted.

'Possibly,' Stone said, 'but also some of them would've bought drugs off Pearce. Lose their visas and be shipped back home if they admitted to buying. Therefore, placing a few local cops in the pub who can infiltrate the pub crowd …'

'Does that mean you won't need my help anymore?' Julian interrupted, his face glum.

'Not at all. We're very grateful for your assistance and if you want to continue going to the Regent, that would be much appreciated. As long as you don't place yourself in danger,' Stone soothed.

Sensing the meeting needed to be called to order, Jim stated, 'Let's recap. Siobhan *won't* meet Zervos wearing a wire as it's too dangerous but plain-clothes police will go to the Regent to mingle amongst the patrons. The only problem with that is the English crowd will probably be suspicious of Aussies trying to become part of their group.' He paused. 'How about Alan and I approach the English bloke, Terry, and see if he's willing to help? He wouldn't be so obvious. And it's not like he has to dob in mates, just listen for any references to Mark or Pearce and their connections. Alan, I gather you're not out to arrest anyone for buying drugs?'

'That's the least of our worries.'

CHAPTER THIRTY-SIX

When Siobhan stood up, excusing herself as she had to go to work, Julian leapt to his feet to accompany her. Her attempts at declining his offer fell on deaf ears and the two, after giving their thanks and saying goodbye, left together. Julian's desperation to be with Siobhan was not lost on those remaining.

Jim, eager to refocus on the purpose of the meeting, asked Ray and Alan how they could contact Terry and how to convince him to act as an informer. They knew the word informer had negative connotations, but in this case it was finding out about the death of a fellow Pom, and although Pearce didn't have the same personal connection, he'd been a part of the Regent. Plus, Terry may know something about the AC/DC man.

'Do we go back to the Viceroy and hope to bump into him?' Jim suggested. 'It'd be better than at the Regent. Less obvious.'

'Yes, but if he's not there then we'll still have to send some of our own to the Regent,' Alan argued.

'Can you ring him?' Jim asked.

'Don't have his number.'

Jim's next question was whether informers were paid.

'No, but there are certain advantages especially if they are … how can I put it? Up to no good.' Alan sighed knowingly.

'Didn't get that impression about Terry, but then you never know. What was the night we met him in the Viceroy?'

'Can't remember. But I think tradies and ex-pats go to the pub most nights of the week. Look how many were there on Monday night when Pearce was killed. Perhaps Terry alternates between the two pubs.'

Ray, looking bored, said suddenly, 'Look. Why don't I go to the Regent with Siobhan, and she can point Terry out to me? If he's there. I'm nearer her age than either of you. It's unlikely the crowd at the Regent would know I'm with the police.'

'Jeez, thanks *mate*. Didn't know we look so bloody old,' Alan replied, causing Ray to grin apologetically. 'Anyway,' Alan stressed, 'you might get some info regarding this AC/DC bloke.' They sat mulling over the coincidence of two drug dealers in the same pub until Alan said, 'Siobhan has never mentioned Terry so does she know who he is?'

'If he's part of the crowd, she'll have some idea,' Ray justified.

'Will Daphne mind?' Jim asked.

'What?'

'Your going to the pub with Siobhan, a pretty stripper?'

''Course not. It's part of the job,' Ray explained, glowering at Jim.

'Fair enough,' Alan calmed. 'How about Jim and I go to the Viceroy while you go to the Regent?' He turned to Anh who'd been sitting silently, sipping her wine. 'Would you like to join us? Be lovely if you did.'

Anh, clearly surprised by the invitation, declined.

'Your observations could really help us,' Alan persuaded.

'Well, it has been a while since I've been to a pub,' she answered, glancing at her husband.

A wave of guilt washed over Jim. Was he becoming like his father who'd taken his mother for granted? His father was of the generation which assumed their wives were happy to stay at home, bring up the children and sacrifice their own lives and opportunities for the family. 'Yes, please come. The boys will be okay on their own and as Alan says, your observations will be really useful. You have a much better understanding of human nature than any of us.'

Anh rubbed Jim's arm. 'Thanks, darling. Very happy to help. So, when are we going to the Viceroy?'

Jim wondered if Anh were taking the mickey. He didn't blame her.

'Is tomorrow night too soon for us to go to the Viceroy and you to go to the Regent?' Alan asked Ray.

'I'll check with Siobhan.'

249

'You sure it'll be okay with Daphne?' Jim persisted. 'I don't think she's the jealous type, but Siobhan *is* young and pretty and …'

'What the hell are you trying to say, Jim?' demanded Ray.

'Nothing. Just don't want Daphne to feel left out.'

'She won't. She knows what the police have to do.'

Attempting to deflect the tension, Alan said to Ray, 'Didn't want to say this in front of Julian or Siobhan, but I called into Kings Cross station.'

'Oh?'

'I was in the area so thought I'd pop in and say gidday, but as you weren't there, spoke to that Demetriou fellow.'

Ray grimaced. 'How'd you get on with him?'

Alan rolled his eyes. 'Bit of a prickly chap. Said he'd had dealings with Zervos but reckons he's hard to pin anything on. He knew about Pearce's death but nothing about Mark's.'

'Mmm? Not sure I'd believe a word the bugger says. Could be wrong but I think he plays both sides.' Ray waggled his head slowly.

'Really? I mentioned the AC/DC bloke and he got the shits saying I was being racist when I said the bloke could have been Greek and he may know him.'

'That's typical. Got a huge chip, or he plays the race card when he doesn't want to let on what he knows.'

'Right. Thanks for the tip,' Alan said, before suggesting they call it a night and he quickly summarised the plans for the following evening. 'Ray, let me know if Siobhan is happy to go with you and keep me in the loop re any developments.' He was about to stand up when Anh said, 'Before you go, do you mind if I ask a question?'

'Of course not.'

'You know how Jim had to say it was Mark in the morgue, did that happen with the other man?' Anh looked at her husband. 'The one who was killed in the pub?'

'Trevor Peace,' Jim prompted.

'Yes. Him. Did anyone identify him?'

'Good question, Anh,' replied Stone. 'He *was* identified. Took us a while to track down a family member. His sister came. Very different sort to Pearce. He must have been the black sheep of the family.'

Anh nodded sadly. 'And to be stabbed to death.'

'Well, we know he was stabbed but forensics are still confirming the weapon … On that note, we'll leave you to enjoy the rest of the evening.'

Jim firmly closed and locked the front door, before returning to the lounge.

251

'My God. That was a bit tense,' Jim sighed, as he sat down next to Anh.

'Yes, it was.' Anh took a sip of her wine. 'Do you think Ray likes Siobhan? He was a bit touchy feely.'

'That's exactly what I thought. I hope he hasn't got plans for the two of them. It'd be terrible for Daphne. And for Julian. He's obviously keen on her.'

'I agree. But we are not responsible for what Ray does. Perhaps he was just flirting. Siobhan *is* pretty so it's normal.'

'It is?' Jim queried.

'In Saigon, the American soldiers were always flirting with the girls even though some were married or had a girlfriend back home.'

'But that was during the war when most soldiers didn't know if they'd ever see their partners again.'

'James! You know men are attracted to pretty women, and it doesn't matter how much they *love* their wives or girlfriends. War has nothing to do with it.'

'Gosh my dear. You're sounding very cynical. Hope you're not including me in this theory.'

'Of course not, darling. You'd *never* be attracted to a gorgeous woman,' Anh answered with a smile.

'Only you, sweetheart.'

Anh laughed. 'So? What is our role for tomorrow night?'

252

'I'll confirm with Alan tomorrow morning and double check what time to meet and the plan of action.'

Anh began to gather the plates and glasses. 'But how do you or Alan approach this man Terry, and persuade him to give information to the police?'

'If he cares about Mark, or even Trevor Pearce, he may be willing to help.'

Anh looked doubtful. 'Is it legal how we're involved with the investigation?' she asked on her way to the kitchen. Jim, picking up the remaining crockery, followed.

He thought about her question as he placed the dirty dishes on the bench. 'I don't really know, but I suppose because I've been involved with Alan before, at the school with Bentley, and in Rarotonga, he knows he can trust us. Not so sure about Julian and Siobhan.'

Anh stopped loading the dishwasher and straightened her back. 'It's just an idea, but do you think Ray was flirting with Siobhan for a reason? I know we haven't seen much of him and Daphne lately but whenever we have they've always seemed happy and compatible, even with the age difference.'

His lips pursed, Jim asked, 'What reason?'

'Perhaps he doesn't trust Siobhan and thinks if he can win her heart she may confide in him.'

253

'Bloody hell. I think you're giving him too much credit. He's a pretty simple bloke. Can't imagine him being that Machiavellian.'

'As I said, just a thought,' Anh murmured and continued to stack the dishwasher.

CHAPTER THIRTY-SEVEN

The day passed slowly for Alan, while Jim and Anh were in a state of subdued anticipation until they could join him in the Viceroy later that afternoon. Josh and Daniel had been informed that their parents were going out; they wouldn't be late home, homework was to be completed and to put dinner in the microwave. As a single man, Alan had no one to tell, while Julian, miffed by Siobhan's flirting with that police prick, decided to have a night in. Ray and Siobhan agreed to meet at the Regent the following afternoon if Terry had not shown up at the Viceroy.

Jim arrived at the pub to find Alan already ensconced at a tall table by the wall with an unobstructed view of the bar. A number of young men, a few older women and regulars were present, but the pub was by no means full. Alan got to his feet enquiring about Anh's whereabouts. She'd be joining them soon, once the boys were home.

Once settled with a drink, the conversation was immediately about the plan of action. 'No real plan. Just hoping Terry turns up, and if he does then you or me or all of us will talk to him,' Alan advised.

255

'Really professional,' Jim laughed.

'Maybe it should be Anh who talks to him. She has more tact than we do,' Alan suggested. 'Anyway, let's keep our eye on the crowd. With luck, he'll come and talk to us like he did last time.'

Anh finally arrived but there was still no sign of Terry. How much longer should they wait? Two bowls of chips were ordered as well as more drinks. At the bar, Jim observed the growing crowd of drinkers. A figure near the door looked vaguely familiar. Was it Terry? He surreptitiously signalled to Stone and pointed in the man's direction. Stone peered around and seeing who it was, gave Jim a thumbs up.

'What do we do now?' Jim asked, as he placed the drinks on their table.

'We should wait a few minutes. If we rush up to him we'll scare him off.'

'Let's chat amongst ourselves,' Anh suggested with a laugh.

'Okay,' Stone agreed, reaching for the last chip. 'Rhubarb, rhubarb, rhubarb,' he muttered, causing Jim to chuckle at the reference to old British comedies while Anh looked puzzled. Jim was about to explain when Terry suddenly appeared at their table.

'Here again,' he greeted. 'Has this become the coppers' new hangout?'

'Couldn't keep away,' Stone replied. 'How're you?'

'Sound,' Terry answered. 'You?'

'Good.'

'Can I buy you a beer?' Jim asked quickly. 'Name your poison.'

'Toohey's New.'

Jim strode to the bar, grateful that not many punters were ahead of him. He returned, placing the cold, frothy schooner in front of Terry, wondering if he'd missed anything of interest.

'You from Vietnam?' Terry was asking Anh.

'Yes, I came to Australia as a refugee after the war. Well before your time,' she flattered.

'Don't know about that. Must have been awful,' Terry sympathised.

'It was. But Australia let me stay and then I met Jim. We now have two sons.'

'Brilliant.'

Anh touched Terry on the arm. 'Thank you. Not everyone here wants us.'

'Well, the people who don't want you here sound like numpties to me. Ask anyone in the pub at the end of the night, they'd love to pull an Asian chick.'

Unsure how to respond to Terry's compliment, Anh smiled.

Stone and Jim who'd been listening to the conversation were waiting for their moment to join in. Jim, impressed by his wife's ability to put Terry at ease, didn't want to interrupt, and he could tell from Stone's silence he felt the same.

Terry picked up his glass. 'Nice to meet you, Anh. Better leave you guys to it. Thanks for the beer,' he said, causing Stone to say quickly, 'Hang on a minute, mate. We've got something to ask you.'

'Jesus. What have I done?' Terry rolled his eyes, chuckling through his beard.

'Nothing. At least not yet.'

'Sounds mysterious.' He put his drink down, staring expectantly at Stone.

'You can say no but we need your assistance.' Stone paused. 'We obviously know you frequent the Regent as well as the Viceroy. We want a regular to be our eyes and ears. You're English and …'

'Hang on. You want me to spy on me mates?' Terry picked up his glass again and made to move away.

'Just give me a minute. Please. We're not interested in anyone's social activities, if you follow me? You knew Mark Dunlop and Trevor Pearce and now both are dead.' Stone stopped to let the importance of what he was asking to sink in. 'I'm certainly not implying you'll be next, it's just that if we send the local police to the pub, no-one is going to let anything slip to a bunch of strangers, but as the regulars know you, you can go there as usual.

258

You know that what happened to Pearce, and what happened to Mark is suspicious.'

Jim could see Terry was being swayed by Stone's logic. He'd seemed a decent bloke when they'd met him in the Regent, and Alan was appealing to Terry's sense of fair play. 'Did you know Mark well?' Jim asked before Stone had a chance to say anything more.

'Not very. But I did know who he was. A Scouser and friends with Siobhan. He was alright.'

'Yes, he was. He lived with us for a while when he first arrived. We liked him a lot. We really want to know if someone killed him. We want to be able to explain his death to his family when they come to Sydney. They're waiting to hear. Must be dreadful for them.' Jim stopped, worrying he was laying it on too thick.

Terry nodded solemnly. 'The tyranny of distance. Know the feeling. So, what do you want me to do?'

Stone took over. 'I'll give you my phone number and you can ring me anytime. The main thing is to listen to conversations and hopefully someone will let something slip. Don't ask questions. We don't want you to attract attention to yourself and put yourself in danger. Don't let anyone know, including your mate, Scott. Just act normally.'

'What am I actually listening for? Don't think anyone is going to say, 'Oh by the way, heard that blah blah killed Mark or Trev.''

259

They all chuckled. He was right.

'If I do hear anything useful, and only if it's about some arsehole who deserves to be put away, I don't want anyone to know I'm involved,' Terry stressed.

Stone held out his hand and they shook vigorously. Jim couldn't help but think of the quote, 'A gentleman's word is his bond'. In Shakespeare's day a handshake was a legal promise. It certainly wouldn't be in this day and age.

'The man we're interested in is Jason Zervos. He's a king pin in the Cross so we're wondering if he had anything to do with Pearce's death. We're not sure who Pearce worked for. Maybe Zervos, so Trev could have done something to piss him off. Perhaps he was trying to set up his own little empire,' Stone explained carefully.

'What about Mark?' Terry asked.

'Unfortunately, we haven't had any leads. So again, if you hear anything.'

Jim butted in. 'There's another bloke, wears an AC/DC T-shirt. He's a pusher and was there the night Trevor was killed.'

To Jim, the grimace on Terry's face was ambivalent. He wondered if it indicated Terry's disapproval of drug dealing, or if he knew this particular dealer.

Terry looked at the three of them in turn. 'Why do you trust me? I could inform this Zervos bloke and tell him what you've told me.'

The three remained silent for a moment till Jim, glancing at Stone, said, 'Remember when we met you in the Regent?' Terry nodded. 'Well, you seemed like a decent chap. That's basically it.'

Terry smiled wryly. 'Can I put that on my CV?'

CHAPTER THIRTY-EIGHT

The next morning Stone rang Ray to tell him they'd met up with Terry at the Viceroy the previous evening and as he was willing to be their eyes and ears there was no need for him to go to the Regent with Siobhan.

'We're still going,' Ray stressed. 'Being with Siobhan might be useful. I get the impression she knows everyone in the pub and as she was connected to Mark and Pearce, she might trigger some action.'

Stone hesitated. Was Ray only going so he could see Siobhan? His reaction to her at Jim's home had made him feel uncomfortable. And what about Daphne? 'Well, as long as you know what you're doing?'

'What the fuck does that mean?' Ray asked. The annoyance in his voice told Stone he'd hit a nerve.

'Siobhan's a very pretty girl.'

'Jesus. You sound like bloody Jim.'

'Come on, Ray. You know what I mean. I'm thinking about your relationship with Daphne.'

'This has got nothing to do with Daphne. Siobhan is someone who has lots of connections and if I'm with her, you never know what I'll discover.'

Ray's reasoning appeared correct but Stone knew how many relationships had fallen apart, his own included, because of the demands on the police, their working hours, mixing with criminals and an eclectic assortment of people. It often led to the loss of living in reality.

When the call ended abruptly, Stone couldn't help but wonder if Ray was up to no good. He hoped he was wrong.

Bloody Stone. Interfering Kiwi prick, Ray thought as he told Daphne he was going to the Regent later that afternoon so wasn't sure what time he'd be home. As usual, she'd been understanding. She'd probably enjoy the free time to ring her mates without him in the background. The plan was to meet Siobhan at three-thirty in the hope that the regulars would go to the pub after their shifts on the building sites finished.

Ray looked through his wardrobe, searching for clothes which wouldn't give him away as a member of the police force. What should a bloke wear to the pub when he wanted to fit in with a bunch of backpackers? Jeans and a T-shirt were the most neutral. The trouble was, so many pub goers seemed able to smell a cop

263

from miles away. Finally dressed in what he hoped was appropriate attire, Ray left the house and hailed a taxi.

Siobhan was standing outside the Regent smoking when Ray pulled up. He walked straight up to her, kissing her on the cheek as if he'd known her for ages.

'How're you?'

'Grand. You?'

Without bothering to reply, Ray placed his hand on her back and gently pushed her towards the entrance. 'What'll you have?' he asked, once they'd entered the public bar.

'A Toohey's Old would be grand.'

He ordered the same and both stood attempting to look as if they knew each other well.

'I'm going to follow your lead,' Ray told her. 'You know the crowd. Say I'm a mate down from Brisbane.'

'Never been to Brisbane so how about I met you at one of the clubs in the Cross? We got chatting during my break as your girlfriend is Irish and a mate of mine. Her name is Ciara. She couldn't come tonight as she's got a girls' makeup party.'

Ray's eyebrows rose. 'Jeez, you're pretty good at this. Hope I can remember the details.'

'As my mammy used to say, 'Lie like a tomb stone.''

He couldn't help laughing. 'Ever thought of joining the police?'

Siobhan nudged him, instructing him to call her Shiv, and with a nod of her head strode towards the regulars she knew.

Hanging back till she introduced him as her friend's boyfriend, Ray shook hands with Steve and Brian.

'How's it going?' Ray asked, sipping his beer, looking over the schooner glass at the two men.

'Where's Julian?' Steve asked, smirking at Brian.

'Julian?' Ray questioned.

'Shiv's mate.'

'No idea. Should I know him?'

'He's a Pommie guy from London, but don't hold that against him,' Steve explained wearily as if everyone should know Julian.

'Nah. Never met him but I heard another friend of hers met an untimely end.' Ray raised the glass to his lips.

Steve lifted his glass in salute. 'Yeah, Mark. Poor sod.'

Ray couldn't decide whether or not to continue the conservation as the last thing he wanted was to be accused of being nosey.

'You never met Mark?' Steve asked.

'No but heard a lot about him from Siobhan …Shiv. Sounded like a good bloke.'

'He was okay. You know he was a woofter?' asked Brian with a wink.

'Really?'

'Maybe his boyfriend done him in,' Brian stated, grinning.

265

'Bloody hell. For real?'

'No idea but wouldn't put it past some of them queers.'

This bloke's a fucking pain, Ray thought, wishing Brian would bugger off. He was about to join Siobhan who was busy chatting with other members of the group when Steve said, 'Don't listen to this nob'ead. He's just a jealous twat. Fancies the pants off our Shiv. Wants to empty his dirty water.' He shoved Brian on the shoulder then turning to Ray said, 'Fucking terrible what happened to Mark.'

Ray, not sure how to reply, asked cautiously, 'What did happen?' He was pleased when Brian stomped off to another group of mates.

'He went down to Bondi Beach and ended up dead.'

'Jesus. How'd he cark it?'

'Well, rumour has it, someone filled him with drugs then pushed him in the water,' Steve explained.

'What a way to go.' Ray took another gulp of his beer. 'Speaking of drugs,' he looked around to see who was within earshot, 'anyone here who can supply a bit of Mary Jane? Nothing heavy.'

The frown on Steve's face made him think he'd put his foot in it. 'Sorry, shouldn't have asked. I could be a cop for all you know,' Ray apologised with a laugh.

'Where d'ya live?' Steve asked suddenly.

'Parramatta. Why?'

'Ah, well, if you lived 'round here, you'd know what's been goin' on.'

'What? Sounds heavy.'

'Hasn't Shiv told you a bloke got stabbed in this pub a few days ago?' Steve stared at Ray.

'No. We haven't caught up for a while,' Ray responded quickly, aware his cover could be blown if he didn't sound convincing.

Steve's eyes narrowed, 'How d'ya know her?'

'Through my girlfriend. She's Irish too. Knew each other back in Ireland.' Ray stopped. He didn't want to be asked any more questions.

He could see how Steve was weighing him up. Did he look young enough to have a girlfriend who'd be a similar age to Siobhan?

Steve watched him closely, then his face relaxed. 'Like the younger chicks?' he asked.

'Fucking hell, mate. How old do I look?'

'Not as young as our Siobhan.'

'Ah, yeah, well Ciara's a bit older than her. Anyway, good to meet you.' Ray turned to see where Siobhan was.

Steve, sensing Ray was about to walk away, said, 'The geezer who sold the goods was bumped off. Stabbed in the pub. Nobody saw anything,' he said with a roll of his eyes. 'Maybe someone muscling in on his territory. I'm sure Shiv will let you know.'

'Siobhan? Didn't think she took drugs.'

'What? She loves a bit of charlie.'

Ray realised he'd made a blunder.

'Thought you'd know, seeing as you're a mate of hers,' Steve stated, shaking his head.

'You know what women are like. Only tell each other important stuff.' He felt Steve's eyes following him as he walked away to join Siobhan. Ray reprimanded himself. He'd better watch what he said, especially in front of the Liverpudlians who were more cluey than he'd given them credit. He stood next to her hoping to listen to the conversation but those in the group seeing his arrival stopped talking.

'Can you get me another beer?' Siobhan asked.

Realising she was trying to get rid of him, Ray did as he was ordered. He stood at the bar watching her interaction with the men. From the body language it was obvious she had admirers and now he'd moved away they'd started talking again. Ray was relieved the barmaid was busy serving other customers. Take as long as you want, he mentally instructed. Siobhan could tell him what was said later.

Siobhan knew she had to get Ray away from her circle. He was a stranger, and an Aussie. The conversation wouldn't have continued with him hanging around, particularly as there were comments about Trevor and if anyone was going to take his place. She was pleased Trev wasn't missed, except for his supplies. It was assumed that the other bloke who'd also been selling that evening and on previous occasions would continue supplying. No-one appeared to know where Trev had got his supplies from. Her mention of Jason Zervos hadn't resulted in any comments, or at least they weren't saying.

'Let me buy *you* a beer,' she suggested to Ray who was now standing on his own watching one of the large screens which was showing a league game. 'I'll have to leave soon. Get ready for my show.'

'What time do you start?' Ray asked, his voice cool.

'Nine. But have to get my face on and organise my outfit, or lack of.' She laughed and was pleased when Ray grinned. His miffed attitude towards her was thawing. 'I'm sorry about before but I knew there was no way they'd talk in front of you,' she told him.

'Fair enough. Did you find out anything useful?'

'Not really. Nothing about Mark. Maybe I'll find out more tonight at the club.'

'Don't you go doing anything stupid with Zervos,' Ray warned.

269

'Worried about me?' Siobhan asked, cocking her head to one side, smiling.

'Yes! He's a dangerous character. I don't think you appreciate who you're dealing with. Drugs are worth a lot of money and … well, you know what I mean.'

'Yes, Da.'

'Can't you stay for one more? Then I'll put you in a cab,' Ray suggested.

'Twist my arm.'

Ray did as instructed, took her arm and gently held it behind her back. 'What would you like?'

'Whatever you fancy.'

As promised, Ray made sure Siobhan caught a cab and handed the driver enough money to cover the fare to the Cross.

In the taxi Siobhan thought about their time at the pub. Ray wasn't much help as he didn't know how to play the game with the Scousers and the rest from the UK. Aussies were far more open than the British and Irish. Julian had been more successful as he knew the score. She should continue going to the pub with him, but then Ray was nice looking even if he was a bit older than the usual fella she'd go for. Jesus, Mary and Joseph. She couldn't believe what she was thinking. He was bloody married. This should be all about Mark.

The cab pulled up outside the Love Hut but it wasn't guaranteed Zervos would be in attendance. Occasionally, he was on the door as he liked to keep an eye on the guests and she'd noticed how he wanted the punters to have a good time and not be threatened by aggressive behaviour from drunken gobshites. Sometimes fights broke out but were soon stopped as all the clubs' bouncers in the area came to each other's rescue.

The friendly Tongan was on the door and she asked him if Mr Zervos was in the building. He was. Siobhan made straight for the dressing room. She wanted to look her most alluring. Should he see her in normal clothes or in her dance outfit again? Her hope was he'd still be at the bar and as the show didn't start for at least half an hour, there wouldn't be too many guests this early. Stone's words of warning rang in her ears but she wasn't wearing a wire or doing anything dangerous.

After deciding on her outfit and disguising it with the same long drab cardigan, Siobhan made her way to the bar. Relieved, although nervous, she saw Zervos was there with the usual minders. There didn't seem to be much conversation happening.

'Hello Mr Zervos,' she said, standing behind him.

He turned, looking her up and down. 'Hope you're not wearing that on stage?' Siobhan shook her head. This wasn't going as planned.

'Anyway, how are you?' he asked indifferently.

'Grand. How are you?'

'Okay. Well, now we've got the niceties over, what do you want? Hope it's not a pay rise.'

'Not at all. You pay us very well, thank you.'

'Glad to hear it. So?'

'You don't sound very happy, if I may be so bold.'

Her boss shrugged lazily. 'Sweetheart, I'm a busy man. What *do* you want?'

This definitely wasn't going well. The last time she'd spoken to him he'd been much more accommodating. Something was obviously pissing him off.

Siobhan ignored the two minders and whispered to Zervos, 'I was hoping to have a word with you in private. You know? That friend of mine who was killed recently?'

'Do you think I know everyone who gets bumped off? What the fuck.'

'Sorry … I didn't mean that. It's just that you seem to know what goes on. I thought as nothing gets past you, you might be able to help me.'

Zervos stared at her, his eyes heavily hooded. 'Not in the mood right now. Try me tomorrow. Maybe I can help you then. … Who was this *friend* of yours?'

'Mark Dunlop. English. From Liverpool. Gay.'

His eyes glazing and the slight yawn indicated the conversation was over. Siobhan returned to the dressing room. She had thirty minutes to kill.

CHAPTER THIRTY-NINE

'You're back early,' Daphne stated when Ray arrived home. 'Thought you'd be gone for hours.'

'No. The Irish girl had to go to work. She's a stripper so had to be at the Cross for her show,' Ray explained as he took off his shoes and threw himself onto the couch, facing the television.

'You okay?'

'Oh yeah. Just felt a bit useless at the pub. So different dealing with Poms compared to Aussies. If it hadn't been for Siobhan, I wouldn't have found out anything. Even though she's Irish, the Pommie crowd seems to trust her. Same part of the world.'

'Did she find out anything?'

'Sort of. Apparently, their biggest concern is who will be the next supplier now that Pearce has gone and the other dealer isn't in the pub every night. No-one has any idea who killed Pearce, or at least they're not saying. He wasn't well liked but whether it was enough to attack him?' Ray shrugged despondently. 'One of the guys did mention Mark. He said Mark could have been filled with drugs and pushed into the water, but didn't have any details about who or why. Doesn't look as if there's any point in me going to the pub again.'

'Oh, darling. Maybe the next time they'll open up a bit more.'

Ray puffed out his cheeks. 'Don't think so. Bloody Poms are so suspicious of anyone who isn't from fucking England.'

Daphne wasn't sure how to deal with the mood Ray was in. She'd not seen him like this for ages. The last time was when he'd first been promoted to detective and he'd been full of insecurities. 'I'm sure Alan will understand. He probably feels the same.'

Grunting, Ray muttered, 'I'll talk to him tomorrow. Can't face it now.' He reached into his pocket, pulled out a packet of cigarettes, lit one, inhaling deeply. 'That bloke Julian seems the best bet as he's one of them. I felt bloody useless.'

'Oh darling. You are not useless,' Daphne reassured, sitting down next to him. 'You must have work mates and connections in Kings Cross who can assist you?'

'You make it sound easy, but it's not. The Cross is full of crims and some of my *mates*, as you call them, are in their pockets and certainly won't be willing to share anything. They don't want to end up dead like that Pearce bloke.'

Not knowing how to respond, Daphne remained silent. She'd rarely seen Ray this upset. She stood up to walk back into the kitchen. 'Can I get you a beer? A coffee?' she asked.

275

'A beer would be great. Thanks.' Ray switched on the television.

Daphne returned, handing him the stubbie. 'Are you sure there's nothing else wrong?'

Ray looked up at her. 'No. Why are you asking?'

'You've just seemed a bit distant over the last couple of days … And, to be honest, for a while.'

'Sorry, don't mean to be. Things on my mind.'

'I hope it's not another woman,' stated Daphne with a hesitant smile.

'What the …? Why the hell would you think that?'

'Just aware I'm getting older. Not quite the woman I was when we first met.'

'For fuck's sake. I'm no spring chicken either,' Ray argued. 'Wish I was, but I'm not. And you still look bloody good.'

Accepting his somewhat backhanded compliment, there seemed nothing more Daphne could say. Ray obviously had the shits, so there was no point in continuing. Perhaps he was going through mid-life crisis. Being older than him had its positives but also its drawbacks. Was there some younger woman who appealed to him? Siobhan? Although he'd said he wasn't bothered about having children, perhaps now he wanted them and didn't want to be an elderly father. Pushing her own insecurities aside, Daphne asked if he'd learned anything more from the visit to the pub.

There was no response. Ray drank his beer, finally saying, 'Just hope Siobhan doesn't do anything stupid. She seems very self-willed so God knows what she'll say to Jason Zervos tonight. I don't think she realises how easily she could put herself in danger.'

'What's she like, apart from being self-willed?' Daphne asked nonchalantly.

'Irish, obviously, and is pretty tough. Seems nice enough and is determined to find out what happened to Mark Dunlop. But she's being bloody naïve when it comes to Zervos. He's a dangerous man.'

Daphne listened to his description. He'd never shown such interest in a colleague before. If one could call Siobhan a colleague. 'Oh well, I'm sure you'll do your best to protect her.'

Ray looked up from the couch, frowning.

CHAPTER FORTY

'Tezza! How's it going, mate?' Brian greeted. 'What's happening? Long time no see.'

'Things to do, mate. Things to do.'

'Anything of interest?'

'Nah. What's going on? Any juicy goss?' Terry asked, looking around the bar.

'Not much. Siobhan was in last night with some Aussie bloke. Must have given that Julian bloke the flick. She's definitely a goer, that one.'

'Don't suppose *you* want to have a go?'

'Fuck no.'

'So, you wouldn't give her the time of day if she asked you?'

Brian considered Terry's question. 'Nah. Not my type.'

'Me thinks the gentleman doth protest too much.'

'What the fuck? Speak bloody English.'

Terry changed the subject. 'Any news about Dunlop?'

'Nowt. Word has it his death is a bit suss. Probably some jealous boyfriend who done him in.' Brian flapped his hand in the air.

'Didn't think he had a *boyfriend*,' Terry commented, 'seeing he was always with our Irish lass.'

'Yeah, but a poofter if there ever was,' Brian dismissed.

Terry nodded. 'What about Trev?'

'He wasn't a fag!'

'Mate, I know that. Just wondered if there was any update on his demise?'

It took a few moments for Brian to digest Terry's meaning 'The regulars got interviewed by the bizzies. Were you?'

'Me? Wasn't here that night. Thank the Lord.'

Brian laughed. 'Yeah. You'd have to tell them about your favourite drugs.'

Playing along with Brian's inaccurate insinuation, Terry asked if there was a new *friend* who'd be able to supply them with goods for the weekend. Seeing the rest of the group were deep in conversation, Brian stepped closer saying how there'd been that other bloke in the pub that night, selling in the toilets, with the usual heavy outside.

'Jesus! Really? The same night Trev was killed?'

'Yeah.'

'Know who he was?'

'He's been in the pub before but not every night. Must of scarpered before the police got there.'

'Oh well, keep me in the loop. Wouldn't mind a bit of blow.'
He knew Brian had a loose mouth but didn't want to press him in
case he blabbed about him as well, especially as he wasn't into
drugs. Alcohol was his choice of relaxation.

'Get you a swifty?' Terry offered.

'Cheers.'

Terry was pleased he'd talked to Brian, but he had his doubts
about him. He couldn't put his finger on what it was but somehow
Brian seemed too willing to please. Who to try next? There was an
animated conversation going on between the Scousers. No doubt
about football but worth an eavesdrop. They might know who the
other dealer was. Trev had been a right pain, but he didn't deserve
to be bumped off.

As expected, the conversation was about Liverpool FC and
Everton, but after a while it reverted to Siobhan. Her bringing a
new bloke to the pub added fuel to the fire that she was a player.
She was Trev's girlfriend, but 'mates' with Mark, then Julian, and
now some Aussie called Ray. And two of the buggers were dead.

'You know what Irish girls are like,' one said knowingly.

'Fuck off, ya goose. What's that got to do with being Irish?'
another accused.

'Well, she's a fucking stripper.'

'So? Jesus, what century are you in? A girl has to earn money.'

'Should get a normal job.'

The majority of the group groaned in despair and the topic was changed.

Terry was about to go to the bar when Jimmy the Scot sidled up. 'Terry, you've lived in Sydney for fucken ages. Is it normal what happened to Trev?'

'Depends what you mean by normal? Hardly knew the bloke.'

'Come on, mate. We all knew him. Heard anything on the grapevine?'

'Nah.' Terry shrugged. 'Maybe someone wanted to take over his patch.'

'Or the police had him malkied?'

'Why the hell would they do that? … Arrest him maybe?' Terry suggested.

Jimmy scowled.

'Well, what do you think?' Terry asked. 'Get rid of Trev and then the market is open sesame?'

Still appearing dubious about Terry's theory, Jimmy questioned, 'But who'd take over? Shiv? What about that dafty, Julian? He's been hanging around like a bad smell. Or the bloke who sells in the gents every now and then?'

'The mystery supplier? That is the question. To sell drugs, you have to have a source.' Terry opened his mouth, downed the dregs and made out he was going for another beer when Jimmy said, 'I heard there's some guy in the Cross who supplied Trev. Had a funny name. Zavos? Something like that. Perhaps he wanted Trev out of the way so he could use the other dealer who isn't here all the time? Or maybe Trev overstepped the mark? Wanted his own little empire.'

'No idea, mate. Time for another beer,' Terry excused himself.

CHAPTER FORTY-ONE

Despite feeling knackered after a long night entertaining rowdy crowds of businessmen visiting Sydney for conferences and meetings, Siobhan woke up early. Her mind was filled with thoughts about Zervos, his minders and some of his customers. Zervos was the sort of man who could call on favours. And, was the crowd at the Regent really so unobservant that no-one noticed a punter who'd stuck a knife into Trevor? Or was it one of the bouncers who maybe worked for Zervos as well as at the pub? But what about Mark? There was still nothing which gave her any clues about who or why he was killed.

Siobhan rolled over, trying to go back to sleep, but her mind was whirring, and everything went back to Zervos. Had he supplied Trev with the drugs and if so, what had Trev, the eejit, done to get himself killed? Skimmed the profits? He was always making out he was important, the 'big man', but he had a natural talent for putting people off-side. In some ways she wished she hadn't been so nasty to Trev but it was too late now.

Jason Zervos's reaction to her the night before had been disturbing. Perhaps Stone and the others were right, and she *was*

283

placing herself in danger. One minute Jason was friendly, the next he was a gobshite. Took too much coke? Perhaps a word with Tongan Joe on the door might lead to some answers. He was always chummy with a lovely big smile on his face.

Taking a gulp from the glass of water next to her bed, she started thinking about Ray. He'd seemed flirty 'round at Jim's place but last night he'd been different. Not exactly dismissive but certainly not coming onto her. He'd proved to be useless as the English lot were suspicious of him, but luckily they didn't twig to him being the police. She wondered if it was worth returning to the Regent with him, maybe they'd be more accepting the next time? Doubtful. It was too risky for Ray to come to one of her shows as Zervos was bound to know all the coppers in the Cross. And what about poor old Julian?

Forget Julian, what about poor old Mark? Her mind drifted back to how they'd met in the Regent and the conversations they'd had about their lives and loves. She couldn't believe how much she missed him.

Realising she'd never get back to sleep, Siobhan dragged herself out of bed, wandered into the small kitchenette and opened the fridge. As usual, it was virtually empty. She found a crust in its plastic bag and popped it in the toaster. At least she wasn't going to put on weight if this was all she had to eat.

The piece of toast popped and after finding a bit of butter and a nearly empty jar of marmalade, she was biting into it when the phone rang. 'Siobhan?' the voice asked before she had a chance to say hello.

'Yes?'

'It's Ray. Got a minute?'

Struggling to swallow, Siobhan gurgled that she did.

'How did you get on with Zervos?'

'Asked him about Mark. Flattered his ego. King of the Cross and all that shite.'

'But what about Pearce and his replacement?'

'Fuck, Ray. What's up *your* arse?' She paused to let her annoyance sink in before she continued. 'He was in a grumpy mood, but he did say I should talk to him again tonight.'

'About Mark or Pearce?'

'With luck, both.'

'Do you want me to come?' Ray asked.

'Where?'

'To meet Zervos.'

'With me? No. Better if I'm on me own. Surely he knows who you are?'

'Don't think so. Never met the bugger.'

'But what about the bouncers and the doormen?'

285

Siobhan could almost hear him thinking. 'Ray, what's up your arse?' she asked again.

'Nothing. Even if he does know I'm the police, I might still turn up.'

'Why?'

'We often pop into local venues to see how things are going. What time is your boss usually there?'

Ignoring his question, Siobhan asked, 'Is that a good idea? You can't let on you know me.'

'Of course I won't. What do you take me for?'

'A bad-tempered twat, if you must know,' she told him. There was no response. 'Zervos was there when I arrived last night, a bit after eight. But there's no guarantee he'll come tonight or be there at the same time.'

'No, but I might as well give it a go. And don't worry, I'll completely ignore you.'

Siobhan laughed. 'That won't seem right. Most of the guys can't take their eyes off the girls. You'd look weird if you didn't have a quick perve.'

'Yeah, okay. I won't recognise you if that makes you feel better.'

She laughed again. 'What are you going to ask him?' His intake of breath was cut short when she exclaimed, '*I'm* meant to be meeting him tonight so won't it be odd if you're there too?'

'If you talk to him before your show and I turn up about eight-thirty, that should give you enough time.' He paused. 'I'll look like I've popped in for a quick drink at the end of a long day.'

'Are you going to stay for my performance?'

'Do you want me to?

'Not if you're in the same mardy mood.'

'I'll do my best to perk up. See you tonight, stranger,' Ray said and hung up.

Jesus, Siobhan thought. Miserable sod. She hoped his acting skills were better with Zervos than how he'd acted at the Regent.

CHAPTER FORTY-TWO

Ray checked his watch to see if it was a suitable time to ring Daphne at work. She usually went into the staffroom at the morning break and if she wasn't in her office then he could leave her a message which might actually be easier. No questions asked. He didn't want to tell her he was going to a strip joint that evening.

He held his breath while the phone rang, hardly believing his luck when it went to the answer machine. He left a message saying he'd be home late as he was on a case but didn't go into further details and with a guilty sigh put the receiver down. Why *did* he feel guilty? he asked himself. It was work and he often had to do late hours.

The day passed slowly; meetings, phone calls and paperwork, but Ray spent much of his time thinking about how to approach Zervos. Should he look like he'd just popped in for a drink at the club before heading home? It wasn't exactly the end of a working week. Or should he be upfront and ask the man directly what he knew about either of the deaths? Perhaps it could be a mixture of both. As I'm here could you answer a few questions? … Or just play it by ear. See what mood the bloke was in and who else was hanging around.

He was about to leave the office when his phone rang. Daphne? Should he answer it? It might be important. He picked up the phone. It was Daphne.

'Hello, darling,' she greeted. 'I heard your message but just wanted to say goodnight as I'll probably be asleep by the time you get home. Hope it won't be a big job.'

Ray reassured her it was the usual and he'd be home as soon as possible but if he was really late he'd sleep in the spare room. Daphne's acceptance reinforced his guilt. Deep down he knew it was because he was attracted to Siobhan, but it was hard to admit. It had nothing to do with Daphne's age. She was wonderful as well as beautiful, but there was something about the Irish girl that overwhelmed him. He couldn't understand why he'd been so off hand with Siobhan on the phone and she'd certainly put him in his place. For some reason he found her spunky attitude a turn on.

Putting his internal questions aside, he made his way to Darlinghurst Road to find somewhere to have a bite of dinner. If he was going to have a few drinks at The Love Hut, he wanted to have something in his stomach. Didn't want to give anything away. Loose lips and all that.

In the end he went to MacDonald's. Ray couldn't believe what he was doing but it seemed easier. He hadn't eaten Macca's for a long time and to his shame he enjoyed the burger and chips. Once finished, there was still time to kill so he wandered up to the Bourbon and Beefsteak. Even though it was early evening there was already an eclectic mix of people seated at the tables and around the bar. He enjoyed the Bourbon as its clientele was varied, the rich and the poor, the young and the old.

Ordering a beer, Ray stood by the bar listening to the band playing the quieter of the latest hits. He knew they'd become much louder as the evening wore on.

'Alright?' a voice said at his elbow. Ray turned to see it was one of the Scousers he'd met at the Regent.

'Gidday,' Ray greeted. 'You're a long way from Bondi. Thought you Poms got a nosebleed if you left the area.'

The Scouser rolled his eyes. 'Meeting some of the lads for a few jars and maybe watch the odd girl do her bit to help the right hand.'

Ray acknowledged the inference with a smirk. 'Which club?' Before the young man had time to answer, Ray said, 'Sorry, forgotten your name.'

'Morgo. Mates with Paddy, Brian, Steve, Harvey and the rest.'

'Oh, yeah … Ray,' he said, holding out his hand. 'Met some of your crowd the other night, but don't think we met properly. I

went with Siobhan. Felt a bit out of place with all you …
Scousers. Isn't that what you're called if you're from Liverpool?'
Morgo confirmed he was correct then asked Ray if he liked The
Beatles. 'Shit yeah. Who doesn't?'

Morgo's nod of approval showed he'd given the correct answer,
although he didn't have to lie as he'd always liked The Beatles.
His mother was a huge fan so had grown up listening to their
records. But why had Morgo come up to him? His voiceless query
was answered when Morgo said, 'Heard you'd been asking
questions in the boozer.'

'Who told you that?' Ray asked, trying not to show his
annoyance at being sprung.

'Come on, mate. Word gets around.'

'Bloody hell. I just wanted to buy a bit of dope so was
wondering if I could get anything now that … what's 'is name has
gone.'

Morgo looked sceptical. 'You a rozzer?'

'What?'

'The police.'

'No way.' Ray held Morgo's gaze.

'Well, you're an Aussie, and suddenly turn up with our Shiv.
Seems a bit coincidental … unless you're thinking of taking over
Trev's patch?'

'God no. Far too risky. Why don't you take over?' Ray suggested.

'Tempting, but not worth the risk.'

'Lose your visa?' Ray grinned. 'Out of curiosity, who did Trev get his supplies from? And no, I'm not the fucking police.'

Morgo's eyes narrowed as he scrutinised Ray's face. Satisfied, Morgo explained how Jason Zervos owned the Cross and supplied every dealer in the Eastern suburbs. 'How come you haven't heard of him?' He looked closely at Ray. 'Oh, that's right, you're not from 'round here. Must love this neck of the woods to be here again.'

Ray was starting to think he'd overplayed his hand by telling the others at the pub he was from out West and yet here he was again in the Eastern suburbs. He'd dug himself a bloody big hole.

'Fancy a beer?' he asked, playing for time.

'Wouldn't say no,' Morgo replied, and Ray signalled to the barman. What excuse could he make for being in this part of Sydney again?

Handing Morgo the beer, Ray grinned guiltily. 'If you ever meet Ciara, my girlfriend, don't tell her I was here. I fancied seeing Siobhan perform tonight. Even though Ciara and her are good friends, I doubt if she'd like me to have a close up of Siobhan's lovely body.' Ray winked theatrically at Morgo, hoping he sounded convincing.

'You sly bugger,' Morgo said with a grin. 'What time is our Siobhan doing her stuff? Wouldn't mind seeing her meself.'

'Not sure. That's why I'm here killing time. Don't think the show starts till late. Come along. Should be *entertaining*.' Ray hoped his invitation would have the reverse effect and with luck Morgo would be meeting his mates soon. He could see the lad was tempted. 'Bring your mates with you.'

Morgo, clearly not wanting to look like he was under the thumb of his friends, said he'd tell them about Siobhan's show, and they'd see him at The Love Hut.

'Great. See you later but don't ever let on to Ciara you've met me before.'

Morgo tapped his nose, grinning. 'No worries, mate.' He swilled his beer and left.

CHAPTER FORTY-THREE

Ray remained at the Bourbon until he felt he'd given Siobhan enough time to chat to Zervos. It was nearly nine and her show would start soon. He couldn't deny he was keen to see her 'dance'. She was definitely sexy and had a good body. Her tits could have been a bit bigger, but he couldn't ask for everything. Guilt waved over him again. What was he thinking? This was just a job. Yeah, right.

Leaving the Bourbon, he made his way towards the strip club which was upstairs in a nondescript building with a kebab shop underneath. A longish queue was waiting to get in. He was glad he'd eaten Macca's as he'd already consumed a few beers and needed to keep his wits about him.

The queue gradually shortened as the doorman vetted each guest making sure he or she wasn't too drunk and might cause trouble. The big Islander greeted Ray with a glimmer of recognition and with a nonchalant wave of his hand allowed him entry. Thanking him, Ray made his way upstairs and was met by a wall of sound. Def Leppard was singing *Pour Some Sugar on Me*, accompanied by cheers and cat calls. Siobhan was prancing erotically around the small stage, teasingly removing her few items of clothing. As expected, the majority of the audience were men but there were a few couples who were perhaps wanting to add a bit of excitement to their sex lives when they got home.

Ray peered around the semi-dark venue. Only the stage was lit, with the spotlight on Siobhan. All faces were upturned to watch her every move, while waitresses wove between the audience supplying drinks. He noticed how a few women wended their way to the men who were on their own, whispering in their ears. The reactions were mostly negative but occasionally there was a taker and attempting nonchalance he followed the woman out of the venue. Ray knew there were rooms in the floor above for prostitutes to ply their trade.

Dragging his eyes away from Siobhan, he aimed for the bar, took a seat, and ordered a beer from the pretty, scantily clad barmaid. He was about to pay when a male voice from further down the bar interrupted his attempt, saying to the barmaid, 'I'll get that.' Ray looked around. It was a swarthy man in a flash outfit flanked by a couple of large blokes dressed in dark suits. Nodding his thanks, Ray figured it was better to wait and see what happened next.

He raised the schooner in the man's direction but before he had a chance to put it to his lips, one of the large blokes walked up to him. 'Care to join us?' The way he asked left no chance of refusal unless Ray had balls of steel. Saying nothing, Ray slid off his seat and walking towards the man held out his hand. 'Ray O'Shea.'

'Jason Zervos. Having a quiet drink after work?'

'Could say that,' Ray responded. 'Been a busy day.'

'I can imagine. Keeping everyone on the straight and narrow.' Zervos sniggered smugly. 'Enjoying the performance? Daniella puts on a good show, despite being Irish.'

'Irish? Oh well, everyone has to earn a living.'

Zervos drank before turning back to Ray. 'But I'm sure you're not here just to watch the pretty lady.'

Ray laughed. 'I have needs like everyone else. Be off home soon.'

The grunt from Zervos was ambivalent. Ray remained silent. 'Apparently there's been a couple of *accidents* down at Bondi. Surprising in such a lovely neighbourhood. As you're with the Kings Cross cops, I assume you know what's going on?'

Ray nodded. He wasn't sure how to continue. How much should he tell Zervos, or should he play dumb and hope Zervos let something slip? Finally he said, 'One might have been a gay hate crime. There's been a lot of them over the last few years.'

'Yeah. But are the police bothered by the death of a few queers?'

Ray didn't bother to answer. He knew the man was trying to rile him. He drank some of his beer. It was obvious Zervos was waiting for a reaction. Speaking as neutrally as possible, Ray asked what else he'd heard.

Zervos scratched his chin as if in deep thought. 'Some bloke got knifed in the Regent. A dealer from what I've heard. Tut-tut. Shouldn't be selling those dreadful drugs.'

Ray couldn't help smiling. 'Of course not. But there's always a market. The average punter likes a bit of escape from the realities of life.'

'And you're a policeman! You'll be saying drugs should be legalised next.'

'Not a bad idea. Stop a hell of a lot of crime and the government could get the sales tax.'

'Do me out of … 'Zervos began then stopped when one of his minders gave him a not-so-subtle nudge.

'Out of what?' Ray asked, wondering if Zervos was pissed.

Zervos didn't answer.

'Did you know the bloke who got killed in the pub?' Ray asked quietly.

The King Pin remained silent for a long time. Finally, he admitted he did know Pearce. He was well known as a dealer.

'Not one of yours?'

Ignoring the question, Zervos waved his hand, dismissing the minders who did as instructed and shuffled further down the bar. Zervos leant towards Ray. 'If I tell you something, I hope you'll remember me when the investigation starts.' He pushed a hand through his gelled hair. 'I had nothing to do with Pearce's death, but I have a good idea who did.' Zervos paused dramatically. 'There's a new group on the block, if you understand me, and they're fucking ruthless. Take no prisoners.'

'Can you tell me who?'

Zervos whispered in Ray's ear then said, 'But this never came from me.'

Shit, he must have had a lot to drink, Ray thought, as he downed his beer. Why was he being so informative, and what did he hope to gain?

Ray was shocked by the information. This was a bigger deal than he'd imagined. The news was so important he left the club as soon as his conversation with Zervos was over even though Siobhan was still performing. Any sexual thoughts had vanished.

The usual trail of taxis were driving slowly along the main drag of the Cross, waiting for passengers to exit pubs and clubs. Within seconds Ray was in one and heading home. Daphne should be asleep by now and it was too late to ring Stone. He wanted to share his news, but the hour was wrong. It would have to wait till morning. He was also keen to talk to Siobhan and find out if she had managed to have a chat with her boss before he got there but her work didn't finish for hours. It was not surprising how fit she was, going from one club to the next. Her show, from what little he'd seen of it, was very physical. She certainly earned her money. Some compensation for all those sleazy blokes trying to grab her.

Entering his home, he tiptoed to the spare room and got into bed. He wished Daphne was awake so he could tell her what he'd found out, however, after numerous beers, it wasn't long till sleep arrived.

When he opened his eyes, Daphne was peeping around the door. 'Didn't want to wake you but have to get off to work soon. Cup of coffee?'

'You're an angel,' Ray complimented, struggling to sit up. She was back in no time with the coffee, asking how his evening had gone.

'Very interesting. Let me get my thoughts in order and I'll tell you all about it.'

The coffee helped him get his head together and after a quick visit to the loo, he joined her in the kitchen.

'So, tell me. What was so interesting?' Daphne urged.

'Hang on. Want another coffee?' Ray asked, smiling at her.

'No. Hurry up! You certainly know how to keep me hanging on ... sounds like a song,' Daphne joked, watching him closely.

Ray finally began his story.

Daphne, with elbows on the kitchen table, sat absorbed and all thoughts of getting to work early were forgotten. 'Do you believe him? Zervos obviously knows you're with the police so why would he give you such information? He must want something.'

'My thoughts exactly. I did wonder if he'd had a lot to drink and it loosened his tongue or there was some other motive. Has he done something dodgy and thinks by winning favour with us, we'll go easy on him? He admitted he knew Trevor Pearce but insisted he wasn't his supplier.'

'I'm not surprised. It's an admission to drug dealing.' She picked up her empty mug. 'Perhaps Pearce intimated Zervos was his boss to put everyone off the scent and all the time he was working for that other mob.' Daphne was about to stand when she said suddenly, 'Or maybe Zervos got rid of Pearce because he was saying it was Zervos who supplied the drugs instead of the other lot … Putting Zervos in danger when he's actually innocent. It's not surprising since the criminal class, if I can call them that, know each other so for him to know Pearce is not unusual.' With eyebrows raised at Ray, she challenged him to disagree. He didn't, instead asking, 'What's the time? Think I should call Stone and see what he has to say.'

Daphne turned to look at the kitchen clock. 'It's only just after seven.'

'Bugger it. I'll ring him at home. This is too important to wait.' Ray stood up, fumbling in his work bag to find Alan's number. He tapped the numbers, raising his thumb at Daphne when the phone was answered. 'Gidday, Alan. Ray. Is this a good time? Got something to tell you.'

CHAPTER FORTY-FOUR

Jim wondered how he could approach Julian about Alan's surprising suggestion without hurting his male ego. Alan had rung to pass on Ray's news and out of the blue had put forward the idea that Julian go to a certain gay bar in an attempt to find out more about Mark Dunlop. This placed Jim in a quandary. He knew that Alan was frustrated by the lack of progress regarding Mark's death, but how would Julian react to Alan's suggestion?

Although Jim found Julian irritating at times, he felt sorry for the young man after observing the frisson between Ray and Siobhan and he hoped that Julian would still be glad to be involved in the investigation even if it was not with Siobhan. Should he propose two options; Julian to continue going to the Regent, or visit the Oxford Street gay bars? It was a big ask and Julian may say no to both. Perhaps he should say he'd go with Julian to Oxford Street? He'd gathered age difference wasn't an issue for gay men, and many younger men had older boyfriends. Or should *he* go without Julian? He doubted he'd look out of place or was he kidding himself?

The bell ringing for morning break dragged Jim back to reality and he wove his way down the corridor between the teachers and students to the staffroom. Julian was already there making himself a cup of something. 'Gidday,' Jim greeted. 'Got a minute?'

Julian finished making his beverage and joined Jim on one of the large couches placed around the room. 'What's up?'

Jim glanced around to make sure no-one was listening and once reassured the teachers were involved in their own conversations told Julian about Alan's suggestion.

The puzzled expression on Julian's face dampened Jim's hopes. 'I was even thinking I could go by myself,' Jim said.

Julian began to laugh. 'Oooooh, ducky. I'm sure you'll fool them into exposing their secrets.'

Jim pursed his lips. 'I've got to do something and as you've done so much to help, I can't lay it all on you.'

Julian shook his head vigorously. 'Jim, I haven't felt put upon. If anything, I'm glad to help, and it gives me something to do. I've enjoyed mixing with the other Brits.' He drank some of his tea. 'I'm happy to go with you to a gay bar. We'd pass for a couple, and it might make the others feel more relaxed. Better than a single bloke asking questions.'

Stifling a sigh of relief, Jim didn't tell Julian he'd already thought the same. 'Great idea. Obviously, I'll have to get Anh's

303

approval but I'm sure she'll agree. She's desperate to find out what happened to Mark.'

'So I've gathered. We'll have to think about what to wear. Ooooh, it's exciting.'

'Steady on. Remember I'm the deputy principal. What night suits you? Tomorrow?'

Julian grinned at Jim's eagerness to get cracking. 'Tomorrow is fine. We don't want to get there too early so is seven okay? Which bar will we start with?'

'I have no idea … How about I ring Alan and see if he has any pointers? He talked to Mark's chap, Darcy, about where they were meant to meet the night Mark died. That might be a good place to start.'

The bell rang and Jim stood up. 'I'll let you know when and where.'

'Thanks, my dear,' Julian whispered, tapping Jim on the arm. Trying to keep a straight face, Jim quickly walked away.

'What the hell have I done?' Jim asked, as he headed back to his office. Julian seemed to be getting too much enjoyment out of this. He hoped Julian would keep his mouth shut, especially as the English loved taking the piss out of authority figures.

The first thing he did when he entered his office was pick up the phone and ring Alan. 'Do you remember which pub or club Mark and his chap were meant to meet on that Saturday night?'

'The Albury.'

'Ah yes. Well, Julian and I are going together to see what we can find out about Mark.'

'Something you're not telling me?' Stone asked, with a theatrical cough.

'That'll do,' Jim warned. 'I thought it'd be more convincing if we went as a couple and hopefully get chatting to the clientele … and don't make any comments about what to wear.'

'Wouldn't dream of it, but are you having your chest waxed?'

'Piss off. You're worse than bloody Julian. Anyway, we're going there tomorrow night if Anh is happy.'

'Remember Mark's chap is called Darcy and he's a hairdresser, so if you come across him, be careful what you say.'

'Will do, and not a word to anyone.'

Stone a hemmed. 'Your secret's safe with me. I'll only tell … no, don't worry I won't. Keep me in the loop.'

Jim hung up.

Anh couldn't hide her smile as she listened to Jim's explanation about his plan for the following evening. 'Never in my wildest dream did I think you would go to a gay bar and pretend to be homosexual,' she said, trying not to laugh.

'Alright, alright,' Jim retaliated, although he too couldn't resist a grin. This was something he'd never envisaged either, but at least he was being proactive.

'What are you going to wear?'

'You sound just like Alan.'

'Well, you need to look convincing.' Anh thought for a minute. 'Mark didn't really wear anything different to what most men would wear so maybe smart casual. Make sure you have a decent shave and put some gel in your hair.'

'Bloody hell, Anh. Really?'

'Yes. If you look like straight man, everyone will ignore you and wonder what you are doing in their territory.'

Jim agreed. She was right. He'd ring Julian and confirm their going to the Albury the following evening.

Neither man had ever made such a fuss of their appearance and by the time both left to go to the Albury, their nerves were shattered. Julian was waiting outside the pub on Oxford Street having a cigarette when Jim pulled up in a taxi. Eying each other up and down, they gave a nod of approval, then Jim insisted that Julian go in first. He couldn't believe how nervous he felt.

The sound system was belting out *I Will Survive* by Gloria Gaynor and many in the bar were singing along. How appropriate, Jim thought. Would he survive the evening? Looking around, he saw how there was a cross-section of patrons. There were a few cross-dressers, with others looking as if they'd just come from work in an office, and some in brief shorts and T-shirts. He'd expected to see over-the-top outfits, something like The Village People or *Priscilla, Queen of the Desert* but it was a mixture of all – the staid to the flamboyant.

'What's your poison?' Julian asked, pulling out his wallet.

Jim hesitated. Should he order something exotic or stick to beer? He glanced at those nearest and was glad many were having a beer. 'Toohey's New,' he ordered, and to his relief Julian was soon back with two schooners.

Both stood drinking self-consciously, feeling very out of place. Luckily, the popular songs playing in the background disguised their lack of chat. Their beers quickly finished, Jim went to the bar and once served by a friendly barman, found Julian in conversation with an attractive, tanned young man.

Julian asked the man his name then introduced Jim as his partner.

'So lovely to meet you,' Diego greeted in an accent which definitely wasn't Aussie.

'You too,' Jim agreed. 'Where are you from?'

'Chile.'

'Ah. South America. Would love to go there,' Jim flattered. 'Enjoying Sydney?'

'It's okay. Very expensive and many no like us here.'

Neither of them knew how to respond. Better to change the subject.

'Do you come to this pub often?' Jim asked, conscious of his trite cliché.

'Many nights of the week I come,' Diego answered. 'Not seen you before.'

Putting his arm around Jim's shoulders, Julian explained, 'My partner is a teacher, and it can be a bit risky to be seen in places like this. There's still a lot of prejudice despite it being 1995.'

Diego waggled his head vigorously in agreement. 'Like my country. Torture. Prison.'

'Goodness,' Jim said, shocked. 'Is that why you're in Sydney?'

'Si. Yes.'

'Well, I hope you enjoy your time here and I hope you can stay,' Jim comforted. He drank, wondering how long they could keep this chat going till it occurred to him Diego may have met Mark. Both strangers in a strange land. 'Just wondering, Diego, if you ever met an English guy called Mark Dunlop? And his partner Darcy?'

The Chilean leant his head to one side, thinking. 'Many people come here. How does he look?'

'Young, dark haired, nice looking. Quite tall. Bit like you,' Jim flattered.

Diego laughed. 'Sound like many here.'

'What about his partner, Darcy? He's a hairdresser and older than Mark.'

'Ah, si. I talk to him one night about having my hair cut. In Kings Cross.'

Jim nearly cuddled the man but held himself back. 'That's him. That's Darcy. Did you meet his boyfriend, Mark? He was a friend of mine. Would love to know if he was happy.'

'Happy?' Diego questioned, frowning. 'If he the man you mean, he seemed good.'

Jim quickly turned to Julian. 'Darling, could you get us all another beer? What are you drinking, Diego?' They both watched Julian as he went to the bar.

'Here you go, pet,' Julian said on return, handing Diego a schooner.

The conversation ground to a halt and the three stood in awkward silence. Jim knew he had to say something or Diego might go elsewhere. 'I'm sorry to keep asking, but can you tell us what you remember about Mark? I really miss him.'

309

Diego pouted at Julian as if to ask why. Jim realised how he'd sounded and jumped in, explaining Mark was considered a member of the family. He wiggled his finger around family hoping to clarify their relationship. Diego rolled his eyes, saying, 'I no like threesomes. Have partner. Too dangerous.'

'Oh my God, that wasn't what I meant,' Jim blustered, thinking how this conversation was a bloody minefield. 'I just meant Mark was a very good friend. Nothing more. Because he died suddenly, I just hope he was okay. I hadn't seen him for a few weeks.'

Seemingly unfazed by the news of Mark's death, Diego gazed into the distance. Julian and Jim waited, mentally crossing their fingers, hoping he would come up with something useful.

'Mark was English, no?' Diego asked.

'Yes. Yes he was.'

'He always with Darcy. Seemed to love him. Many people here wanted him but loyal.'

'You mean Mark was loyal to Darcy?' Julian asked.

'Si, si.'

'Was there anyone in particular who wanted Mark?' Jim asked carefully, hoping his meaning was clear.

Diego shrugged dramatically. 'Many, many.' He lifted his schooner taking a gulp before saying, 'One man always here. English, the same. But Mark not interested.'

Jim looked at Julian, thinking, Was this the man who rang the police the night Mark died? 'Do you remember where that man was from in England?' Jim asked slowly.

'Ah no. All sound same. Difficult to understanding what they say.'

Julian laughed. 'I hope you understand *me*?'

Diego rubbed his arm. 'Si. I understand *you*.'

'Do you remember his name?' Jim asked abruptly. Diego shook his head. Jim stared around the bar. 'Is this man in the pub now?' Again Diego shook his head.

Sensing he was becoming the third wheel, Jim decided to use his non-existent acting skills and put his arm possessively around Julian's shoulders. 'Darling. Do you think it's time to make a move?'

'Ooooh. Do we have to? I'm enjoying myself.'

'Yes we do. I have to be up early in the morning.'

'You spoilsport. It was so nice meeting you,' Julian complimented Diego and gave him a kiss on the cheek. 'I hope we'll meet again.'

Diego agreed and watched as Jim grabbed Julian's hand, leading him out of the pub.

'Is there something you haven't told me?' Jim asked, conscious he was mimicking Stone's words as they stood in the street waiting to hail a cab.

Julian threw his head back and laughed. 'No, mate. I was just playing along. Didn't want our man, Diego, to think we were asking too many questions. Hopefully, I gave him a bit of an ego boost. And you weren't too bad yourself, calling me darling and holding my hand.'

'That'll do. Don't fancy yourself ... At least we found out something. The English guy who was hanging around Mark sounds of interest. Could be the one who rang the police.'

'Yes, darling, you might be right,' Julian said, slapping Jim lightly on the wrist.

Jim waved frantically for a cab.

CHAPTER FORTY-FIVE

Siobhan felt at a loss. She hadn't been able to talk to Zervos properly. He'd seemed grumpy, too busy drinking and obviously didn't want to talk to her. Then Ray arrived but left before she'd finished her show. It was hard to admit, but she'd wanted him to see her perform. See how good she was at her job and find her a turn on.

What the hell was she thinking? She knew he was in a relationship, and he had a few years on her. Plus, he was the police. It was like dating the enemy. But why did he leave so quickly? What had Zervos said to him? Questions. Questions. No effing answers.

The only good thing about the day was she'd managed to get some sleep. A shower was in order. The thought of going down to the Regent before heading to work had no appeal. Julian hadn't been in touch, and it was unlikely Ray would go there again. Also, she could do without the sly looks she got whenever she walked in.

The shower lifted her mood a little. Perhaps she could try to talk to Zervos again tonight? While dressing in jeans and a tight T-shirt, the phone rang. It was tempting to let it ring but curiosity won, and she managed to pick up before the call went to the answer machine.

'Hello.'

'Siobhan?'

'Yes.'

'It's Ray.'

'Ah, hello. To what do I owe the pleasure?' she asked, unable to resist sounding flirty.

'Don't know if it's a pleasure,' Ray doubted, 'but I was wondering if you could spare me a few minutes tonight before your shift?'

'Of course. Unless you're going to tell me something terrible. Where do you want to meet?'

'Not at the strip club. What about the Kings Cross Hotel? Neutral territory.'

'This is sounding most mysterious.'

'Just want to keep you up to date regarding my chat with your boss,' Ray explained.

'What time?' she asked, annoyed at his dismissive attitude.

'Eight o'clock. Upstairs on the balcony.'

'See you then.' Siobhan hung up.

With a few hours to kill, Siobhan went into the bedroom and lay on the bed. One minute Ray had seemed interested, the next distant. Bloody men. It was impossible to work them out. Julian hadn't been in touch over the last few days. Had he found out what he wanted from her and now couldn't be bothered? They always wanted something. Well, the bastards could all get fucked.

A couple of hours later, she was awakened by the phone ringing. She looked at her bedside clock. It was already five. The phone had stopped by the time she pulled herself out of bed. Yawning, she wandered into the lounge to see if there was a message. The answer machine was flashing.

Siobhan pressed play. There was no greeting and although the voice was muffled, it sounded like a man. It was difficult to make out what was being said. There was something about Trevor and him being attacked and … she was responsible. If she wanted to live she had to …

What the hell? Siobhan rewound the tape and pressed play again. Holding her ear nearer to the machine she still couldn't decipher much more. It sounded as if the person had rung from a noisy venue. There was some sort of music in the background, although it didn't sound like the sort of music a pub would play.

With shaking hands, she ejected the tape and put it into her bag. This was something Ray and Stone needed to listen to. Who knew her phone number? She was always cautious about who she gave it to and certainly never to the men who came to watch her show. Was it someone from the Regent? Julian, Stone, Jim and of course Ray, now knew her phone number, but it was hardly likely to be one of them. Her girlfriends wouldn't play such a shitty game unless it was one of their boyfriends. But why would they be so daft?

The worst part of the message was the threat. The caller seemed to imply she'd had Trevor attacked and now he wanted to murder her unless she did … what? Grabbing the phone book she scanned the numbers for Kings Cross Police Station.

'Kings Cross Police Station,' a neutral female voice answered. 'How can I help you?'

'It's Siobhan Greene here and I want to speak to Detective Ray O'Shea. It's urgent.'

'I'm sorry, he isn't in his office at the moment. Can I take a message?'

'Yes, please. When he comes back can you ask him to ring Siobhan Greene as soon as possible. Tell him it's very urgent. He knows who I am.'

'Your number?'

'He has it, but I'll give it to you.' Siobhan dictated her number and hung up.

The minutes while Siobhan waited for Ray to return her call seemed like hours. She tried to distract herself by getting ready to go to work but nothing could take her mind off the threat to kill her. She knew how her so-called relationship with Trev had made her unpopular with some of the crowd at the Regent but for this person to threaten her life was completely unexpected and worst of all, really scary. A couple of hours remained until she'd catch a taxi to the Cross. She poured herself a wine. Food was out of the question. It was doubtful if it would remain in her stomach. Perhaps she should ring Alan Stone? Yes, better than nothing. Another search through the White Pages and she found Waverley Police Station. A similar answer and the same request, except this time it was for Detective Alan Stone. Thank God he was in the station.

'Alan, it's Siobhan.'

'You okay?'

'No. I had a call about an hour or so ago, someone threatening to kill me.'

There was a short silence then Stone instructed, 'Stay calm and tell me what was said.'

'It was hard to hear as it went to the answer machine and there was a lot of noise in the background, but it was some guy saying I was responsible for Trevor's death, and I was next. Or maybe it was I had to do something, but I couldn't hear properly.'

317

'It was definitely a man?'

'I think so. It was really muffled and there was lots of noise.'

'What type of noise?'

'It didn't sound like a pub, but there *was* music. Nothing I recognised.'

'You didn't delete the message did you?'

'God no. I've put the cassette in my bag as I'm meeting Ray tonight at a pub in the Cross before my show.'

'Oh … Well make sure you give it to him, and we can listen to it and hopefully learn more. And if you don't mind, we'll make a copy of it.'

'For sure … Alan, do you think I'm safe?'

'Good point. Whoever rang you obviously knows your phone number and maybe your address. Do you have a friend you can stay with over the next few days? If not, we'll put you up in a hotel.'

Siobhan didn't answer immediately. She'd been so busy with work, earning money and just going to the Regent, she didn't have a close girlfriend she could ask. Fucking Trev blackmailing her with the visa.

'I sound tragic but a hotel is probably best. Don't have many close friends in Sydney.'

'Fair enough. I'll get back to you soon with a hotel you can go to. Somewhere in the Cross as you work there.'

'Grand. Thank you, Alan.'

'Thank you for the information. Take care.'

CHAPTER FORTY-SIX

The taxi dropped Siobhan in front of the Kings Cross Hotel and after thrusting cash at the driver, she dashed inside carrying a holdall. Despite having lived in Belfast where The Troubles still lingered, she found this new situation upsetting. At least in Belfast the enemy was more obvious. You were either Catholic or Protestant and you lived in separated areas of the city.

She raced upstairs to the smoking balcony of the pub and found it full of drinkers, making it hard to find Ray. She didn't have long to tell him her news. Stone had already informed her which hotel to go to after she finished work and it was right behind this pub. Her bag was full of clothes and toiletries. Luckily, her outfits for the shows were minimal and some of them were already in the dressing rooms of the different clubs.

Ray was finally found sitting with a beer, the dispassionate expression on his face changing quickly when he saw Siobhan.

'You okay?'

'No.'

'Can I get you a drink?'

Yes! A whisky.' She could see Ray flinch at the request but fuck 'im. Placing her bag underneath the table, she took a few deep breaths. Stay calm. Stay calm, she mentally chanted as she waited while he went to the bar.

'What's up?' he asked on his return.

Her hands were shaking as she lit a cigarette before picking up the whisky and knocking it back in one gulp.

'Jesus. Steady on. What the hell's the matter?'

'I had a horrible phone call. Scared the bejesus out of me. Some bloke, at least I think it was, rang and threatened me.'

'What? Calm down and start again. When did he ring and what did he say?'

Seeing Siobhan lift up her empty glass to see if a dribble was left, Ray dashed back to the bar. 'Take this one easy,' he ordered as he handed her the glass. 'Right, now start again.'

Taking a deep breath, Siobhan began, 'It was about five this afternoon. Woke me up. There was all this noise in the background, so it was hard to hear. It had gone to the answer machine.' She opened her handbag and took out the tape. 'This is it. Can you give it to Alan? You guys might understand more than I did.'

'What did you understand?'

'He mentioned how Trevor Pearce was attacked and something about how I was responsible, so I had to do something. ... but it

321

wasn't clear what. The worst thing is whoever it was, has my phone number, and probably knows where I live.' Siobhan picked up her drink and was about to neck it then changed her mind and took a sip. 'Ray, I'm fucking scared. Trev was killed so easily.'

'Am I the only one you've told about this?' Ray asked, putting a hand on her arm.

'No. I rang Alan. He's booked me into a hotel here in the Cross.'

'Good idea. Is there anything else on the tape that stands out?'

'The music. It didn't sound like a pub, more like a restaurant but not a normal one. Or maybe a party?'

'Did the guy have an accent?'

'Hard to tell. Nothing was really clear.'

'When I get home I'll listen to it, and tomorrow I'll pass it on to Alan.'

'Cheers. Thank you, Ray. … What's the time?' Siobhan asked, prompting him to look at his watch.

'Ten to eight. Is it time for you to go?'

'In a minute.' Siobhan drank more of her whisky before asking, 'Have I done something? You seem a bit bullin with me since we went to the Regent.'

'Pardon?'

'Pissed off with me.'

'Didn't mean to. I just find you …'

'What?'

'Nothing … We'd better get going. I'll walk you to the club. Which one is it?' Ray asked, standing up.

'You don't have to.'

'I want to. And when you've finished your shows, get a taxi to the hotel, even though it's close.'

'Yes, sir!' Siobhan picked up her holdall from underneath the table. 'Oh. You never told me why you rang to meet.'

'It doesn't matter,' Ray replied, and led her to the lift which took them to the ground floor.

CHAPTER FORTY-SEVEN

'You're back early,' Daphne said, taking her eyes off the television as Ray walked into the lounge. 'Everything okay?'

'Not sure. I caught up with Siobhan. She's had a call from an anonymous bloke making threats because of Trevor Pearce's death. She gave me the tape. Do you mind if I listen to it now? It should work on our answer machine.'

'Not at all. Can I listen as well?'

'Of course. You may have ideas that haven't occurred to me.'

They walked into the kitchen where the telephone and answer machine were positioned on the divide. Ray inserted the tape and pressed play. Both listened intently to the message. He replayed it, then turned to Daphne. 'Any thoughts?'

'The voice doesn't sound Australian. Someone who hasn't been here very long and English isn't their first language?' Daphne suggested.

'Yes, that's what I thought. Any idea which country?'

'Play it again. The music in the background may be a clue.'

Ray did as he was told.

Daphne listened closely. 'It reminds me of when I went to Saigon with my ex, Michael. It's definitely got an Asian feel to it.'

'Do you think the caller is Vietnamese?'

'It's hard to tell because it's so muffled, and with the music in the background. Do you think the person who rang was in a restaurant coincidentally, or wanted to give a hint about their origin? Is there a Vietnamese, or maybe a Chinese gang trying to break into the drug scene?'

Ray tightened his lips. 'Good point. But how did they get Siobhan's phone number?'

Daphne opened the fridge and took out a bottle of white wine. She quizzically held it up to Ray who nodded in agreement. After taking two glasses out of the cupboard above the bench, she handed the bottle and a corkscrew to Ray. 'It's been a while since you and I had a drink together. This is nice.'

Ray pulled out the cork and poured the wine. 'Yes, I'm sorry. My job definitely gets in the way. Cheers.' They clinked glasses.

'Getting back to Siobhan's phone number. Is it that difficult to find? The phone book? Or ring Directory Assistance?' Daphne suggested.

'Why would she put it in the phone book? But I suppose if they knew Trevor Pearce it wouldn't be hard to get her number … although as he was so possessive, it's doubtful he'd give it to some random guy.' Ray picked up his glass, took a sip then said,

325

'Perhaps Trev belonged to this gang and then when he was killed they contacted Siobhan.'

'Maybe.' Daphne raised the glass to her lips, then put it down. 'But what exactly are they threatening?'

'Something about if she doesn't … that's the bit I didn't get. Something like she was responsible for his death but …?'

'Do you think they wanted her to know who they are? Preparing her?'

'For what?' Ray asked.

'To be the dealer, now Trevor's out of the way? Or to keep her mouth shut?'

Ray thought about Daphne's suggestions. 'Don't want to sound sexist but asking a young woman to sell drugs seems highly unlikely.'

'The times they are a changing,' Daphne quoted Bob Dylan with a knowing smile.

'True, but if the threat is there and they know she was associated with Pearce, she's in danger.'

'Perhaps she shouldn't have bought drugs off Trevor?'

'Daph … you're being a bit judgemental.'

'It sounds like she can do no wrong in your eyes.' Daphne drank her wine, staring at Ray.

'What do you mean? I'm not interested in Siobhan.'

326

Daphne shrugged. 'Maybe not. But if you do find yourself interested in someone else, I want you to tell me. Don't want to spend years with someone who doesn't want to be with me. Wasted enough years on my ex-husband.'

'Where did all this come from?' Ray asked, frowning.

'Ooh, let me think. Never see you. Always at the pub on a job. I'm on my own most of the time.'

'I can't help it. It's work.'

'I understand that, but this Irish girl has been mentioned a lot lately. Honestly, if you don't want to be with me, just say. I totally understand. I'm older than you and if you want to have kids …' Daphne stopped and poured them another drink. 'Anyway, where were we?'

Ray dragged himself out of bed, leaving Daphne asleep. Her words from the night before hung over him. Was she right? He couldn't face thinking about what she'd said. Now, he just wanted to speak to Stone and give him the tape.

Was it too early to ring? He wanted to get rid of it. The tape was a reminder of his thoughts about Siobhan. He knew he'd been offhand towards her because he did find her attractive and he could tell she liked him as well. Or, was it because she flirted with him, flattering his ego, but then he too had flirted with her at Jim's place. He couldn't help himself and last night when he'd walked her to the strip joint, he was so tempted to kiss her. What the hell was he doing? He loved Daphne. She'd changed his life. Without her he'd have gone nowhere.

He looked at the kitchen clock. It was only seven-thirty. Far too early to ring Alan. He made a cup of coffee and for something to do, listened to the tape again. What was this bloke threatening? He pressed play. '… you responsible for Trevor's death … you have to …'

What the hell was Siobhan supposed do? …You responsible … not, *you're* responsible. A simple mistake but was it someone who wasn't a native English speaker as Daphne had pointed out? He'd heard rumours there was a Vietnamese gang on the move. He and Stone had been so busy focussing on Zervos when maybe it was this lot from out West?

Bugger the time, he had to talk to Stone. He rang the station only to be told that Detective Stone had not yet arrived. Did he want to leave a message? Yes he did. Straight after he rang Stone's home number and thanking God, Alan answered.

'Sorry to ring so early, but Siobhan gave me the tape of the message she received yesterday, and I want to drop it off to you as soon as possible. Need you to listen and see what you think. Played it to Daphne and we have a variety of opinions. Are you around today?'

'Steady on, Ray. You sound stressed,' Stone said. 'Yes, I'm around. Do you want me to come to the Cross? Save you the bother.'

'No, I'll come to Waverley.

'Okay. See you shortly.'

Being early, it didn't take long for Ray to drive to Waverley Police Station and of course, he could park in one of their designated parking spots.

He hardly listened to the desk sergeant telling him Detective Stone had just arrived. A quick knock on Stone's door, allowed him entry.

'My God, Ray. Everything alright?'

Ray sighed. 'Yeah. Just keen for you to hear the tape. Glad you booked Siobhan into a hotel.'

'Well, it seemed the best thing to do from what she told me. Anyway, let's listen to it,' Stone suggested, pointing to the answer machine next to his phone.

Quickly inserting the tape, Ray pressed play. Both listened then Stone asked for it to be played again. 'What do *you* think?' he asked Ray, once the tape was stopped.

'Sounds like a threat to me. Siobhan's connection with Pearce has put her in danger. Got the impression they want her to work for them, but it's not very clear. Who do you think is speaking?'

329

'The type of music and the accent indicate an Asian of some sort.'

Ray agreed. 'That's what Daphne thought. She said the speaker sounded Vietnamese. She's been to Vietnam.'

Stone nodded. 'Is there a Vietnamese gang trying to muscle-in on the Eastern suburbs?'

'That's what I was thinking. We've been assuming it's Zervos who supplied Pearce, but when I spoke to him the other night he insisted it was a bikie gang with powerful connections.' Ray scratched his unshaved chin. 'The voice and music don't sound like bikies. Unless they're pretending to be Asians. Throw us off the scent. And maybe Zervos is doing the same?'

'That sounds a bit far-fetched. Didn't know you'd spoken to Zervos. How did it go?'

'To be honest, I wondered if he was pissed as he was telling me all this info which seemed out of character for someone like him. Also he was hinting for police protection.'

Stone's eyes widened. 'But why murder Pearce? Or is Zervos acting all innocent and helpful to win favour with the police?'

'Buggered if I know,' Ray answered.

'I'll give the tape to the guys who look into this sort of thing and see what they come up with. If it is a Vietnamese voice, it doesn't necessarily dismiss the bikies as there could be Asians in their gang. Or as you said, they're trying to throw us off the scent.'

Ray shook his head. 'Nothing's bloody easy.'

'No! How's Siobhan coping?' Stone asked. 'Hope she's staying at the hotel and not doing anything stupid.'

'She's frightened. I insisted she did, and I'm assuming she played ball after she finished her shows last night. Told her to get a taxi no matter how close she was to the hotel.'

'Let's hope for her sake.'

Stone waited impatiently for feedback regarding the tape. Even if there was no new information it would be good to have their own analysis confirmed. Finally, there was a tap on his door and the sergeant who dealt with computers and technology stood holding the tape.

'Come in, come in,' Stone urged.

'Thanks, sir.' The sergeant placed the tape on Stone's desk. 'Very interesting. Managed to play it on a better gadget than the average answering machine so heard quite a bit more.'

Stone opened his notebook and grabbed a pen from a jar on his desk. 'Let's have it. Sit down.'

'It appears the phone call was made from a restaurant and on close listening, the music in the background *is* Vietnamese and there were noises of cutlery and plates being moved around. The voice was muffled because a tissue or hanky may have been placed over the mouthpiece to disguise the voice, but it was definitely a man. I'm no authority on Asian accents but judging by the way he didn't end some of his words, he sounded Vietnamese.'

Stone busily wrote down the sergeant's analysis. 'Anything else?' he asked hopefully.

'The man seemed to be threatening the woman because of her connection to Pearce, but it didn't sound like she would be next. More like she has to work for them. He appeared to know that she is familiar with the Regent and the Cross.'

'But they must know she works for Zervos as a dancer. Not as a dealer,' Stone interrupted. 'Why would they want her to work for them? Is it because she is known to frequent the Regent and work in strip clubs?' His questions were rhetorical as the sergeant had no clue to as to the activities of Siobhan Greene except for what was on the tape.

'Do the Vietnamese gangs have any links to the bikies in the Cross? The Lebs do but I'm not aware of any other ethnic group muscling in,' Stone puzzled.

'Perhaps they want to establish themselves in the Cross, as well as out west,' the sergeant suggested.

Stone agreed. 'Any idea how they got Siobhan's phone number?'

The sergeant thought for a moment. 'Directory Service?'

'Sounds too simple,' Stone said with a sigh.

CHAPTER FORTY-EIGHT

As Julian wasn't a proper boarding master, he didn't have the same duties to fulfill but sometimes he wished he hadn't taken the offer to live at the school. He wasn't exactly lonely, but the evenings could be boring. Going down to the pub at Bondi had certainly given him something to do and although most of the crowd were merely acquaintances, he felt more at home hearing familiar accents, the British references and expressions. Deciding he no longer cared if Siobhan were present, his mission now was to find out more about the chap wearing the AC/DC T-shirt.

He entered the Regent, pausing to listen to the music playing over the sound system, and was glad it was a British band as it made him feel less homesick. He bought a bevvy and checked out who was in attendance. As he gazed around the bar, he wondered who of the regulars had been allowed access to AC/DC man on the night he'd been refused. Then he remembered. It was Jimmy! Jimmy had bought drugs off AC/DC man that night. Spotting the Scotsman standing amongst the usual suspects, Julian wove his way through the crowd.

'Any luck with our Siobhan?' Brian asked as soon as Julian drew near.

'No. Wasn't really my type,' Julian replied with a shrug, causing the Scouser to laugh. 'Didn't fall for your southern charm then?' Brian smirked.

Julian couldn't be bothered getting into a verbal ribbing. 'You win some, you lose some.' Should he ask Brian about AC/DC man? Even if he didn't buy drugs, he might know something.

'Speaking of luck, did you have any with the geezer selling in the gents the other night? I couldn't get into the bloody toilets. Can't believe management doesn't know what's going on.'

Brian acknowledged Julian's disbelief before saying, 'Mate, with the hours I work, don't take any of that stuff. Hoping to score?'

'Wouldn't have minded a bit of something for the weekend … Remember going to the barber and he would ask sooo politely, 'A little something for the weekend, sir?' as he cut your hair? Must have lost a fortune when the vending machines started selling condoms.'

'Fuck!' Brian exclaimed, laughing. 'Haven't thought of that for donkeys.'

Eager to return to the main topic, Julian continued, 'Who was that guy in the gents? The one who wore the AC/DC T-shirt. Hadn't seen him before.'

Brian turned to Jimmy, who'd moved closer. 'What's the name of the bloke who sells stuff in the bog? You know who I mean. Nudge, nudge, wink, wink.'

'NFI,' Jimmy answered dismissively.

'Something Greek. Stavos?' one of the group butted in and grinning at Brian said, 'Want a little something for the weekend?'

'Not me, ya tool. Julian here,' Brian explained, scowling.

'After buying a bit of charlie?' another asked Julian, forcing him to join in the conversation. 'Not tonight. Tried to when he was here last time but couldn't get past his big beefy *friend*.'

A few muttered in understanding and Steve who'd been listening, stated, 'That nob'ead. Bit of power goes a long way. Didn't ya know how to play him?'

'Was just hoping for something for the weekend … not condoms,' Julian grinned at Brian, 'but wasn't allowed entry. Wondered what I had to do to go to the bloody toilet.'

He knew he'd scored a point against Steve when the others laughed.

'Probably thought you was a copper,' Steve retaliated.

'Well, if I *am* a copper,' Julian stated sarcastically, 'how come that bloke was selling drugs in the toilets? Has he taken over from our man, Trev?'

Those around Julian pulled back, then realising he was taking the piss, a couple chuckled. Steve glared at the two who'd

335

laughed. 'Look, mate, we don't get involved in the politics of the pub. The less we know the better and you'd be safer if you stopped asking fuckin' questions. And the bloke you're talking about, that wasn't his first time in the pub.'

It was clear to Julian that Steve wanted to keep control of the conversation. 'Don't you want to know who killed Trev, or Mark for that matter?' Julian asked forcefully. 'There's something going on in this pub that's not right. I don't give a shit who takes whatever drugs but there's been two deaths in as many days. The whole thing is bloody dodgy.'

'What do you expect *us* to do? We could lose our effing visas, end up in Villawood or worse,' Steve argued.

'Yeah, but Mark was a mate of yours and he's ended up dead.'

'I thought he'd just drowned,' a voice interjected.

'Come on. Not likely,' Julian replied, looking around at the men.

There were grumblings showing their doubt about the inference to foul play.

'I can't tell you how I know, but he *was* killed, then pushed into the water.'

Steve rolled his eyes, indicating to the group that Julian was full of shit. 'Well, if you're not a copper, how do you know so fuckin' much?'

Wearily pulling his shoulders back, Julian eyed them. 'I'm *not* a copper but I *do* want to know what happened. I want to find out why Mark died and why Trev did as well and you blokes could help me.'

He knew he was taking a risk, but despite the reputation Scousers had for being robbers, they were known to be loyal and had a developed sense of what was right. Also, no-one had said anything about his being a teacher so it looked as if Siobhan hadn't betrayed him.

Suddenly, Steve fronted him, holding out his hand. 'What do we do?'

Most of the guys had wandered off, not keen to be involved, but as well as Steve, Paddy and Jimmy remained. Julian bought them a beer before leading them to a quieter corner of the pub. He was surprised Steve wanted to be involved, yet at the same time pleased.

'Thanks, guys. I promise I am not the police and I will do nothing to jeopardise your visas. And I certainly won't tell them you've bought drugs off either chap. If you trust me, and I hope you do, I want to tell you that I work at a school nearby, in Bellevue Hill, and Mark was a friend of one of my work mates. That's why I'm involved. Even though I'm a Londoner … just like the song,' he laughed, 'I want to help my colleague, Jim Cameron.

337

He's the Deputy Head at St Cuthbert's. Mark stayed with his family when he first came out from Liverpool. They got on really well even though they'd never met him before. His death has been a real shock and they want to find out the truth.'

Julian's small audience nodded vigorously.

'Do you think Mark's death is linked to Trev's?' Steve asked. 'Seems too bloody coincidental not to be.'

'I don't know,' Julian answered. 'It could be because Mark was a homo …'

'Why?' Paddy interrupted.

'Apparently, there've been a number of gay killings and bashings in Sydney over the last few years.'

'Thought Sydney was meant to be the gay capital of the Southern Hemisphere?' questioned Jimmy.

'So did I, but there've been lots of murders.'

The men looked at each other in surprise.

'AIDS hasn't helped the prejudice,' Julian continued, then seeing the worried expression on Paddy's face, added, 'Don't worry, you can't catch AIDS by talking to someone who is gay. What we need to find out is who supplies heavy drugs, not just the odd E or weed.' Julian stared at them. 'Did Trev sell heavy drugs or anything like that or was it the bloke in the toilets? You need to think about who Mark associated with. Siobhan and Mark were mates, so it seems highly unlikely she was involved.'

'That's bollocks,' Steve doubted.

'I know it looks suspicious because of her connection with Trevor, but from what I've heard, she and Mark were good friends. And, she certainly wasn't Trev's girlfriend, despite the rumours.'

Steve grunted in disbelief and Julian could see he was about to argue. 'Yes, it's hard to believe she wasn't as you saw them together a lot, but I think he had some hold over her, and it wasn't just buying the odd bit of charlie,' Julian justified.

Frowning, Steve asked, 'If you're right, where do we go from here?'

'Yes. Where to from here?' Julian looked at the tradies intently. 'Firstly, how come Trev was killed in front of everyone and yet no-one saw anything? Secondly, where did this bloke, … AC/DC man, come from and who are his connections, and thirdly, was Mark murdered?'

Seeing their engrossed expressions, he continued, 'Did you see someone not usually in the pub hanging around Trev? Or did someone disappear straight after Trev was attacked? And is there anyone you can think of who wanted him dead?'

'You sure you're not a copper?' Steve asked with a sly grin. 'You fuckin' sound like one.'

'Watched too many episodes of *The Bill*.' Julian's reply caused another laugh. 'You've got your homework,' he said with a smile.

'I really appreciate your help and I know the family who had Mark to stay will as well.'

'Yes, sir, no, sir,' Paddy joked, saluting.

'Sorry to sound like a teacher, but we're dealing with organised crime so we have to be bloody careful.' Julian grabbed a few coasters off the nearby tables and wrote down his phone number. 'Please ring me if you find out anything if I'm not in the pub. And if you've had a few too many bevvies, keep your mouths shut.'

CHAPTER FORTY-NINE

Thrilled by the reaction of the two Scousers and the Scotsman, Julian couldn't wait to tell Jim his news. Surely he'd be pleased by the help they could give the investigation. They knew virtually everyone in the pub so they should be able to find out more information than he could. The other backpackers would trust Steve and the other two far more than him. That bloody divide in England.

The bell rang for recess and Julian was about to head to Jim's office when he stalled. Should he tell Jim? He knew that Jim was already worried about him and now there were three more guys who could be in danger. Maybe better if he kept their involvement to himself. See if they come up with the goods, and then tell Jim and Alan Stone.

'Shite,' Julian swore. Had he done the right thing? This whole situation had become so engrossing. Should he just pack his bags and head back to London? … No. He had to admit the investigation was exciting and as he'd said before, gave him purpose. Being involved helped keep his homesickness at bay. Before he came to Australia, he'd thought that as many here were of English origin he'd feel more at home, but since he'd been in Sydney, there was little affinity between him and Aussies. They seemed to dislike people from the UK especially England.

Walking swiftly away from Jim's office, Julian entered the staffroom and made himself a coffee. As he drank the school's Nescafe Instant, he wondered if he'd been too trusting of Siobhan. Had she played him, knowing he fancied her? Was this the Profumo affair all over again? A pretty girl and a weak man falling for her charms.

Don't be daft, he warned himself. His negative thoughts were interrupted by the sudden presence of Daphne. 'Hello,' he greeted. 'How are you?'

Daphne didn't reply.

'You alright?'

She hesitated. 'Can I ask you something?'

Julian's stomach swirled. Siobhan came instantly to mind. 'Of course.'

Daphne checked no-one was in earshot. 'You know that Irish girl … Is something going on between her and Ray?'

This is exactly what he'd dreaded. 'Siobhan?' he asked, playing for time.

'Yes. Her.'

Not enough time. 'What do you mean?'

'What I said. Are they having an affair?'

'Oh my God, Daphne. I don't think so. What on earth makes you think that?'

He could see she was struggling not to cry. Julian reached out, putting his hand on her arm.

Ignoring his reaction, she stated, 'I get the feeling you know something. Weren't you interested in her as well?'

Julian thought quickly, removing his hand. 'I was, but we're not the same type.'

'So? Men don't always like the same class of women. From what I gather, she's a stripper. Must be very sexy.'

Julian decided to change tack. Discussing Siobhan's sexual appeal would not help Daphne's mood. 'I only wanted to meet her so I could find out about Mark. I knew they'd been friends. I was doing what I could to help Jim.'

Daphne seemed doubtful. 'Ever since Ray met her at Jim's he's been offhand and I know he met her at a pub near the hotel Stone organised for her.'

Julian looked into her eyes. 'I think you're imagining things. It's part of his job. Odd hours. Meeting all sorts of people.'

'You're being kind. I'm sure you've noticed I'm older than him and if he wants a younger woman I understand, but I just want to know so I can get on with *my* life.' She stared at Julian. 'My ego doesn't need it.'

343

'No-one needs it,' Julian responded softly, surprised by Daphne's honesty.

'I know I shouldn't put pressure on you, but please tell me if there *is* anything going on.'

Julian's heart sank. 'I will, but I'm sure there's nothing.'

'I'm sorry if I'm putting you in a spot, but I have no desire to be taken for a fool.' Daphne gave Julian a weak smile before leaving the staffroom.

Meanwhile, Stone decided it was time to have yet another catch up. There were so many people involved in the two cases including the Bondi Police, Jim, Anh, Julian, the new bloke Terry, Siobhan, and of course, Ray. Rather than being drip fed information he wanted to hear from all of them at the same time. See what matched, what didn't, and anything new. But, perhaps he should talk to the Bondi police separately as they may find it odd for so many civilians to be included in the investigation.

He flipped through his filo-fax to find Bondi Police then dialled. Detective Miller answered the call and agreed to organise a meeting with his colleagues. Stone, about to hang up, changed his mind and asked if Miller could join the group meeting instead. He could. That done, Stone then rang St Cuthbert's to speak to Daphne.

'Hi Daphne, Alan Stone here. How're you?' There was a slight pause. Surely, she knew who he was?

'Fine thanks, Alan. How can I help you?' Daphne finally responded.

'Sorry to bother you but I'm hoping you can pass on another message to Jim, Julian and Ray.' He waited for her to speak but as she didn't he continued. 'We need a meeting to keep everyone up to date. Better than phone calls. Whether we meet at a pub or at Jim's again, I want as many to attend, including Siobhan, so we can share our knowledge. And of course, you are more than welcome to join us.'

'Siobhan?' Daphne asked abruptly. 'Hasn't she talked to Ray already?'

Stone flinched at her tone. 'You okay?'

'Yes. Fine. So, you want me to tell the three of them to contact you and you will tell them when and where to meet?'

'Got it in one. If it's too much trouble I can ring them. Just thought as you see them ...'

'It's no problem, Alan. I'll get onto it today. Lunch time soon so I can speak to Jim and Julian and will tell Ray this evening. If I see him.'

'Thank you, Daphne. I really appreciate it and as I said, you are more than welcome to join us. Be lovely to see you.'

345

The lunch bell rang and a few minutes later Daphne made her way to the staffroom. Jim and Julian were already there deep in conversation.

'Sorry to interrupt,' Daphne began, 'but I just had a call from Alan and he wants to have a meeting with you two, Ray … and the others involved in … well you know who.'

'Did he say why?' Jim asked.

'He wants to get everyone together to share their information, rather than his hearing about it bit by bit.'

'Fair enough,' Jim replied. 'My place again?'

'Yes, I got the impression he was hoping it could be at your place.'

Jim peered around at the teachers in the staffroom. There was animated chatter amongst the different groups 'Oh well, be better than in a pub. Too noisy. I'm sure Anh will be okay.'

'Did he mention Siobhan?' Julian asked Daphne carefully.

'Yes. Everyone who's involved.'

'I'll contact her,' he said. 'So Jim, if it is at your place, we'll need to meet early again so she can get to work on time.'

'Yes, and what about that bloke, Terry? The one in the pub. Wonder if Stone has heard anything from him?'

'No idea. Anyone else?' Julian asked.

'Obviously Ray, but you'll be keeping him in the loop,' Jim assumed, glancing at Daphne.

'When I see him, I'll tell him.'

Daphne was about to go when Jim remembered her house guest. 'Do you still have your backpacker? Forgotten his name.'

'Sean. No. Bit too dull at our place so he's gone to a hostel. Wants to party and meet other people of a similar age.'

'That's a shame. It sounded like you enjoyed his company.'

'I did.'

Once she'd gone, Jim, with furrowed brow, stared at Julian. 'Is it me, or is Daphne not herself?'

Julian could only shrug.

CHAPTER FIFTY

Once home from work, Jim began to explain to Anh how Alan wanted another catch up with all involved when she interrupted saying she was happy to host and tomorrow night was suitable. Better sooner than later. Hugging his wife, Jim kissed her with gratitude.

Ending the call to Alan to inform him of the arrangement, Jim then rang Daphne and once the brief conversation was over, he thoughtfully replaced the receiver, saying to Anh, 'Something's up. She's not herself. *And*, she's coming tomorrow night.' Jim looked quizzically at his wife whose brow was wrinkled in thought. 'Maybe she's picked up Ray's interest in Siobhan?' Anh wondered. 'He seemed very taken with her when they were here last time.'

'I noticed that, but I just thought he was playing silly buggers. Do you think that's why Daphne's coming? Keeping an eye on him? Bloody hell, we're dealing with Mark's death and Pearce's and now Ray is behaving badly. Can it get any worse?'

'As long as *you* are not interested in Shiv …Siobhan,' Anh warned, putting her arms around him.

'No chance,' Jim reassured, kissing her lips.

The bus took Julian to Bondi Junction and dropped him close to the Viceroy. After Jim's call he decided to go to the pub in person and see if he could track down Terry. As he walked into the pub, its punkah moving back and forth above the bar reminded him again of India and its colonial past. It was surprising how something so Asian could be in Bondi Junction. The public bar was already busy and it occurred to Julian that he had no idea what Terry looked like. He ordered a beer and looked around. There were tables of tradies towards the back of the bar while older regulars sat at tables by the windows which overlooked one of the main shopping streets in the Junction.

Julian decided to stand near the entrance to the hotel so he could see the punters entering as well as those seated at the tables. He needed a believable excuse if he asked anyone if they'd seen Terry. It was obvious he wasn't a tradie so what else could he be? A teacher? A relative out from England?

'Looking for Terry,' he said to the nearest table.

The silent frowns told him to move on.

Better to go to a different part of the pub, he decided and wandered over to the section where numerous screens were showing sport and horse racing. 'Seen Terry?' he asked those seated staring at the screens.

'Bristol Tezza?' one answered, not taking his eyes off the current race. 'Over there by the T.A.B.'

Turning, Julian saw there was a small section of the bar where customers were lined up, holding betting slips. Thanking the man, he made his way over to the queue.

Julian decided to be direct. 'Looking for Terry. From Bristol,' he said to the line. Most were intent on their next bet and paid no attention, but one man with a beard glanced at him. 'Who's asking?'

'I'm a mate of Jim and Alan's and would like to have a quick word with him.'

'And you are?' the man asked, squinting at Julian.

'Julian Butterworth. I work with Jim and he's a mate of Alan Stone's,' Julian repeated quietly.

Terry slid out of his place in the queue and stood next to Julian. 'What's the Bobby Moore?'

'Are you the bloke they spoke to in here the other night? If so, Alan Stone …' Julian paused to see if Terry had registered the name and satisfied with Terry's reaction, he continued. 'Alan Stone wants to have a catch up with you and some others tomorrow night.'

'How do I know you're who you say you are?'

'You don't, but if you ring St Cuthbert's School and ask for me and Jim Cameron, they'll tell you.' Sensing Terry was becoming convinced, Julian offered to buy him a drink. To his relief, Terry said cheers and Julian was soon back with two schooners. 'Look, I won't keep you but I wanted to let you know that there's a few of us who're helping with the investigation. We're meeting at Jim's place tomorrow night to pass on any relevant information to Detective Stone. That's why I've come to the pub to see if you want to join us. I can give you the address. Starting early. Around six o'clock.'

Terry stared into his drink then at Julian. 'What am I meant to be *investigating*?'

'Anything to do with Mark Dunlop's or Trevor Pearce's deaths.'

Terry scratched his beard. 'Think you've passed the test. Where's the meeting?'

Julian gave him the details. 'You sure you'll remember?'

'Memory like a sieve. No. I'll remember. See you tomorrow.'

'Cheers,' Julian farewelled, as Terry hurried off to place a bet.

CHAPTER FIFTY-ONE

Anh and Jim, and Julian who'd cadged a lift with Jim, were nervously waiting for the rest of the group to arrive. Each of them had their own concerns and the common denominator was the Irish girl. The situation now seemed more serious than ever. Drinks and nibbles had been bought as if for a party, but there was no party atmosphere.

Stone and Detective Miller soon arrived, followed by Ray and Daphne, and not long after, Siobhan. Julian had told Jim that Terry may come so when a knock indicated another visitor, he rushed to the front door.

'Terry! Thanks for coming,' Julian greeted. Holding a slab of beer, Terry followed Julian into the lounge. Jim hid his surprise at seeing Terry and thanked him for bringing the beer while Anh, sensing the situation was awkward, held out her arms to take it. 'That's very kind. Can I put it in the fridge?'

The men stepped forward to prevent Anh from carrying the heavy slab, but Terry held the Reschs protectively. 'Let me. Kitchen through here?' he asked. Anh led him into the kitchen while the others raised their eyes at each other inferring that Terry seemed a decent bloke.

Stone waited till everyone had a drink and were settled before making introductions. 'Detective Miller is a member of the Bondi Police. Dave and his colleagues are part of the investigation into Pearce and Dunlop's deaths. The Bondi Police received the phone call from the English bloke telling them about Mark Dunlop's body at the beach.' Next, Stone indicated Ray. 'Ray O'Shea is a detective working in Kings Cross and beside him is his partner, Daphne who is a colleague of Jim and Julian's at St Cuthbert's.' He faced Daphne. 'You've assisted us before so it's wonderful you're here.' Daphne bowed her head. 'Don't think you've met Terry or Siobhan?'

'No, I haven't, although I've heard a lot about you, Siobhan. Do hope I'm saying your name correctly?' Daphne asked politely. Smiling, Siobhan assured her she was.

Stone couldn't put his finger on it but there seemed to be a shift in the atmosphere. Turning to Miller, Stone explained how Siobhan was linked to Dunlop and Pearce, how Terry was the ears in the Viceroy, and that Julian was a colleague of Jim and Daphne's and was also assisting in the investigation.

After hearing Stone's description of his role, Terry huffed through his beard stating, 'Only helping to catch the killers, not to

353

dob, as Aussies say, on me mates.' There were mumbles of understanding.

'Anyway, let's get down to business. If anyone has to leave soon, let's start with them.'

'Grand. That'll be me,' Siobhan replied, including everyone in her gaze.

'Okay,' agreed Stone, taking a notebook out of his jacket pocket. 'What do you have to report?'

All sat in silence waiting to hear her information. 'I'm staying in a hotel in the Cross because some man rang me.' Siobhan glanced at Ray and Alan. 'We don't know how he knew my name or my number. It was someone with an Asian accent and it sounded like he wanted me to work for him as I knew Trevor. Very threatening. Alan ... Detective Stone, can tell you more about it.' She paused. 'I've tried to have conversations with my boss, Jason Zervos, about Mark's death but he wasn't willing to share. He owns the clubs where I dance and from what I've heard from my fellow strippers,' she stared at Daphne as if challenging her, 'he has his fingers in the drug business although he says he hates drugs. Trevor gave me the impression Mr Zervos was his boss, but now I don't think it's true.' Siobhan stopped.

'Why not?' asked Stone.

She thought about the question. 'Zervos seemed to know who he was but said he was small fry, of no account and I believed

354

him.' Facing Ray, she said, 'You and Alan have listened to the tape so you can fill everyone in on the craic.'

It was obvious to Stone that Jim and Julian were watching Daphne watch Siobhan as she spoke, especially when she turned her attention to Ray. The expression on Daphne's face was disturbing.

Ray explained how Siobhan had given him the tape the night before and he'd listened to it, then given it to Alan who'd passed it over to someone who was a whizz with technology. He gestured for Alan to take over. 'There's not much more to add but I felt that Siobhan could be in danger so she's now staying in a hotel in case whoever sent the message knows where she lives and decides to pay a visit. We're still not sure who it was but it could be a Vietnamese gang who's trying to muscle in on the drug scene in the Cross and Bondi ... The accent of the voice on the tape definitely sounded Vietnamese,' he added.

'What about the guy who was selling drugs in the pub the other night?' Julian butted in. 'He wasn't Asian, and the big bloke with him vetting who could go into the toilets where the deals were happening, definitely wasn't Asian.' Julian peered around at everyone.

'Can you describe this man and his minder in case anyone else has seen him?' Stone directed.

'The main thing about him was he wore an AC/DC T-shirt. Possibly of Mediterranean background. He appeared to know the regulars and his minder was a really big chap with huge hands.' The titters from the others at the description made him pause. 'He wouldn't let me into the gents to make a purchase because he didn't recognise me.'

'But the minder recognised other people?' Stone asked, but before Julian had time to answer, Siobhan raised her hand stating that she'd seen both men in the Regent on previous occasions and lots of the regulars knew there was dealing going on.

Stone acknowledged her information before returning his attention to Julian who said, 'The heavy looked Aussie, but as I've said the dealer looked of Mediterranean background, Greek, Italian. Definitely not Asian.'

'Thanks Julian. Who's next?'

'Can I continue for a minute?' Julian asked rhetorically. 'You may know Jim and I went to the Albury the other night and got chatting to a South American, Diego.' He looked at Jim for confirmation and receiving a frown, said with a cheeky smile, 'Jim was a lovely partner, most convincing, and our Diego told us how he'd met Mark and his boyfriend, Darcy.'

'And?' Stone asked, while the group glanced at each other, grinning at the thought of Jim in a gay bar.

'Unfortunately, Darcy wasn't there, so perhaps we should go again?'

'Maybe,' Jim doubted. 'Anh, no need to worry. I'm a very straight man but I had to put on an act so we could convince the crowd to accept us.'

Anh giggled. 'Wish I'd been there.' All, including Daphne, grinned.

'And,' Julian interrupted emphatically. 'Diego told us there was an English bloke who hung around Mark. He didn't know who this bloke was but he was aware of how much interest he'd showed in Mark.'

Seeing Stone make a note, Jim suggested, 'It could have been the man who rang the police the night Mark died?'

Agreeing, Stone instructed, 'You should definitely go back to the Albury and with luck that bloke will be there and if the chap … Diego is there, he can point him out.'

Jim, clearly eager to change the subject from the Albury, asked, 'Alan, is there any news of what was on Mark's mobile phone?'

'Ah. Yes. I've got Sergeant Harris on to it. He's contacted Telstra as they are the main, what's the word? … Provider. And he's waiting for them to fax through a copy of Mark's calls. Apparently, all calls made and received are recorded so once we get the fax we can check who he spoke to. With luck it shouldn't take too long.'

357

Stone swivelled towards Terry. 'This might be the time to bring in Terry. Jim and I approached him in the Viceroy in Bondi Junction, and he kindly agreed to pass on any information which may lead to the apprehension of Mark's killer.' He gazed at the group sadly. 'Apparently, Mark died from a large dose of amphetamines and combined with alcohol would have helped him drown, but it's becoming more doubtful that he took them by himself. According to Darcy, and from what you've said, Siobhan, Mark wasn't into heavy drugs … Terry, any luck overhearing anything? Oh, and thanks for bringing the beer.'

Terry brushed off the thanks. 'My local boozer tends to be the Viceroy as it's nearer my gaff but go to the Regent occasionally. I want to make it clear I'm not going to name names. However, as one of my compatriots was done in, maybe for being gay, then I'll pass on any info I can.' There were nods of approval. 'From what I've heard via the grapevine, Trevor Pearce was known as the dealer down at Bondi.'

'We know that,' Julian dismissed.

'Yeah, but as Siobhan said, his supplier wasn't Zervos.' Staring at Stone, Terry confirmed, 'You're right. It seems a Vietnamese gang wants to take over Bondi and possibly the Cross.'

'But what about Mark?' Jim asked impatiently.

'Jiiiiim,' Anh warned.

'Sorry, mate. Nothing to report regarding Mark,' Terry answered.

'How do you know they're Vietnamese?' Stone pressed.

'Only going by what I heard. Word has it this gang is on the move. They can get cocaine, heroin, amphetamines into the country bloody easily.'

'Jesus,' Stone exclaimed and staring at Miller said. 'We need to get onto Customs. Check the noodles coming in.' No-one laughed.

There was silence till Stone spoke again. 'The other big question is, how come *nobody* saw Pearce being attacked? We keep thinking it's because the regulars don't want to admit seeing anything as they may have bought drugs off him, but was it someone who works for the Vietnamese gang? The AC/DC man? Or someone who works at the Regent? Someone no-one would have noticed?' The collective muttering reflected Stone's frustration. Miller lit a cigarette and sucked deeply before suggesting another visit to the pub.

'We've already talked to the manager and a barmaid, and the bouncers have been interviewed, but no-one knows anything. As if …' Stone huffed.

'Worth another try,' Miller persisted.

Stone shrugged. 'Anybody got anything else to add?'

'What about the AC/DC bloke?' Julian asked.

'We'll talk to the staff at the Regent again and they may tell us who he is.' Stone rolled his eyes. 'It's bloody coincidental he was there the night Pearce was killed, and from what's been said, he's been dealing there for a while.' There were nods of agreement.

Turning to Siobhan, Julian asked if she'd ever heard Trevor mention this man.

'Not at all. Himself made out he was the only one working at the Regent, but the gobshite was full of bullshit. Constantly big-noting.'

Stone was about to call it a night when it occurred to him that Siobhan had been a regular at the Regent long before Julian arrived and why was she always with Trevor Pearce? How could he ask her about him without putting her offside again? 'Siobhan, don't take this the wrong way, but can I ask why you were friends with Pearce when you obviously didn't like him? It seems odd, if you don't mind my saying.'

The group sat nervously waiting for her to answer. She appeared absorbed by a painting on the wall above the television set. Finally, she spoke, 'Trev was a possessive hoor so most of the time when we were in the pub, we went outside. He hated me talking to any of the other fellas.'

The frown on Stone's face showed his disbelief at her explanation. 'But you seem a pretty strong woman, how come you let him control you like that?'

All watched her, holding their breath. Siobhan picked up her drink then put it down. 'He knew something so I had to ...'

'What?' Stone asked quickly.

'He knew my visa had run out and he threatened to tell immigration if I didn't do what he wanted.' She blinked at the group with reddened eyes. 'I don't want to go home. I want to stay here. The last time I saw him I told him I'd tell the police about his drug dealing even if he did *dob* me into immigration. I'd had enough of his control.'

There were noises of understanding and the shaking of heads. Ray leant towards her, placing his hand on her arm. Siobhan tightened her lips and picked up her drink.

Stone breathed out. 'Siobhan, you have to get to work, and I'm sorry about what Pearce put you through. Thanks so much for coming. Don't forget to ring me or Detective Miller if you have any news.' She picked up her bag and made a quick goodbye. The others followed suit not long after.

The atmosphere in the car was frosty as Daphne drove home, the silence finally broken when she asked Ray. 'Is something going on between you and Siobhan?'

'Pardon?'

'You know what I mean. You can't seem to take your eyes off her. Touching her on the arm.'

361

'Daphne, that's bullshit. I only have eyes for you.' Ray attempted a laugh.

'Very funny. Is there?'

'Of course not. It's part of the job to watch people closely. See if they give anything away. Their body language, contradictions in their stories. She works for Zervos so I'm a bit suspicious of her motives.' Ray was about to pat Daphne's leg but quickly retracted his hand.

'Why are you suspicious of her?' Daphne asked, ignoring his hand movement. 'She told us why she let the Pearce chap control her, and isn't she just helping to find out more about Mark?'

'Yes, but because of the visa issue, she had a reason to get rid of Trev That's the point,' he paused, 'I know that she and Mark were supposedly good friends, but her connection with Zervos and Pearce makes me wonder if she's a plant. She can report back to Zervos what the police know and what we're doing.'

'Really? Would she risk her life, and the visa for her boss?'

Ray didn't reply. Daphne sensed he was thinking about what to say next.

'You know what,' he said at last. 'She might be willing to do anything so she can stay in the country. She knows overstayers end up in Villawood and then get sent home.'

This made sense to Daphne. 'Where in Ireland is she from?'

'Belfast. Northern Ireland. Obviously not busting to go back.'

362

'No … Although isn't it better, more peaceful than it was?'

'Maybe, but to be forced to go home …' Ray rubbed her leg. 'Believe me. I love you. I don't want to be with Siobhan or anyone else.'

'You sure?'

'Absolutely. Why are you so insecure?'

Daphne was about to argue that she wasn't insecure then stopped herself. 'It's hard when you're an older woman, especially when there are pretty strippers around. I hope you still find me attractive?'

Ray groaned. 'You know I do. You're gorgeous. I'm amazed you've stuck with me. My long hours, the stress. I wouldn't blame you if you found someone else. Happens all the time in the force.'

Daphne took one hand off the steering wheel and placed it on Ray's leg. 'I love you, despite your grumpy moods and never being home.'

'Thank God for that,' Ray murmured, placing his hand over hers.

CHAPTER FIFTY-TWO

Detective Miller was having a quick ciggie outside the Regent while waiting for Detective Stone. It was a replay of their previous visit and finally someone opened the door. This time Stone had decided on a heavier approach. The pub must have known about the drug dealing and if they didn't want to lose their licence, they'd better come up with some decent answers.

'Mr Carter,' Stone greeted firmly when the manager finally met them. 'A few more questions if you don't mind.'

Carter, unable to hide his anxiety, immediately invited the detectives into his office away from the prying eyes of the bar staff. 'How can I help you?' he asked as he indicated for them to take a seat.

'We're enquiring about a certain man wearing an AC/DC T-shirt, and his 'minder' who was controlling those who could enter the toilets. Were you aware of the drug dealing that went on in the gentleman's toilets a few nights ago?'

Carter shook his head vigorously. 'No. Not at all.'

Stone frowned in disbelief. 'Come on, mate. Everyone knows this pub is a source of supply. You *must* have known.'

The manager gulped quietly and shook his head. 'Honestly, I had no idea. I'm a busy man. I have to look after the front of house, the cellars, admin, the staff and all their issues …'

'Mr Carter, I don't believe a word of it. There was a bloke on the door to the gents' toilets to keep people out. If you want to help yourself, I'd like you to tell us who the dealer was, and I'm not talking about Trevor Pearce. We already know he was a regular supplier but this other bloke … Who was he and who did he work for?' Stone stared intently at the young manager. 'Don't give us any bullshit.' Carter remained silent, his forehead now covered in a sheen of sweat. Stone continued, 'Who owns this pub?'

'A guy in the Cross. If I tell you anything, he'll kill me.'

'Don't worry, you'll get protection. Who?'

'Oh fuck. I can't. I don't want to …'

'Do you want to go to prison for withholding vital information?' Stone threatened.

'Nooo. He's a scary man,' Carter wailed.

'And so am I.' Stone warned before changing to nice cop. 'Jeff, if you work with us we'll look after you.'

'That's what he said.'

'Just tell us who he is. As I said, the police will protect you.'

'Yeah, right. How? He has the police in his pocket.'

Stone turned to Miller. 'Have you heard about this?'

Miller shook his head. 'Probably saying that to get everybody to do what he wants.'

'Everyone knows the police are paid off by the drug lords in the Cross,' Carter despaired.

'Okay, putting your theory aside, you need to tell us what you know. If you don't, then …'

The young man's face had gone blotchy, and tears were brewing. 'It's Jason Zervos. Please don't tell him I told you. He'll kill me.'

'Zervos owns the Regent? You sure? I've heard he doesn't deal in drugs. Prostitution, strip clubs, protection rackets but not drugs. Who's the licensee? You're the manager so you must know,' Stone persisted.

'Yes, but I've only dealt with the company who has the licence, not Mr Zervos. Trev told us that if we didn't do as he said, Zervos would have us bumped off.'

'So you're saying that Trevor Pearce told you that if you didn't do what *he* wanted, he'd inform Zervos who would then have you killed?'

'Yes.' Carter clasped his hands together, the tightness turning his knuckles white.

Stone spoke grimly. 'Let me get this straight. Did Pearce know the other supplier who was in the pub the night he was killed?'

Carter nodded vigorously, a beaten look on his face.

Grimacing, Stone suggested, 'Or did you just assume Pearce knew about the other guy and thought he must work for Zervos as well? Did you ever wonder if *Trev* was power-hungry and needed to control you and the pub?'

'We thought he was one of Zervos's men, because of what he said,' Carter answered, rubbing his eyes.

'Mmmm,' Stone doubted, leaning over and patting Carter on the shoulder. 'Well done. Don't worry, we'll take care of you. But don't go anywhere.'

The manager, looking slightly relieved, thought for a moment. 'It was Alex Stavros who was selling the drugs that night, but I don't know the name of his … whatever you call those blokes.'

'Bouncer, heavy, muscle, minder,' Stone listed while jotting down the dealer's name.

Carter shrugged despondently.

'Any idea who did supply Pearce if it wasn't Zervos? Was it Stavros?' Miller asked.

'I don't really know, but you hear things. There were rumours Trev was trying to set up his own business or join another supplier.' Carter blinked nervously at Miller. 'You sure I'll be okay? From what I've heard, Zervos is a mean bastard.'

Miller reassured Carter that he would be okay. 'As the manager, have you heard any rumours regarding who killed Pearce? Do you think Zervos was behind it?'

'I don't know. It's possible.'

'Was there anyone here that night who you'd never seen before?' Stone asked.

Scratching his head, Carter said, 'Obviously there were the regulars and some customers we see every now and then, and of course the tourists, but no-one stands out.'

'Is there a regular who hated Pearce?'

'No idea. The only person I can think of who didn't like Trev was Siobhan. But she can't have done it.'

'Why not?'

'She's a girl.'

'Oh? So you don't think women can kill?'

Carter's expression showed he realised how his assumption was naive, then he shook his head. 'I'll ask the staff again if they saw anyone who stood out.'

'Only one more question,' Stone said, as if to relieve the manager of his discomfort. 'I've already asked you, but did you see Mark Dunlop in the pub on the night he died?'

Carter admitted that he had seen Mark and was with Siobhan.

'Apart from Siobhan, did he talk to anyone else?'

'I was too busy to take much notice. He was there one minute and gone the next.'

Stone fumbled in his jacket pocket and pulled out a business card. 'Ring me if you remember or hear anything. Your assistance is greatly appreciated,' Stone's tone had an underlying threat which Carter didn't miss.

'I will but I don't want to lose my job.'

'We'll keep that in mind,' Stone answered.

He and Miller left the pub.

CHAPTER FIFTY-THREE

Alan Stone was making a cup of coffee in the station kitchen while mulling over the information he and Miller had received from Carter. The feeling of getting nowhere with either death left him wondering what the hell he was doing with his life. Why was he so concerned about other people's misery? Jim had Anh and two sons while Ray had Daphne and although her children weren't his, he was part of a family. Work seemed to have ruined his own chances of happiness. Ngaire and Tammy, his last two loves were well and truly gone, no doubt married to some other jokers. And it didn't help when Anh and Daphne questioned him about his private life.

As he drank his coffee, Alan's mind returned to the conversations of the previous night at Jim's. All roads seemed to lead to Zervos yet it was proving to be a cul de sac. Pearce may or may not have been working with this new Vietnamese gang while pretending to work for Zervos, and now according to Ray, Zervos had mentioned bikies, possibly linked to the Vietnamese, as Pearce's suppliers. He needed to confirm whether Zervos owned the Regent or if it was owned by a company as Carter had said.

It was time for him to talk to Zervos. Although Ray had already done so, he wanted to hear the information from the horse's mouth. He rang Siobhan, hoping he wasn't going to wake her and was thankful when she answered.

'Glad I didn't wake you. Do you know where Zervos might be tonight? I think we need to have a chat and it's probably better in an informal environment.'

Siobhan took her time before replying. 'Not sure. He has so many venues. I'm at three of his clubs tonight but it doesn't mean he'll be there. Can I ring you from work?'

'No point. Won't be contactable.' Stone thought for a second. 'Don't worry, I'll just visit his various venues and hope I find him.' He wondered why Zervos had never visited the Regent if he did actually own it.

Knowing he had time to kill before going to the Cross, Stone caught up on paperwork and worked out his plan of action regarding Zervos. From what Ray had said, Zervos was a bullshit artist which wasn't surprising. He was playing a game with them. On the other hand, it was vital to confirm if there *was* a Vietnamese gang.

Stone considered which of the Western suburbs police stations he should ring to ask if they had any information about such a gang. Parramatta might be the go.

After identifying himself and explaining what he wanted to find out, the desk sergeant put him through to Detective John Lanceley.

Lanceley ummed and aahed after hearing the reason for Stone's call. 'Not sure if I can help you. You're probably better calling Cabramatta. That's where the majority of Vietnamese live. I'll ask around and if I find out anything I'll get back to you.'

Stone hung up. That was a waste of time. He'd try Cabramatta. Repeating his request, he was put through to Detective Tam Nguyen.

The detective listened silently while Stone explained the reason for his call and was about to ask if Nguyen was still there when the man finally spoke, 'A Vietnamese gang trying to get into the Cross? They'd be bloody obvious.'

'Maybe, but not if they supply the drugs and have a nondescript person on the ground to do the dealing.'

Another drawn-out silence. Nguyen's lack of response was starting to get on Stone's nerves. 'Look mate, if you can't help me, just say.'

'Hang on. I'm thinking. There are gangs 'round here but haven't heard if they're trying to invade any new territory. The Western suburbs is a huge area to supply so I can't see why they'd want to move into the Cross or Bondi.' He paused. 'Let me ask around and I'll get back to you.'

Stone thanked him and ended the call. Another bloody waste of time. Was Nguyen protecting his own? Stone asked himself, frustrated by the detective's seeming unwillingness to assist.

The afternoon wore on. Stone was about to leave his office and head to the Cross when the phone rang. 'It's Tam Nguyen here.'

Stone couldn't hide his surprise. 'Tam, didn't expect to hear from you so soon.'

'Said I'd get back to you.'

'You did. Thanks. Any news?'

'Yes. Rang around and found out there's a local gang who has connections to a bloke who works around your area. Apparently, he's already dealing in Bondi, but as it's controlled by some big shot, he has to pick his moments.'

'Not sure what you mean?'

Nguyen sniffed. 'There's a dealer who regularly trades at a pub in Bondi, but this other bloke goes to the same pub to build up custom and wants to take over.'

'Ah. You don't happen to know who he is?'

'Alex Stavros is the name I was given. Apparently, he gets his supplies from here. Cabramatta.'

Stone was shocked. If Zervos owned the pub why would he allow Stavros to do his trade there? And, if Stavros was AC/DC man then why wasn't he always in the Regent? Yet from what he'd gathered the locals knew who he was. 'Do you know who the suppliers are?' he asked.

'Shouldn't be too hard to find out if it's someone from around here,' Nguyen reassured.

'That'd be great. You've been a big help. Really appreciate it,' Stone gushed.

'No problem.'

Turning off the light in his office, Stone made his way out of the police station and headed to Bondi Junction to catch the train to Kings Cross.

It wasn't as late as Stone would have liked, but he couldn't hang around work any longer. He felt frustrated with the lack of progress regarding both deaths and despite Nguyen's information he couldn't see a connection between either one. One victim was gay and the other was a drug dealer. With luck, a chat with Jason Zervos might throw a bit of light on the connection, if there was one? Ray's meeting with him had produced a few items of interest but he wanted more. If Zervos didn't show up at the Love Hut then he'd have to go to the other venues which meant a bloody long night.

The bouncers on the door gave him a cursory look as he walked in, although the Islander doorman made him welcome. Stone made his way to the bar which had a clear view of the low stage. He bought an overpriced drink, took a seat at the bar and lit a cigarette. He hoped Siobhan wouldn't see him and come over to say hello. However, she was a worldly woman so he doubted she'd 'recognise' him.

His beer was nearly finished when a couple of burly men walked in and ordered drinks. Were they Zervos's minders? No. They wandered off to sit at a table nearer the stage. Another beer was ordered and as Stone paid and thanked the pretty barmaid who was wearing a very revealing top, three more men arrived. One sat down while the other two stood protectively next to him. This had to be Zervos. The expensive suit, flashy gold watch and chain reeked of money but no class.

Stone wasn't going to introduce himself immediately and was willing to wait for an appropriate moment. The three ordered their drinks and seeing the barmaid didn't charge them, he felt certain as to who they were.

Suddenly, the man who was seated, leaned towards him asking loudly, 'Here to enjoy the show?' Stone said he was. 'The girls put on a great performance,' the man praised, running a hand through his dark gelled hair. Stone nodded obligingly.

'You don't look like the normal punter,' the man continued. 'I'd say you're the police, but not from around here.'

'Got it in one,' Stone said, leaning over to shake hands. 'Alan Stone, Waverley police.' His hand was taken and given a weak shake. 'Jason Zervos. How can I help you? I assume you're not here to watch the girls do their stuff?'

'It wouldn't go astray.' Stone raised his eyebrows, relieved to see Zervos twist his lips into a slight smirk. 'I'm hoping you can help me.'

'Don't you blokes have a home to go to? Another one of your lot was in here the other night,' Zervos complained, looking at his colleagues who grinned on cue. 'I'll help you if I can, although I might want something in return. No such thing as a free lunch.'

Stone grinned. ''Course not.'

Zervos leaned back on his stool. 'Let me guess. It's to do with the guy getting bumped off down at the Regent and do I know who did it?'

'You're a mind reader. That was my first question and my second is what do you know about a Vietnamese gang trying to muscle in on the drug trade in Bondi and possibly the Cross? Oh, and do you know a bloke who wears an AC/DC T-shirt as his business apparel?'

'Fuck me. You're not asking for much.'

Stone stared at Zervos. The two minders were looking concerned and one whispered into Zervos's ear. His words were brushed aside with a dismissive wave of a hand.

'As I told your mate, Pearce didn't work for me. He may have said he did, but he fucking didn't. Met him once and the guy was a wanker.'

'How come you met him?'

'Wanted to work for me but I don't sell drugs. Not my thing.'

Stone was about to question the validity of this statement but decided not to, instead asking, 'Do you know who supplied Pearce?'

'Mate, there are so many. The bikies maybe? Or the Lebs?'

'What about the Vietnamese?' Stone asked.

Zervos turned to his two heavies. 'Have you heard anything about the slopes dealing?'

One shrugged but the other who'd muttered something to Zervos said, 'Heard they're trying to take over the Cross. They don't come here, stick out like dogs' balls, but they've got workers to do the dirty work.'

Mentally making a note of the information, Stone then asked, 'So, in regards to Mr Pearce, do you think he could have been attacked by this gang as they want to take over Bondi as well?'

Zervos rolled his head from side to side. 'Maybe it was the man in the T-shirt. AC/DC you say? Not keen on his choice of music.' He laughed and the two minders joined in.

Stone, beginning to think he'd hit a brick wall, reached into his jacket pocket to extract a business card then remembered Mark.

'One more question and I'll leave you to enjoy the entertainment. Have you heard of a man, Mark Dunlop? He drowned down at Bondi under suspicious circumstances. He was a Pom and hadn't been here long but may have been involved in drug dealing.'

'Christ, mate, do you think I know every drug dealer in Sydney? I run night clubs. That's enough stress for me.'

Stone was about to mention the Regent but he didn't want to put Carter in a dangerous position by revealing he'd talked to him. Zervos was obviously used to getting his own way and was probably only willing to reveal information which would benefit him. Stone was sure that Zervos had a vindictive streak.

Despite thinking it futile, Stone handed his card to Zervos, gave the usual instructions, thanked him, said goodbye and left the building.

On returning home that evening, Stone couldn't resist ringing Ray. 'Hope I'm not ringing too late?' he asked when Ray answered the phone.

'All good. What's happening?'

'Just got back from meeting Jason Zervos. Wanted to compare notes. Do you believe a word he says?'

'Depends what he told you,' Ray responded with a laugh.

'He said he's not in the drug business. Yes? No?'

'God knows. Said the same to me. Seems anti-drugs although has no problem with prostitution and women taking their clothes off. Or charging like a wounded bull for drinks,' Ray sniggered.

Stone agreed then told Ray how one of Zervos's minders had said he was aware that the Vietnamese were trying to get a grip on the Eastern suburbs although the *slopes*, as Zervos called them, don't actually go to the Cross. Stone then quoted Detective Demetriou and one of Zervos's minders who'd both said they'd stick out like dog's balls.

Ray snorted in agreement.

'Zervos said he had no idea who killed Pearce. What did he tell you?' Stone asked.

'Much the same. I did wonder how much he'd had to drink when I spoke to him as he seemed quite willing to tell me stuff. About the bikies.'

'Do you feel he's playing games with us?' Stone asked.

'For sure. Bit of power goes a long way.'

'Absolutely. I spoke to Tam Nguyen in Cabramatta and he said Alex Stavros works for the Vietnamese. Think we need to find out more about the AC/DC man and see if he *is* Alex Stavros.'

'Have a quiz about musical tastes?' Ray suggested.

'Yeah, right. Anyway, better let you get to bed. Say hi to Daphne.'

'Will do.'

CHAPTER FIFTY-FOUR

Stone went to the station bright and early the following morning, keen to find out more about Alex Stavros. He gave instructions to one of the sergeants, instilling into him the importance of finding out any details about Stavros and to tell him immediately if he discovered anything. The sergeant sensing the urgency rushed back to his desk and began the search.

The next job was to ring the Bondi station and speak to Miller. 'Gidday, Dave. Alan Stone. Wondering if you've found out any more about who's selling amphetamines in your area?'

'Nah. I know who's selling a bit of weed, cocaine and other drugs but not amphetamines. Someone must know but it ain't us. Let me know if you manage to find out.' Miller gave a dry laugh.

They were about to end the conversation when Miller suddenly said, 'Shit, sorry. Nearly forgot to tell you. My head's up my arse. Had a bit of a biggie last night. The wife's birthday.' Stone mumbled his sympathy. 'Got the final report from forensics about Pearce. Interesting reading.'

'Ah, tell me more.'

'He was stabbed, but it's been confirmed that it wasn't with a knife but a work tool. A screwdriver. The wound is different to that of a knife. Whoever did it managed to hit a major artery and Pearce bled to death.'

This was not what Stone had expected. 'Who carries a screwdriver in order to attack someone, especially in a pub?' he asked. 'Makes me wonder if whoever stabbed Pearce did it on the spur of the moment. Used whatever weapon was handy.'

'Yeah. Lots of tradies in the pub so any one of them could have had a screwdriver on them,' Miller confirmed with excitement in his voice. 'Although I'd have thought they'd leave their tool bag at work.'

'True, but it looks like we need to change our focus. Maybe Pearce's death had nothing to do with drugs?' Stone hesitated. 'Or … was one of the tradies sold a dud deal?'

'Jesus. Nothing is simple. We'll have to re-interview everyone. This puts a different slant on our questioning.'

'It certainly does.'

After checking if the sergeant had made any progress regarding Stavros, which he hadn't, Stone returned to his office. The frustration was unbearable. He understood why Jim couldn't sit by and do nothing. At least there was a lead regarding Pearce. The phone rang, jerking him out of his gloomy thoughts.

'Detective Stone,' he answered glumly.

'Cheer up, mate. Got some news for ya.'

It was an English accent which sounded vaguely familiar. 'Who's speaking?' Stone asked.

'Vice Squad Terry.'

'What?'

'Terry from the Viceroy,' Terry translated, with an exaggerated sigh.

'Ah, right. Thought I recognised the voice. I'm all ears.'

'Well, I kept *my* ear to the ground and heard the amphetamine dealer is a bloke called Stavros. He's not from 'round here but comes into the East occasionally and sells all sorts – not the sweets.' Terry coughed theatrically. 'My sources tell me he's due to visit the Regent again in the next day or two.'

'Jesus. That *is* good news. Well, you know what I mean.'

Terry laughed. 'Yeah. Know what ya mean. He's from somewhere out west and wants to enlarge his territory, especially after poor old Trev's demise.'

'You don't happen to know if he's connected to a Vietnamese gang?' Stone asked hopefully.

'Sorry, my sources,' Terry coughed twice, 'didn't go that far. But do with my information what you will.'

'I definitely will.' They both chuckled.

'With luck you'll catch the bastard who done Mark in.'

382

'Hope so. Thanks, mate. Really appreciate your assistance. Anything else, … well, you know the story.'

'Cheers.'

Stone's mood improved instantly. A direct reference to Stavros. He finally felt like they were making progress. He'd have to organise undercover cops to go to the Regent. Maybe Julian as well. With fingers crossed in the hope that Jim would answer, Stone immediately rang his office. 'It's Alan. Just had a call from Terry, from the Viceroy, or the Vice Squad if you're a Pom, and he told me that Stavros is apparently going to the Regent to do some dealing in the next night or two. Apparently, he sells amphetamines.' He could hear Jim swallow. 'Terry's definitely done his homework. Funny bloke in a good way and obviously keen to find out who killed Mark.'

'What do you want me to do?' Jim asked eagerly.

'Have a word with Julian and see if he's willing to go to the pub tonight and the following ones until this Stavros bloke turns up. We need to know if Stavros and AC/DC man are the same person. Julian's had a good look at AC/DC man, but he won't be alone. I'll send some young sergeants to keep an eye on him. Not in uniform, of course.'

'Won't it be obvious if a group of strangers turn up?' Jim asked.

'It *is* a pub, and we'll work out their story if anyone asks. Up from Melbourne for a work do et cetera.'

'Okay. I'll talk to Julian at morning break.'

'Good oh. Tell him to keep his eyes peeled for Stavros and to let our blokes in situ know if he sees him.'

'Before you go, any other news?' Jim asked.

'Ah yes! Miller down at Bondi got the report from forensics and it looks like Pearce was killed by a screwdriver, *not* a knife. That changes our focus as tradies carry screwdrivers so there's a chance it was one of them. Any of them could have a screwdriver in their work clothes.'

'Good grief. That puts a different slant on things.'

'Totally.'

Julian, after receiving the news from Jim, was weighing up whether to inform Stone that he'd got the support of Steve, Jimmy and Paddy. He'd found the detective a little intimidating, no doubt due to the position he held and like a schoolboy, Julian didn't want to get into trouble for taking things into his own hands. Girding his loins, he decided to ring the Waverley Police Station.

'Hope you won't mind what I'm about to tell you?' Julian warned Stone after confirming that Jim had passed on the news about the need to go to the Regent. Stone urged him to continue and listened to Julian's explanation of how he had three of the regulars on hand to help and they would all be at the pub that evening. He could hear Stone scribbling down their names.

'We'll have plain-clothes police there as a backup. I'm assuming your mates know what Stavros looks like and may have dealt with him before, but I want to stress, that they and *you*, must not take any risks,' Stone enforced.

Julian couldn't deny he felt nervous as he jumped into a cab to go down to Bondi. What if the AC/DC man, or rather Stavros, did turn up? Stone had instructed him what to do if he did. He was not to acknowledge anyone he didn't know in case they were the police. However, the police would know who he was from the description Stone had given them and if they detected he or his mates were in danger, they would take action.

The cab soon pulled up in front of the Regent and Julian dashed towards the building and once inside walked straight to the bar. He ordered a whisky, downing it in one gulp then ordered another.

'Busy day?' the barmaid asked.

'You could say that,' he replied, then changing his mind ordered a schooner instead. He needed to have his wits about him.

Beer in hand, he could see Steve and the rest of the crew. He wasn't sure whether to join them in case they gave something away but he had to let Steve, Paddy and Jimmy know that this Stavros bloke might come in and … and then what? The decision was made for him when Steve called out, beckoning him over.

'Alright?' Julian gave him a curt nod. The Scouser frowned. 'Siobhan bin-bagged *you* this time?'

Julian didn't bother to retaliate. Should he tell Steve about Stavros? Fuck it, he would, as Steve and the other two had seemed willing to help the other night. 'A quick chat without all the ears?'

Steve sauntered away from the group with Julian close behind. 'What's going on?' Steve asked, trying to appear as if they were having a normal conversation.

'You know what we talked about the other night?' Julian reminded. Steve nodded. 'Well, it appears the AC/DC bloke is going to come to the pub any time soon. Maybe tonight. Detective Alan Stone at Waverley police has been in touch, that's why I'm here and there are plain-clothes coppers here as well,' Julian explained, glancing around.

'What do ya want me to do?'

'The police want to know if he is actually the bloke, Alex Stavros. Ever heard his name?' Steve's shrug implied he hadn't. 'We watch what's going on. Act as normal.'

Steve pulled at his lips. 'Erm,' he doubted. 'If he does turn up, do we order some dope and hope your police mates bounce in?'

Julian wavered. 'Are you willing to do that? … I'd hate you to get into trouble. Shit, I sound like a teacher. Anyway, if you could tell Paddy and Jimmy to keep their eyes and ears open and mouths shut and let me know what's going on. We don't know if he is the bloke who was in here the other night, but *if* it is him, he may be in league with a Vietnamese gang from the Western suburbs who're trying to take over the East.'

'Jeez, and I thought Sydney was a quiet little town,' Steve grinned. 'I'll have a word to the lads.'

Julian crossed his fingers, hoping he'd done the right thing.

As usual, waiting for something to happen made the time drag. It was now seven thirty and Julian remembered that AC/DC man was already in the pub by the time he'd arrived much earlier that previous evening. It seemed like ages ago. Looking around, a few of the customers could be the police but as there was no action, he felt it was inappropriate to approach them.

Half an hour passed and still nothing was happening. Some of the Scousers and other Brits were starting to leave, an early start in the morning. Julian wished Siobhan was here, but he knew that was impossible as she was holed up in the hotel in Kings Cross. He hated to admit that he missed her. He'd thought there was a chance of a relationship, but after seeing the way she'd flirted with that Ray bloke, he'd given up any hope she was interested in him.

Julian was brought back to reality when Steve gave him a nudge. 'Wakey, wakey. We're doing the off. Doesn't look like your man is turning up.'

'No. Won't be long behind you. Bit of a wasted evening.' Placing his hand on Steve's shoulder, Julian said, 'Bloody grateful for your help, mate. Are you happy to try again tomorrow night?'

'Nothing better to do and seeing we live in the pub, it's not exactly hard work.' Steve was about to move off when Brian made his way over and stopped in front of Julian. 'Haven't seen you here for a bit? No luck with our Siobhan?'

Unsure how to answer, Julian laughed. 'Bigger fish to fry.'

'Can't see Shiv as a fish but it takes all sorts.'

'You'd have her even if she was a fuckin' shark,' Steve accused.

'Okay, Mr Lothario, where's *your* bint?' sneered Brian.

Shaking his head, Steve repeated he was doing the off and with a nod at Julian, walked away.

'Fuckin' tool,' Brian said, as he watched his friend depart.

'Trouble at mill?' Julian asked.

'Yeah, Ste can be a real nob'ead. Up his own arse.'

'Nowt so queer as folk.'

With no desire to get involved in an argument between friends, Julian said he was leaving as well. He swilled the last dregs in his glass and was putting it on the table when it occurred to him how this was an opportunity to ask Brian about Siobhan and her connection with both Mark and Trev. 'You're on the money when it comes to Siobhan. I couldn't compete with Trev. Jealous twat,'

Julian stated, picking up his empty glass. 'I got nowhere. How about you?'

Brian scowled. 'Couldn't be bothered … Trev was a total blert. Understood how she wanted the odd bit of charlie, but the way she let him rule her life is beyond me. Anyway, mate, shooting the moon. Ta ra.'

Julian said his goodbyes. He almost felt sorry for Brian. Perhaps Siobhan had played them all. On that note, time to leave.

CHAPTER FIFTY-FIVE

Assuming Detective Stone had been informed that the previous night had been a non-event, Julian made his way back to the Regent the following afternoon once his school duties were completed. It crossed his mind whether the info that the AC/DC man was going to turn up at the pub was actually correct. However, it was worth another try.

The barmaid was the same as the night before and greeted him like a long-lost friend. 'Whisky?' she asked with a big smile.

'Good memory. No, better not. A Reschs. How are you?' Julian asked politely.

'Grand, thanks for asking.'

'Where in Ireland are you from?' he asked, feeling he should make chat.

'Dublin ... England?' she returned.

'London.' Thanking her, he picked up his drink and walked away. Normally, he would have continued the conversation, especially as she was pretty and seemed nice, but tonight he had other things on his mind.

Steve was already in the bar with Paddy and Brian and a large number of the British regulars, but there was no sign of Jimmy. From the look of things, it seemed as if Brian and Steve were on good terms again. They were laughing and clinking glasses. Julian felt relief, while at the same time thinking how women so often caused conflict between men.

'Alright?' he asked. 'What's the joke?'

'Just talking about work and the gobshite of a foreman. Steve gave him an earful today,' Brian explained gleefully.

'Still got your job?' Julian asked, turning to Steve.

''Course. Stupid git couldn't do without us.'

'I should have asked before, but what is your trade?'

'We're sparkies. That's why the bellend needs us.'

Julian grinned. 'Gather you're not fond of him.' The grunts confirmed his comment.

A few rounds had been drunk when suddenly he saw the minder come into the pub, followed not long after by AC/DC man except this time he was wearing a Midnight Oil T-shirt. Eclectic taste in music, thought Julian. Clearly, he preferred Aussie bands to American or British.

Watching surreptitiously, Julian noticed how several of the regulars greeted the now Oils man who chatted as if he'd known them forever. His minder stood close by, eyeing the crowd and nodding to the pub's bouncers. Once the greetings were over, the two men made their way to the gents. Not a particularly pleasant place to carry out business, Julian considered, especially after all the beer that went down the customers' throats. What was his next move? Should he go in and attempt to make a purchase or ask Steve or Paddy instead as he'd had no luck last time? There was no sign of Jimmy. He knew Brian wasn't into drugs so no point asking him, plus Brian hadn't shown any interest in finding out about Trev's or Mark's demise.

'What now?' Steve nudged Julian. 'Our man has arrived. Do you want me to go and ask for some afternoon delight?'

Julian looked around wondering if any of the plain-clothes police were in the bar. He saw a couple of men he didn't recognise. They were standing drinking, looking slightly out of place. 'Wait a second,' he whispered to Steve and walked over to them.

'Hello. I'm Julian,' he said to the pair. 'We've met before.' He thought of winking but that seemed over the top. The look of surprise on their faces caused him to apologise and hurry away. As he made his way back to Steve, a young man dressed in jeans and a short-sleeved shirt stopped him. 'Julian?'

'Yeees?'

'Just wanted to say hello and hope you're having a good night. Alan said to say gidday.'

Julian nodded, quietly saying the target had arrived. The man moved on. Phew. He must have been the police. Thank God for that.

'The back-up?' Steve asked, when Julian returned.

'Yup.'

Sotto voce, Steve said, 'Righty ho. I'll go in and buy some gear. Give your back-up man a nod and don't forget to tell him I'm part of the investigation.' Without waiting for Julian to argue, Steve wandered casually over to the gents, spoke to the minder and was allowed entry.

Julian peered urgently around the room. Where the hell was the bloke, he'd just spoken to? Ah, thank God! There he was leaning against the bar. Striding over, Julian stood as if he were about to order a drink while pretending to mutter something to himself. The man appeared not to have heard but within seconds, a couple appeared at his side. One was a woman, looking like she'd been to the beach and carrying a large bag, the other was a youngish man in jeans and a denim jacket. The three casually walked towards the toilets. The woman waited nearby, nonchalantly sipping what looked like a glass of white wine. When the minder blocked the two men from entering the toilets, police ID was quickly produced. Julian could see how the minder was in two minds: to allow them in or to warn his boss. Or as a third alternative, do a runner. At the same time, the policewoman, sans wine, with ID in

393

hand, reached into her beach bag, pulled out a pair of handcuffs and stated that the minder was under arrest. She told him his rights and spinning the man around, deftly cuffed his wrists, remaining with him while her colleagues entered the toilets.

Both policemen looked around the toilet area. Sergeant Wright began to undo his fly as he walked towards the urinal while Sergeant Hayman entered a cubicle. Over by the wash basins a man of Mediterranean appearance who was busy talking to a 'customer', called out to Sergeant Wright that he would be with him in a minute. Wright hoped he was able to produce a convincing stream of urine while trying to listen to the conversation between the punter and the dealer.

The Mediterranean-looking man suggested that the buyer may like something a bit more exciting than hash. 'Coke would be great,' the buyer answered. Wright, waggling his penis to remove the final drips, registered the buyer's accent as English. He slowly buttoned his fly then made his way to the wash basin. Turning on the tap to wash his hands, he waited for Hayman to emerge from the cubicle.

As Wright pulled paper towels out of the dispenser, he could hear Sergeant Hayman flush the toilet and open the door. Hayman, ignoring Wright, stood next to him at the wash basins, watching in the mirror for the potential transaction to go ahead while his partner pretended to fix his hair. Both waited till the buyer pulled out his money and as he was passing it to the dealer they stepped over with IDs on show, stating, 'You're under arrest for selling illicit drugs.' Hayman took out a pair of handcuffs from the inside of his jacket and both sergeants grabbed the dealer's arms, pulling them behind his back and snapped on the handcuffs.

'What the fuck? I haven't done anything,' the man yelled.

'You were about to. That's good enough for us,' Wright replied, picking up the dealer's bag while the buyer scurried off into one of the cubicles after calling out, 'Detective Alan Stone'.

Wishing he was there to see the action, but at the same time glad he wasn't, Julian waited anxiously. Minutes passed. Suddenly, the door to the gents was pushed open and the two sergeants, one carrying a bag, came out on either side of the Oils man who was in handcuffs. But where the hell was Steve?

The whole pub, aware of the unfolding drama, had gone deathly quiet and stared open-mouthed at the plain-clothes policemen escorting two men to the exit of the venue. The three Māori bouncers who'd joined the policewoman and her charge, were instructed not to let anyone enter the toilets as it was now a crime scene. They stood in front of the swing door with their tattooed arms folded protectively.

395

Julian was in a quandary. What had happened to Steve? It didn't look like he'd been arrested but he hadn't reappeared. Was he okay? Should he try and get past the bouncers? He put his drink down and was heading towards the gents when Steve emerged. He could see Steve having a word to the bouncers who stepped aside to let him through.

Dashing up to him, Julian asked if he was alright. Steve's grin assured him he was. Dragging the Pom back to the bar, thankful that loud chatter had resumed after the dealer and his minder had been frog marched out of the pub by the police, Julian asked, 'What happened? How come you weren't taken away if you were buying?'

'Buy me a VB and I'll fill you in.'

Julian did as he was told. 'Come on mate, what happened?'

'Erm. I was making me order when those two blokes came in and before the guy had a chance to do anything except take me money, they grabbed him and showed their ID's. He didn't even struggle.'

'Where were the drugs?'

'In a bag, bit like a briefcase. The bizzies took it with them.'

'Was it Stavros?'

'Hope so.'

'Did the police say anything to you?' Julian asked. 'Why didn't they arrest you?'

Steve shook his head smugly. ''Course they didn't. I said the magic word and they left me to it.'

'Fuck. What was the magic word?'

'Well, three words. Detective Alan Stone. As soon as they heard his name, they knew I was part of the sting. I'll probably have to give evidence. Might help me get residency. Being such a good citizen.' He laughed.

'But you've only just come out of the toilets. What was going on?'

'Mate, I was dying to do a shit,' Steve explained.

Julian groaned. 'Jesus, you had me worried.'

'About me bowel movements?'

CHAPTER FIFTY-SIX

The Oils man aka AC/DC man, now identified as Alex Stavros, and his minder, were driven in separate unmarked cars to Waverley Police Station and delivered to Alan Stone. He'd been waiting eagerly for their arrival once he'd been rung with the news that they had arrived at the Regent. Their legal rights were explained before sergeants Wright and Hayman escorted the two men to different cells while their lawyers were called and instructed to come to the station.

Stone rang Detective Miller. He'd be there within minutes. There was an excited buzz around the station now the investigation was hotting up.

Stavros's defence arrived within the hour causing Stone to wonder if this man was at the dealer's beck and call. Mr Petros was a youngish, good looking, dark-haired man, wearing an expensive tailored suit. Bit of a cliché, Stone thought before he took the lawyer through to the interview room where Miller and a constable were in attendance with Stavros. Meanwhile in his small cell, Stavros's minder was waiting to be interviewed but it appeared his lawyer was in no rush to see his client. Let him sit there on his own and think about the predicament he was in. Stone knew how sitting in silence could result in confessions.

Stone, Miller, Stavros and Petros sat around the small, rectangular table in the boring, nondescript room. Stone spoke the relevant details into the tape recorder then the interview began.

'At around six-thirty this evening you were in the gentlemen's toilets at the Regent hotel. Is this correct? Stone asked.

Stavros nodded before being instructed to speak his response. 'Yeah.'

'Thank you. Can you explain what you were doing in the toilets at the Regent?'

'Needed to go for a piss. Not a crime, is it?'

Stone sighed. 'Come on mate, you took a bag full of drugs into the gents and when the police entered the toilet, they witnessed you were about to sell drugs to a customer.'

Petros interrupted, 'Were any drugs sold?' His name was stated to the recording.

Miller and Stone looked at each other, then at Petros. 'Why else would your client have so many different types of illegal drugs in his possession?'

'But did he actually sell any?' Petros persisted.

'No, but to have so many we can have him for possession with intent to sell,' Miller jumped in.

'I think you need to revise the reason for his arrest. Possession is a different story to selling,' Petros said smugly. 'It could be for personal use.'

Stone was about to say the amount was obviously not for personal use but kept his mouth shut. He wanted to change the subject. 'Do you work for Jason Zervos?'

'Who?' Stavros asked.

'A kingpin up at Kings Cross. I've heard you work for him.'

'Nah. Never heard of him.'

'Really? Then who do you work for, or do you work for yourself?'

Stone could see Stavros was nearly going to say for himself. This was the way to tackle him, appeal to his ego. Petros leaned towards Stavros, whispering something in his client's ear.

Stone continued, 'Okay, we'll assume you work for yourself, but you have to get your supplies from somewhere. If you assist us the court will be kinder towards you but if you play hard to get, then you'll end up with a very long jail sentence. We want to find out who killed Trevor Pearce and Mark Dunlop. If you help us, we'll help you,' Stone bargained. Staring at Stavros, he proposed, 'If you're prepared to cooperate in finding out who killed both men ...' He let the offer sink in.

Again, Petros whispered into his client's ear. Stavros raised his head, shrugging. To Stone, Stavros appeared to accept he was in a

400

tricky situation because of the amount of drugs in his possession even though he'd been arrested before actually handing them over although money had been exchanged.

Realising he was gaining traction, Stone spoke quickly. 'If you don't work for Zervos, where do you get your supplies from?'

Looking at Petros, Stavros asked, 'You'll give me protection if I tell you?'

Stone reassured him that would be the case.

'It's a gang from out west. Vietnamese. They've moved into the Eastern suburbs, so they asked me to work for them.'

'Because you wouldn't stand out?'

Stavros nodded. 'Not many Asians in the Cross. Except in milk bars and some restaurants.'

'Do you have any names? Who's the boss?'

Petros began to look worried. 'My client will be in danger if the police raid this gang. You must confirm that my client's name will not be mentioned.'

'The police are hardly going to knock on their door and say Mr Stavros sent them. We will do everything in our power to protect him,' Stone stressed. 'Do you know Trevor Pearce?'

''Course. Always in the fucking Regent.'

'Is it normal for two dealers to be in the same venue at the same time?' Stone asked.

Stavros shrugged.

401

Miller fiddled with his pen then asked, 'Was this Vietnamese gang behind his death? Wanted to get rid of the competition?'

'It's possible,' Stavros answered ambivalently. 'But he was small fry. Not worth the bother.'

Stone butted in. 'So where did he get his supplies from?'

Rolling his eyes, Stavros laughed. 'Mate, that's the easy part. Plenty of suppliers out there. The hardest thing is the rivalry between the gangs. The bikies, the Lebs, the Vietnamese. They want the power. The monopoly. Maybe Pearce bit off more than he could chew.'

Stone's expression remained neutral. 'It appears no-one in the pub saw anything when Mr Pearce was attacked.'

'Yeah, right.' Stavros laughed. 'Someone with a blade up his sleeve walks past and bang.'

Miller glanced at Stone whose expression showed he agreed with the explanation.

Slowly riffling through his notebook, Stone stalled for time. He wanted Stavros and his lawyer to feel uncomfortable. Finally, he stated, 'I need the name of the gang and who's in charge. In other words, who supplied you with the drugs.'

'And my client will be protected?'

'Of course.'

CHAPTER FIFTY-SEVEN

Jim and Anh sat around the kitchen table finishing their wine now dinner was over, and the boys had gone into the lounge to watch television.

'I can't believe Mark's parents haven't been told when they can come to Sydney and give Mark a funeral. It must be dreadful for them not to say goodbye.' Anh gulped her wine and wiped her eyes. 'Why is it taking so long?'

'Apparently, when there's foul play, bodies are not released immediately. And if the body is going to be cremated, then that's the end of the evidence. Maybe the parents want Mark's body to be returned to Liverpool for the funeral?'

'Do his parents know any of this? If they don't then they must be wondering what on earth is going on.'

'Alan told me he's already been in touch with them but didn't tell them too much. Only the bare essentials. Although he did say Mark's death was suspicious.'

'Why don't we ring or write to them? Anh asked. 'They must be desperate.'

Jim picked up his glass to delay his answer. He couldn't face having to deal with Mark's parents at the moment.

Once Stavros was back in the cell waiting for bail to be confirmed, and his minder finally interviewed, Stone returned to his office. There was a message on his desk asking him to call Neil in forensics at Glebe. Was it too late to ring back? Worth a try.

To Stone's surprise the phone was answered. 'Thanks for returning my call,' Neil greeted, 'Just thought you'd want to hear what else we've found out about Mark Dunlop.'

'Absolutely, but he's been … dead for a while,' Stone doubted.

'I know, but just thought I'd have another look as something occurred to me. He was a young man and although he had alcohol in his system and a load of amphetamines, I wondered if that was all that killed him.'

'Wouldn't that be enough?'

'Yes, but it was niggling me why he took so many amphetamines. If he wanted to die, he could have just walked into the sea as a lot of people do.'

'But?'

'It turns out he was HIV positive.'

'Fuck me,' Stone moaned. 'What are you trying to say?'

'If he knew he was HIV positive, then he may have taken the amphetamines, and … committed suicide.'

'Oh my God. Do you think the man who rang that night saying Mark was dead was a sexual partner who'd infected him?'

'Sorry mate, that's your area. Just wanted to let you know.'

'Thank you.' Stone hung up.

'Jim, Alan. Have some news. Not good,' Stone uttered as soon as Jim answered the phone.

Jim raised his empty glass at Anh hinting for a refill. She topped up his glass and stood anxiously to listen to the conversation.

Staring at Anh, Jim told Alan to go ahead.

'I've just had a call from Neil in forensics. He'd had an idea to do further tests, and it turns out … Mark was HIV positive.'

Seeing the shocked expression on Jim's face, Anh mouthed, 'What?' Jim waved his hand to stop her asking further questions. 'Are you sure?' he asked.

'Yes. That's what the forensic guy said. He wouldn't be making it up,' Stone confirmed.

'Jesus. So, you think that's why Mark took the amphetamines?'

'Highly likely. From what you and others have said, Mark didn't want anyone in England to know he was gay, so maybe he took the amphetamines to commit suicide after all.'

'Oh my God. To be so frightened of anyone back home knowing.' Jim gulped his wine. 'Do you think the bloke who rang the police was the one who told Mark he might be HIV positive, and then gave him the amphetamines?'

'It's a possibility. Maybe they'd had sex and then this bloke found out he was positive so told Mark. To warn him.'

Jim thought about Alan's information. 'You'll have to tell um … Darcy, that Mark was HIV positive. I can't believe it. He must have had a fling with that other bloke.' In despair, Jim turned to see if Anh was following the conversation. She was. Her clutching a wet tissue said it all.

'Yes. Whether he purposely went to the pub to tell Mark or just bumped into him and then told him once they were at the beach ...' Stone stopped. 'Look, we're jumping to conclusions.'

'But why would this man have so many amphetamines on him?' Jim persisted.

'Perhaps he liked taking amphetamines? From what I've heard, they rev up your sex life as well as making you feel good. Maybe he just shagged around and became infected … then took the drugs so he could cope with being HIV.'

'Christ almighty,' Jim sighed. 'Perhaps that's why Mark had the mobile phone, to talk to this other boyfriend.'

'Maybe.'

The next person on Stone's list to ring was Siobhan. As she was staying at the hotel near her places of work there was a chance she'd still be in her room as there was an hour or so until she began her shows. He wanted to be the one to tell her about Mark. Picking up the phone, he dialled the hotel, dreading what he had to say.

'Sorry to sound brutal but I want to be the one to give you a possible reason why Mark died,' Stone began, relieved she had answered the phone.

'Oh, Jesus and Mary. Why?'

'According to forensics, he was HIV positive and from what I've gathered he didn't want his parents to know he was gay, so it's possible, and this is pure speculation, he took the amphetamines on purpose then went into the water.' Stone waited for a response but all he could hear was crying. 'It looks like he was seeing another bloke, and this chap could have told him he had AIDS and therefore Mark probably had it as well.'

'Jesus Christ. Someone gave him AIDS?'

'Yes. If this bloke was HIV positive, he could be the English guy who rang the Bondi police telling them about Mark down at the beach.'

Siobhan blew her nose loudly before saying, 'To be so worried about what his family would think ... I asked Mark that night if he'd told his parents about Darcy and he said he hadn't dared as they were too religious and wouldn't accept him having a boyfriend.' She thought for a few seconds. 'Do you think he was

407

worried about Darcy as well? Catching AIDS? The guilt he must have felt.'

'Possibly … I just hope he died quickly.' Stone, holding the receiver in one hand, ran the other across his forehead. 'I'm not exactly looking forward to telling his parents how and why he died. I wonder if they'll still come out here once they know the reason?'

'If they're that effing prejudiced, they deserve to go to Hell,' Siobhan answered angrily. 'Why does everyone worry so much about everyone else's sex life? Who cares who it's with as long as it's not hurting anybody?'

Stone didn't reply, conscious that Mark's infidelity had possibly led to his death.

Jim stood with his face buried in Anh's neck, his arms clutching her tightly. She was crying and he wished he could too. Somehow the reason for Mark's dying was almost worse than if he'd been attacked.

'Let's call the boys down,' he suggested, releasing Anh. He walked into the hall and called out to them. The possible explanation for Mark's suicide was something Jim wanted to share with his sons, and he also wanted to discuss the dangers of prejudice. For Mark to be so frightened or ashamed to share his homosexuality with his family and friends back home and to take his own life so he didn't have to tell them about his having HIV, was a terrible indictment on others' lack of understanding and tolerance. And if he were brutally honest, he didn't want his sons to be as prejudiced as he had been.

CHAPTER FIFTY-EIGHT

Now Alex Stavros and his minder had left the police station as their applications for bail had been approved, Stone decided it was a good time to ring Tam Nguyen in Cabramatta. It was early morning and being Saturday it wasn't surprising that the detective wasn't in his office but the sergeant on reception gave Stone Tam Nguyen's home number.

Apologising for ringing him at home, Stone explained how they'd caught Stavros who'd admitted he received his supplies from a Vietnamese gang. They'd used him as he wasn't as noticeable as they would be.'

Nguyen laughed. 'Nothing like a bit of racism to justify who supplies the drugs.'

'Not sure it's racism,' Stone doubted, 'but to be honest, they're probably right as there aren't many Asians in the Cross or the Eastern suburbs.'

'Any luck getting Stavros to tell you who his supplier is?'

'Yes and no. He mentioned a gang, but I want to double check if he's telling the truth.'

'Fair enough. What do you want me to do? I'm assuming you want something.'

'That obvious?' Stone chuckled. 'Yes. I need you and your sources to find out who's supplying the drugs to those who deal in the Cross or around Bondi?'

'Mate, we're already onto it after our last conversation. There are two potential groups. We're planning on paying them a visit very soon. Our sources have given us their whereabouts so we're hoping a surprise raid will find them with the evidence.'

'Great. Let me know when you've done the deed.'

Nguyen thought. 'You realise they may be the suppliers but not necessarily the ones who were behind the death of … what was his name?'

'Trevor Pearce.'

'Yeah. You know it was probably an Anglo as no-one noticed him? If it'd been a Vietnamese in the pub, then surely someone would have seen him? Dogs' balls and all that. I can believe a Nam group would want Aussies to sell the drugs but who would they get to kill Pearce? That's heavy stuff.'

Stone sighed. Tam had a point. What Aussie would be willing to kill one of their own for an Asian gang? … Unless a lot of money was involved or a threat of some kind? 'Fuck mate. No idea. Anyway, do you want reinforcements from our end when you approach the gangs you have in mind?'

'Safety in numbers,' Tam agreed. 'Thanks, but I'm sure we'll cope. Will let you know the outcome.'

'Cheers, mate. Talk soon.' Stone hung up, wondering who was willing to do what the Vietnamese wanted? And from what Stavros had implied, Pearce was small fry, not worth the hassle.

Stone needed some breathing space so decided to walk to a coffee shop for a better takeaway than the instant in the office kitchen. As he walked towards St Catherine's on Bronte Road, his mind was flooded with the new information. It seemed highly likely Dunlop *had* committed suicide but if only they could find out who the Pom was who rang the police station. There had been no information yet from the telephone crew who were meant to track calls. Stavros was dealing for a Vietnamese gang, but it still wasn't clear who'd killed Pearce.

It pissed him off how the undercover sergeants had acted too quickly when Steve had asked to buy drugs from Stavros. It meant he was arrested for possession not for dealing. Why hadn't Wright and Hayman waited till Steve had been given the drugs? Their case against Stavros would have been so much stronger.

Stone stood in the queue for a coffee and was finally served by an Irish girl. Her accent and manner made him think of Siobhan. Like Siobhan she was friendly and engaging. There was something about the way she spoke which was both worldly and innocent. As he put the coffee to his lips, he couldn't help but wonder if Siobhan had pulled the wool over their eyes and had he been naïve in trusting her? Did she have Pearce killed? According to Julian, she was with him in the beer garden, but she could have persuaded someone to do it for her. Promising him God knows what? Did she make Julian go outside so she'd look innocent? Stone's mind was racing. As he strode back to the station, he reviewed Siobhan's comments about Pearce. He needed to talk to Julian, and he preferred to do it in person. He was the one who'd got to know her best, and without his assistance they wouldn't have caught Stavros. A visit to St Cuthbert's was due.

CHAPTER FIFTY-NINE

At nine o'clock on Monday morning, Stone left the police station and within half an hour he was parked in a tree-lined street near St Cuthbert's. Admiring the harbour vista, he was amazed by how so many of the private schools were in expensive suburbs with large grounds and panoramic views.

He walked down the familiar steps to the main building just as the bell rang. Classroom doors opened and boys streamed out, making their way to the next lesson. Stone wove his way through the throng towards Jim's office.

His tap on the door was quickly answered, although Jim couldn't hide his surprise upon seeing Alan standing in the corridor. 'Hello. Everything okay?'

Hurrying into the office, Stone puffed out his cheeks saying, 'If it's possible, I want to have a quick chat with Julian about Siobhan as he knows her better than any of us.'

'Can I ask why?'

'It occurred to me she may have asked one of the pub crowd to bump off Pearce and took Julian outside into the beer garden to provide herself with an alibi.'

'Christ, Alan. That's positively Machiavellian.'

'I know, *and* we've included her in our meetings.'

'Do you really think one of those guys would stab Pearce because she asked them to?'

Stone sighed. 'I don't know, but it's worth looking into. Especially as the weapon was a screwdriver. Money or the promise of sex? Both can be a big motivator. We've started interviewing the pub lot again.'

Jim blinked quickly. He turned to look at the timetables pinned to the wall and traced his finger over the classes. 'Julian will be free at the end of this lesson. That'll be in about forty minutes.'

'No probs. Give us time to exchange notes.'

When the bell rang, Jim was waiting outside Julian's classroom to escort him to his office. Stone stood as they entered and reached out to shake the young man's hand. 'Gidday, Julian. Got a minute? Have a few questions. Oh, and thanks for your help at the Regent. Couldn't have done it without you.'

Julian acknowledged the thanks before stating, 'This seems serious.'

'It is. I've been thinking about Siobhan. I know you were with her outside when Pearce was stabbed … but I'm wondering if she arranged for someone to attack him while she was with you. We all know she didn't like him. Possessive, demanding et cetera.'

'What?' Julian exclaimed.

'Did she suggest going outside?'

'Yeah. So?'

'By being with you, she had an alibi.'

'That seems hard to believe. I know she found him painful, but to have him killed. Really?'

'You'd be amazed by what people can do.'

Julian hesitated before replying. 'To be honest, it has crossed my mind, but after our meetings I put the idea to one side.'

Stone waited for Julian to continue but as he didn't, asked, 'Can you think of anyone who was under Siobhan's spell?'

Julian frowned, shaking his head. 'Oh God, that's hard. She was talked about a lot and some obviously fancied her but there's no-one who stands out. Most assumed she was Trev's girlfriend so off limits.'

'No-one stood out?' Stone persisted.

'I'll have to think,' Julian said. 'Give me a minute … Steve liked her but knew there was no chance. Paddy the same. Jimmy wasn't interested. Brian? Yes, he seemed keen but gave me the impression she was out of his league.'

'What about the other Poms or anyone else for that matter?'

'I honestly can't think of anyone. Siobhan is tough and doesn't take any shit, except of course from Trev, but then he had a hold over her. She was off limits to everyone else. It's amazing she even gave me the time of day.'

'Did you get the impression she was using you?' asked Stone.

'No. If anything, she thought I was using her to find out information.'

Stone nodded and thanked Julian for his time. 'Looks like we'll just have to keep interviewing everyone who was there that night, yet again.'

'Why not try Steve? He was helpful with apprehending the drug bloke and may have an idea about who was obsessed with Shiv.'

'Good idea.'

Julian was walking towards the door when he stopped. 'Actually, don't bother contacting Steve. If it *was* one of his mates, I don't think he'd tell you. One thing I know about Scousers is they stick together.'

Back at the station and feeling more buoyant than he had for a while, Stone noticed a youngish, well-built man wearing work clothes as if off a building site, sitting by himself in the reception area. As there was no-one at the desk, Stone went up to him, asking if he could be of assistance.

The man stared up at him, the distress on his face obvious. He looked about to cry.

'Are you okay?' Stone asked.

417

'No,' he answered, levering himself to his feet. 'I've come to confess.'

At first, Stone wondered if the bloke was a nutter, but hearing the English accent said quickly, 'Let's talk somewhere more private and you can tell me what you're confessing to. I'm Detective Alan Stone,' he introduced, while looking around for someone to accompany them. Seeing Hayman emerge from an office, Stone nodded his head at the sergeant indicating for him to join them for the interview.

As if going to his own execution, the man trudged to the room where he was offered a chair and told that the conversation would be recorded.

'Would you like a glass of water?' The man shook his head so slowly, Stone was worried he'd fall asleep.

Turning on the tape recorder, Stone asked gently, 'Do you mind telling me your name?' He didn't want to stress the bloke by being too formal. His mind was racing at the thought that this bloke might be the one who rang the police about Mark.

Picking at a non-existent spot on his cheek, and ignoring Stone's question, the man whispered, 'I'm responsible for Mark Dunlop's death.'

Stone's eyes widened. 'Could you repeat that?'

'I killed him.'

418

Steadying himself, Stone asked again for the man's name. Closing his eyes, the man gave his name, Michael Charteris, followed by his address and phone number before saying he was a friend of Mark's.

The situation was so unusual Stone was unsure what to ask next. 'When you say friend, in what way?' He didn't want to imply that he'd assumed Charteris was gay from his appearance or by being friends with Mark.

'We had an affair. Mark was with Darcy, but we met at The Albury and things went from there.'

Fidgeting with his pen, Stone remained silent hoping Charteris would continue without prompting. His ploy didn't work. 'So, you met at The Albury and had an affair with Mark Dunlop,' Stone confirmed. 'What does that have to do with Mr Dunlop's death?'

Charteris jerked at the last word, tears beginning to flow. 'We went down to the beach,' he gulped, 'I had to tell him that I'd found out I was HIV positive so there was a good chance he was too.' He wiped his eyes with the back of his hand. 'We'd stopped seeing each other ... Mark didn't like going behind Darcy's back, but I felt it was important to tell him ...' Stone nodded encouragingly, and Charteris continued. 'I was only trying to help him, to save him from dying from HIV. Get medical help.' He looked at Stone for reassurance. 'Diego told me a couple of guys

419

at The Albury were asking about Mark and I realised I *had* to explain what happened.'

The name Diego rang a bell. He was the South American Jim and Julian had mentioned after they'd been to The Albury as a 'gay couple'.

'Were you the person who rang the police the night Mark died?'

Charteris mumbled that he was.

'Were you the person who supplied Mark with the drugs?' Stone asked.

Sobbing, Charteris explained, 'He was so miserable. He hated the thought of his parents and family finding out he was gay, and probably HIV positive, so he asked if I had something to make him feel better. … I didn't know he'd go into the water.'

Stone couldn't help feeling sorry for the man, however, he had to ask, 'How come you had so many amphetamines on you?'

'When I found out I was HIV positive I needed something to help me cope and I was missing Mark. When I saw how upset he was, I just handed him the pills.' His facial expression was begging Stone to believe him. 'I didn't expect him to kill himself. I wouldn't have given them to him if I'd known what he was going to do.'

'Did you try to save Mark?'

'I couldn't. One minute we were sitting on the sand, then he charged into the water and that was it … and I can't swim,' he wailed.

'Why didn't you ring the police or an ambulance straight away?'

Charteris wrung his hands together. 'I panicked. I know how prejudiced the police are against gays.'

'But you clearly felt responsible as you later rang the Bondi Police, but why has it taken you so long to come forward?'

Shrugging his shoulders, he stated tearfully, 'Like Mark, I didn't want my family to learn the truth about me. Or my work mates. I work in a very male environment and if they'd known I was queer, I wouldn't have heard the end of it. Also, I was worried about Darcy.'

'Why?'

Charteris went on to explain how he'd met Darcy with Mark at The Albury and soon realised Darcy wasn't into threesomes, and later when he'd found out he was HIV positive, it all became too much.

'But you told Mark, and Mark, if he'd lived, would have told Darcy,' Stone supposed.

'I know, I know. I was gutless.' Charteris gazed around the room as if searching for the correct explanation for his behaviour.

421

'I didn't expect Mark to do what he did. Honestly, I just thought it was better to tell him so he could get medical help.'

All Stone could do was shake his head. He wondered how he would have acted in a similar situation. To have an affair was bad enough but then to give one person, possibly two, AIDS was mind blowing.

'I'm grateful that you've had the courage to tell me what happened, but as illegal drugs were involved and your being the source, you'll have to make a statement and there's a chance it will go to court.'

'But he asked me for the drugs.'

'I wish it were that simple.'

Seeing the anguish on the man's face, Stone said that as he'd rung the police on Saturday night, and now confessed, he believed he would be treated with leniency. Stone hoped this was the truth. He was about to turn off the tape recorder when he remembered the mobile phone in Mark's flat. 'One more thing, we found a mobile phone in Mark's unit. Do you know anything about it?'

Charteris reddened. 'It was our way of communicating without Darcy knowing. Sounds so underhand … but we didn't want to hurt his feelings.'

Stone made a note. 'And what about Mark's wallet? It wasn't on his person when his body was found.'

Looking plaintively at Stone, Michael Charteris replied, 'No idea. It must have fallen out when he was in the water. He didn't give it to me. Why would he?' Tears had returned.

'You realise by supplying Mr Dunlop with an illegal drug you are under arrest?' Charteris nodded. 'And you'll have to stay here at the station until an application for bail is granted. Is there a lawyer you can call now?'

The man's shoulders slumped even further. 'Don't know any lawyers.'

Stone informed him he would be offered legal aid, and turning off the recorder, indicated for Hayman to escort Charteris to the desk sergeant who would take the necessary details and settle the man in a cell.

CHAPTER SIXTY

Stone, enthused yet saddened by his interview with Michael Charteris, finally had some news for Jim and his family. His call to Jim was quickly answered and he relayed Charteris's confession. Jim's relief at a conclusion to Mark's death was palpable and he agreed to only tell Anh. It was too soon to tell everyone else.

Stone's next call was to Miller at Bondi. Now the focus was just on Trevor Pearce and the interviews were to continue. With luck, the mystery of his death would be solved soon.

Later that afternoon, Detectives Stone, Miller, Sanderson, Bourke, and Roscoe were ready to interview those who still hadn't participated in the second round. They were to arrive straight after they'd finished work which for many would be around four o'clock. However, this time the atmosphere in the reception area wasn't the same as when the first interviews took place. It no longer felt like a party.

The interviews began and the responses were similar to before. No one admitted to seeing anything unusual, there was no-one who seemed out of place, they only realised something had happened when they saw the body on the floor.

Sensing he was getting nowhere and assuming it was the same for the other detectives, Stone decided a break was needed and collected them in his office. He stood fidgeting anxiously with his pen and notebook. 'Someone must know something. Make sure you ask if they were carrying work tools. And stress if they know any of the tradies who are keen on Siobhan and would be willing to do her dirty work.'

'I spoke to Steve Bartlett, but he had nothing new to offer,' Miller added.

'Not surprised.' Stone shook his head. 'Anyway, do your best.'

The detectives wearily made their way back to the interview rooms and Stone returned to his. The desk sergeant soon arrived accompanied by a constable and another man dressed in work clothes, no doubt off a building site. The sergeant read out the name of the man and Stone jerked in anticipation. He'd heard this name before. Turning on the tape recorder, Stone listed those present, then greeted the interviewee, 'Mr Boylan. This shouldn't take long. Can I call you Brian?' He received a nod. 'And please state your answers for the tape.'

Stone, remembering the conversations about Liverpudlians having a grudge against the police, especially because of Margaret

Thatcher's iron rule, spoke in a friendly tone. 'Thanks for coming. I know we've talked to everyone before, but we need more help regarding the attack on Trevor Pearce. Now that time has passed, I'm hoping you might remember seeing someone who seemed out of place in the pub, or with luck if you remember seeing who attacked him?'

The Scouser sat thinking, rubbing his stubble. 'No. Don't remember seeing anything. Had a few jars so the memory's a bit hazy.'

'Can you think of anyone who had it in for Pearce? Someone who got a dodgy deal off him?' He stared at Brian then stated, 'Don't worry, we're not interested in anyone's drug habits. Just looking for a motive for why Pearce was attacked.'

'Don't do drugs. Too busy working.'

'So, you didn't buy anything off Mr Pearce?'

'Nah. But half the pub did. You talking to them?'

Stone said they were. 'I've heard you're keen on the Irish girl, Siobhan Greene.'

Brian frowned in disbelief. 'Shiv? You're blaggin'.'

'I gather you mean I'm making it up. Not from what I've heard. Nothing wrong with being keen on a girl,' Stone comforted, 'we've all experienced unrequited love.'

'What the fuck does that mean?'

'When you like someone, and they don't like you.'

426

'What's that got to do with anything?' Brian argued. 'I thought you wanted to ask about that nob'ead Trev?'

'Did you attack him?' Stone asked quickly.

Brian reeled back on his chair. 'You gotta be joking. He was a gobshite, but I didn't kill the fucker.'

'You didn't want to get rid of him so Siobhan would be free?' He watched Brian's face closely. There was a blink of recognition at Stone's words. 'Come on, Brian. You really liked Siobhan and hated the way Pearce treated her. By killing him, she would be free, and you'd be free to pursue her.'

'Bollocks! She weren't interested in me so why the fuck would I kill Trev?'

'Perhaps you just wanted to help her. You seem like a good bloke.' Stone paused. 'I've heard Liverpudlians are really loyal to their mates and although you couldn't have Siobhan, you saw her as a mate. From what I've gathered, Pearce had a hold over her, so he used it to his advantage. Made her life a misery.'

Brian's face crumpled. 'The prick was always swaggerin' around like King Dick, tellin' Shiv what to do, and everyone else doin' what he wanted cos he sold drugs and was minted. He was a total arsewipe.'

'Did you attack him?' Stone could see how the man was emotionally conflicted but whether it was because he didn't want to betray a mate or …? He waited in silence.

427

'Fuck it … I didn't plan to kill him. It was spur of the moment. I'd just finished work, had a few bevvies and he was standing right next to me.'

'You didn't mean to kill him?' Stone asked quietly.

'Thought I'd give the bastard a fright. That's all I wanted. He was a right twat and treated Siobhan like shit. Just wanted to put the wind up 'im.'

'Hurt him a little, was that it?' Stone continued. 'And you had a screwdriver in your pocket?'

'Yeah. Give 'im a wake-up call.'

'Did you take the screwdriver to the pub on purpose to attack Mr Pearce?'

'No! Like I said, it just 'appened.' He gave a thin smile of acceptance. 'A tool for a tool.'

Stone couldn't resist a sympathetic grin. 'You realise I'm going to have to arrest you?'

'There goes me residency,' Brian sighed.

''Fraid so. But perhaps as you've been helpful assisting the police, you might get a lesser sentence. Can't promise anything but I'll put a word in for you.'

Brian put his head in his hands. He wasn't going back to Liverpool any time soon.

CHAPTER SIXTY-ONE

Rather than imposing on Jim and Anh again, Stone invited the inner circle to a restaurant in Paddington with a private room, all expenses paid. It was time to put both deaths to bed. Siobhan arrived with Julian, and Ray and Daphne followed soon after. Terry came alone although Stone had included Scott in the invitation, and a few minutes later Jim and Anh joined the group. Steve was expected, but it was doubtful whether he would turn up as his mate, Brian was now in custody awaiting trial.

Once all were seated and drinks poured, Stone rose, raising his glass. 'I sincerely want to thank you for the assistance you've given us. If it weren't for you the investigations into … well you know what I'm referring to, would not have had the results we hoped for.'

The noise of the door opening interrupted Stone's speech. It was Steve. 'Alright?' he asked, including everyone in his wide grin. All laughed and responded that they were alright. He quickly sat down in the spare seat next to Anh. 'Pleased to meet you. Sorry I'm late.'

Stone waited until the group resettled. 'Good to see you, Steve. I was just saying how grateful we are for the help you all gave us. Without your efforts, we'd still be scratching our heads.'

Like a student, Siobhan put up her hand. 'Yes Siobhan?' Stone asked.

'Did you ever find out who rang the police the night Mark died?'

'I'm glad you asked. I've been waiting till tonight to tell you.' Stone peered around the gathering with a wry smile. 'The English bloke finally came into the station. I think his conscience got the better of him. He explained how he'd told Mark on Saturday night he was HIV positive and as they'd had an affair there was a good chance Mark was as well. And possibly Mark had unintentionally infected his partner, Darcy.'

There were gasps at the revelation.

'But how come this man had so many amphetamines on him? Jim interjected. 'It's a bit suspicious.'

Stone paused. 'I know it looks that way, but he took them to help himself forget the situation he was in, being HIV positive. When he saw how distressed Mark was that he could have AIDS, he gave some to Mark to make him feel better … he didn't realise amphetamines and alcohol don't mix, although it appears Mark wanted enough to help him die. He couldn't bear the thought of

430

his parents finding out he was gay *and* having the dreaded AIDS. Apparently, his parents are deeply religious.'

'Why didn't this bloke try to save Mark?' Jim asked angrily, causing Anh to give him a nudge.

'According to him, Mark's going into the sea was completely unexpected, plus this bloke, I can't tell you his name, couldn't swim.'

'Oh my God,' Anh exclaimed. 'If only Mark had told us. We could have helped him. Not judged him. What a waste of a young life.'

'He never told me he had that other bloke. We were mates and he didn't say anything,' Siobhan blurted out, her cheeks red with anguish.

A quiet sadness dominated the room. Stone waited for the information to be absorbed. He was also hesitant about how to bring up the news about Trevor as he was conscious of Steve's friendship with Brian. Finally, he said, 'Well, we did find out who attacked Trevor Pearce. Nothing to do with Vietnamese gangs or Zervos, or Stavros for that matter.' He paused, not looking at Steve. 'It was Brian Boylan, one of the English guys at the Regent.' He waited for the revelation to sink in. Julian gasped loudly in surprise, and Stone, seeing Steve's face droop in shock, realised he too had no idea. 'Fuck. I wondered why he wasn't at

431

work,' Steve groaned. 'What the hell was he doing?' Anh rubbed his back in sympathy.

Turning to Siobhan, Stone explained, 'It seems Brian had a thing for you, and was sick of Trev's behaviour, especially towards you, but it appeared to be very spur of the moment. Definitely not premeditated.'

'Jesus, Mary … Siobhan began, tears dripping down her face. She picked up the serviette next to her plate, scrubbing her eyes. 'The eejit.'

Julian handed her another serviette and again all were quiet. 'Poor sod,' Julian stated, breaking the silence.

'Who? Pearce?' Jim asked, abruptly.

'No! Brian. Now he'll face years in prison and probably be deported,' Julian stated.

Siobhan put her hand over his, tears streaming. 'I didn't know how he felt about me. If I had, I could have done something. It's all my fault. Too busy thinking about … meself. So worried about me effing visa.'

Cries of denial echoed around the room. Anh rose from her seat and stood behind Siobhan's chair. She put her hands on the young woman's shoulders. 'We don't always know how other people feel or what they want. What could you have done?' Siobhan listened in anguish then stood up, throwing her arms around Anh. The two clutched each other while the group watched on. Stone, like Jim,

432

had tears in his eyes and as he glanced around, saw they were not the only ones.

In an attempt to lift the mood, Stone said, 'On a practical note, Stavros, the AC/DC man, will be put on trial for drug dealing and the Vietnamese gang who supplied him has been arrested. The police are now investigating the Regent, although Zervos is still a king pin up at the Cross.' He shrugged his shoulders in resignation. 'But on a positive note, Siobhan, you'll still have a job, and there's a strong case you'll get your visa renewed and be allowed to stay.' Stone grinned at the gathering before adding how connections in high places can prove useful. The room clapped.

Jim waited till silence returned. 'Alan, what about Mark's parents? Are they coming for the funeral? If there is a funeral?'

Stone considered how to respond. 'To be honest it wasn't easy telling them about Mark's death,' he admitted, looking around the table. 'I left out many of the details. Obviously, they were very upset, but I'm pleased to tell you that they *are* coming out to view his body and take him back to England.'

There was a collective sigh of relief.

'Also, I was in touch with Darcy soon after the English bloke confessed and told him what had happened to Mark, plus, and this wasn't easy, how Mark was HIV positive.' Everyone drew a breath. 'I suggested to Darcy that he have a test which I'm pleased to inform you was negative.' There was another huge sigh of relief.

Suddenly, the door to the private room opened and a waiter stood with his pad to take the orders. He took a step backwards. 'Is it okay if I come in?'

'Yes, please,' was the unanimous response.

Elizabeth Bankes was born in England then emigrated to New Zealand with her family as a young child. She attended the University of Canterbury and later achieved two Masters at the University of Sydney. One of the Masters was in Creative Writing for which she gained a Merit. This degree gave her the confidence to write and with her extensive experience as a high school teacher, has based The Body Series on personal knowledge – excluding the murders.

As a break from teaching, Liz worked at SBS TV for a few years in the Publicity Department: a change from bells ringing and hormonal teenagers.

Liz lives in Sydney with her second husband, an English 'toy boy', and their dog, Martha. Her two children have given her four grandchildren. As well as writing whodunnits, a memoir, helping with the grandchildren, reading, socialising and walking Martha, she teaches Academic English at UNSW College.